The End of
MASCULINITY

Per Patricia Cusi Pascual, 'let's!'

I wish to make an examination of the capacity of the individual to be alone, acting on the assumption that this capacity is one of the most important signs of maturity in emotional development . . . the basis of the capacity to be alone is a paradox; it is the experience of being alone while someone else is present.

D.W. Winnicott, *The Capacity to Be Alone* (1958)

The End of
MASCULINITY

THE CONFUSION OF SEXUAL GENESIS AND
SEXUAL DIFFERENCE IN MODERN SOCIETY

John MacInnes

OPEN UNIVERSITY PRESS
Buckingham • Philadelphia

Open University Press
Celtic Court
22 Ballmoor
Buckingham
MK18 1XW

and

1900 Frost Road, Suite 101
Bristol, PA 19007, USA

First Published 1998

A catalogue record of this book is available from the
British Library

ISBN   0 335 19658 6 (pb)   0 335 19659 4 (hb)

Library of Congress Cataloging-in-Publication Data
MacInnes, John.
    The end of masculinity : the confusion of sexual genesis and
sexual difference in modern society / John MacInnes.
        p.   cm.
    Includes bibliographical references and index.
    ISBN 0-335-19659-4 (hardcover), –
    ISBN 0-335-19658-6 (pbk.)
    1. Men.   2. Masculinity.   3. Sex differences (Psychology)
I. Title.
HQ1090.M327   1997
305.31–dc21   97-20463
                                                             CIP

Typeset by Graphicraft Typesetters Limited, Hong Kong
Printed in Great Britain by Biddles Ltd,
Guildford and King's Lynn

Contents

Preface and acknowledgements   vii

1 The genesis of masculinity   1
2 The fetishism of sexual difference and its secret   24
3 The crisis of masculinity and the politics of identity   45
4 The paradoxes of sex and gender   61
5 Gender as socialization theory: Freud's *Three Essays*   83
6 The collapse of patriarchy and the origins of gender:
  kinship and the traffic in women   100
7 Thomas Hobbes: social contract and the rise of universalism   112
8 Why the personal is not political   134

Bibliography   155
Index   162

Preface and acknowledgements

Somewhere Donald Winnicott remarks that too strong a need to be believed by others was a sure sign of madness. The last few years I have spent writing this book have probably confirmed the wisdom of this remark to my friends and colleagues who have patiently responded to my need to attempt to convince them (and therefore myself) of the argument I make here. I thank them all for their tolerance. Winnicott also argued that the best way to assess someone's psychological health was to notice whether they bored you. For my sake, may you find this book interesting.

Vincent Duindam, Paul Thompson, Tricia Findlay, Ray Pahl, Jonathan Gershuny, John Holmwood, Barbara Grabmann, Chris Warhurst, Jacqui O'Reilly, Paula Skidmore, Bridget Fowler, John Fowler, Halla Belloff, Sue Yeandle, Jan Webb and David Morgan all read and commented on drafts of various sections of the manuscript. Seminar participants at the Universities of Nottingham Trent, Budapest, Edinburgh, Glasgow, Sheffield Hallam and Trinity College, Dublin gave me valuable feedback as did the students on the Sociology of Masculinity and MSc in Gender Studies courses at Edinburgh University. All my colleagues at the Department of Sociology, University of Edinburgh have provided both an intellectually stimulating and marvellously encouraging atmosphere in which to work. My fellow group trainees and trainers in the Gestalt Trust Scotland taught me just how creatively neurotic we can be in avoiding the capacity to be alone in the presence of another: Bert Anderson, Hilda Courtney, Duncan Heal, Tam McVeigh, Flora Meadows, Marianno Pizzimenti, Andy Pritchard, Rob Ritchie, Maggie Saidler, Elsie Shiel, Jane Steele, Eileen Spence, Dagmar Theison and Beneditke Uttenhal. Kirsta Edlund taught me to look carefuly, get things in proportion, see the whole picture, and know when to stop, while Susan Maclennan reminded me to choose capitalism over patriarchy.

Finally seven magnificent men in particular have been so important to this book that I cannot imagine having written it without them. My uncle, Ian MacInnes, taught me how to argue, and has proceeded to argue with me about gender ever since. He gave me a passion for political debate, and as a lifelong socialist, a practical example of how to translate ideals into practice in his local community. He also introduced me to Mill's *On Liberty* and convinced me of its relevance. John Brady, encouraged me to write this book in the first place and together with fellow men's group survivors Tim Holmes, Alan Swann and Simon Watkins, convinced me early on at a personal level of something which I struggled for a few more years to resist at a political level: the realization that there is absolutely no fundamental difference between men and women as persons. They have also endured every twist and turn in the tortuous development of the thesis about gender which this book sets out, been generous in their encouragement and warm beyond words in their friendship. John Eldridge has shown me, without ever instructing me, how sociology ought to be: relevant, radical and robust but simple and accessible. When the pressures from the Research Assessment Exercise and all the other paraphernalia of the rationalized bureaucratization of higher education pointed in the other direction, he gave me the time that allowed me to start this whole project off, by spending a year immersing myself in the literature of psychodynamics and masculinity. Finally, this book owes a tremendous intellectual debt, apparent in every chapter, to the profound, critical and moving work of Ian Craib.

Given that I pursue some unconventional arguments, let me say that this book is intended as a contribution to the feminist struggle against inequality between men and women, and for proper recognition of the needs of children. Given that the road to hell is paved with good intentions, whether it succeeds in this is for the reader to judge. If it does, much of the credit lies with those I acknowledge here. If it doesn't, the blame lies with me.

Grateful acknowledgement is made to the following for permission to quote copyright material: to Laurence Pollinger Limited, the Estate of Frieda Lawrence Ravagli and Viking Penguin, a division of Penguin Books, USA Inc. for 'To Women, As Far As I'm Concerned' by D.H. Lawrence from *The Complete Poems of D.H. Lawrence*, edited by V. de Sola Pinto and F.W. Roberts, copyright © 1964, 1971 by Angelo Ravagli and C.M. Weekley, Executors of the Estate of Frieda Lawrence Ravagli; to Faber and Faber Ltd and Farrar Strauss and Giroux Inc. for the excerpt from 'This Be The Verse' from *High Windows* by Philip Larkin, copyright © 1974 by Philip Larkin.

John MacInnes
September 1997

1

The genesis of masculinity

While Europe's eye is fix'd on mighty things,
The fate of empires and the fall of kings;
While quacks of state must each produce his plan,
And even children lisp the Rights of Man;
Amidst this mighty fuss, just let me mention,
The Rights of Woman merit some attention.
(Robert Burns, 'The Rights of Women' 1792)

If all Men are born Free, how is it that all Women are born Slaves?
(Mary Astell, *Some Reflections Upon Marriage* 1730)[1]

Gender ideology and gender identity

'A man would never set out to write a book on the peculiar situation of the human male', commented Simone de Beauvoir in *The Second Sex* (1972: 15). Yet half a century later it seems that every man and his dog is writing a book on masculinity. So why so many and why another one? The answer to the first question is that modernity systematically undermines patriarchy (men's rule by virtue of their sex and kin relations to others) and as a result, particularly over the last half century, substantial changes have taken place in the sexual division of labour, by which I mean the process whereby males and females routinely perform different activities or occupy different social roles, receive different material rewards and have access to contrasting amounts of power and status because of their sex. Men have lost a great deal of their power over women, have become more aware of this process, have started to realize that they too constitute a 'gender' and have started to discuss and debate this, usually in response to feminist challenge, rather than under their own initiative, producing books along the way.[2]

The answer to the second question is that I think we can best understand this process if we realize that 'gender', together with the terms masculinity and femininity, is an ideology people use in modern societies to imagine the existence of differences between men and women on the basis of their sex where in fact there are none, and whose existence they at other times deny. This imagination helps individuals make sense of a society which is still marked by substantial inequality between men and women, but which claims to be formally egalitarian, and also provides them with some important psychological defences against the terrors of modernity: what I call below 'psychic insecurity'. This is part of a more general move towards the romance of authenticity. But the terms of this imagination, and of this romance, together with the material sexual division of labour itself, are subject to the constant revolutionizing of social relations ushered in by modernity, such that people are forced towards a conclusion which they try to resist, but cannot escape: gender, in the sense of an actually existing identity or social characteristic of men or women, *does not exist*.

Most discussions of masculinity assume that it is an empirically existing form of identity, set out to analyse its oppressive or exploitative character, show how this results from or reproduces patriarchy, and either suggest alternative models of masculinity men might embrace or urge men to reject masculinity altogether. But this overlooks the fact that what we now think of as masculinity was originally used to legitimate patriarchy, by demonstrating how men were more capable of exercising public power than women. The core thesis of this book, however, is that masculinity does not exist as the property, character trait or aspect of identity of individuals. This means that trying to define masculinity, or masculinities, is a fruitless task, and also that explanations of how men come to have much greater power, resources and status than women in the modern world which rely upon the concept of masculinity used in this way are unlikely to be helpful. I argue that masculinity exists only as various ideologies or fantasies, about what men *should* be like, which men and women develop to make sense of their lives. If this is the case, it can make no sense to argue that men should reform their masculinity to help in the struggle for sexual equality – for how are men to reform something which does not exist? I therefore make no attempt in this book to define different forms of masculinity or trace the social or historical relations of different forms to each other. It will become clear that I think that many current explanations of men's power in gender theory do depend on using the concept of masculinity in this way, by reducing identity too directly to ideology, reducing the personal too directly to the political and producing 'oversocialized' models of men and women as a result. Gender should be seen as the ideological result of a material struggle over the sexual division of labour; to imagine that gender identity *causes* the sexual division of labour is mistaken and ultimately expresses the modern form which patriarchal ideology takes. In turn I argue that this ideology depends on systematically confusing sexual genesis with sexual difference: confusing the fact that we are all born *as* a man *or* a woman with the fact that we are all born *of* a man *and* a woman.

Masculinity and modernity

Instead of trying to define masculinity, I ask a more fundamental, and I hope, more revealing question: what historical conditions encourage men and women to imagine the existence of such a thing as masculinity in order to make sense of their lives in the first place? I suggest that one of the most profound but unanticipated and unintended consequences of the spread of market relations is the rise in modern societies of a formal commitment to the equality of all human beings in principle, and social and material pressures which sustain this – what could be called universalism. Modernity produces societies that are 'transitional', in the sense that they combine the material and ideological legacy of a sexual division of labour produced by the patriarchal era which preceded this, with material and ideological forces which undermine that legacy and create the conditions for a sexually egalitarian order. Gender is the fetishistic ideology inevitably created by this transition and its contradictory social forces.[3]

The origins of modern capitalist society and the nature of the transition from feudal or traditional society is clearly beyond the scope of this book. But I think we can accept as uncontroversial the proposition that three interdependent developments were crucial. One was the rise of the market and exchange, which encouraged people to think in terms of private forms of property – the commodity – and of themselves as owners of different kinds of property, including property in their own capacities, literally their 'properties'. Another was the Enlightenment and the process of rationalization whereby logic, calculation, scientific enquiry and empirical evidence came to be seen as the most important way to understand not only the natural but also the social world; Hobbes, for example, started out from geometry, had conversed with Galileo and saw himself as developing a science of the motion of *human* bodies. Finally there was the idea that as members of a species, human beings shared some essential properties and by virtue of that, were in some sense formally equal one with another.

Each of these three developments is dependent upon the other two, and together they describe the twin processes which Weber called disenchantment and rationalization (1948b: 150, 1948c: 350, 1978a).[4] Disenchantment was the process whereby responsibility for the fate of the world is accepted as a human rather than divine endeavour and its order seen as a social rather than natural or supernatural one. Hitherto men and women had projected responsibility for these relations onto nature or supernature (God, spirits, magic) even though they were their actual authors, by imagining themselves to obey or enforce God's will or the laws of nature. We should not be misled by the way in which the early theorists of this revolution still used the language of divinity and nature. They projected equal rights into nature as 'natural rights' which they had discovered rather than invented and they appealed to the interpretation of the scripture to make their case. But arguments about *how* God guided men can be seen, at least for our purposes, as actually about *whether* He did so.

By 'rationalization', Weber meant the process, visible in every sphere of social, economic and political life, whereby the means chosen to pursue given ends, and even the choice of which ends to pursue, came to be determined by logical and rational calculation. Thus relations between people increasingly came to take the form of calculations about the exchange and use of their properties or capacities through the market place and in bureaucracies. The latter were organizations (such as capitalist enterprises or political parties) where people discharged functions specified in advance according to various rules – they held an office or 'bureau' linked by lines of authority. They could hold such offices only if they had the capacities necessary to perform the functions of the office effectively. The social and economic position of individuals therefore came to be determined more by achievement than by ascription, status or kinship. One result of this process was a continuous drive towards greater rationalization and efficiency, and the erosion of traditional patterns of life and thought: what Marx had earlier described as the constant revolutionizing of both the forces and relations of production.

> The development of bureaucracy greatly favours the levelling of status and this can be shown to be historically the normal tendency. Conversely every process of social levelling creates a favourable situation for the development of bureaucracy by eliminating the office holder who rules by virtue of status privileges . . . The objective discharge of business primarily means a discharge of business according to calculable rules and 'without regard for persons'. 'Without regard for persons' also is the watchword of the 'market' and in general, of all pursuit of naked economic interests.
>
> (Weber, 1978a: 215, 226)

This process went much further than what happened to work in actual offices. We could think of office as a term synonymous with social role or function in all areas of life. What Weber did not explicitly anticipate, but what my argument in this book will suggest, is that part of the levelling of status caused by the rise of bureaucracy and the impersonality of the market, was that of sexual status. Eventually, 'without regard for persons' could include disregarding the sex of the person occupying an office or dealing on the market, in so far as that was irrelevant to the capacities they possessed.

Rationalization liberated social relations from the dogma of traditional magic, superstition or religious faith. But its unanticipated and inevitable consequence, according to Weber, was the increasing subjection of individual's lives to pressures from the public sphere, whether as members of bureaucracies (such as the organizations that employed them) as citizens of states which demanded their loyalty, or as buyers and sellers in markets whose operation lay beyond their individual control. One problem was what Bauman (1991) has called 'moral invisibility'. The holders of offices might concentrate on technical means to the exclusion of ethical ends: they need feel little responsibility for final outcomes. Indeed, precisely because the effectiveness of the system was based on its impersonality, any views office holders had about 'final outcomes' should exert no influence. The requirements of the office determined what happened, not the views of the person occupying it. There need therefore be little fit between the formal rationality of markets or bureaucracies and any substantive rationality of their outcomes. Thus the other side of the tremendous material progress generated by industrial capitalism was the Holocaust and nuclear weaponry: the rationalization of the means of genocide.

The second problem was that the ultimate ends which bureaucracies or market transactions might originally be set up to pursue could themselves be overwhelmed by the force of bureaucracies and markets, which by virtue of their technical efficiency, were liable to dominate all social life. Thus the overall direction of society might be reduced to the incalculable and unanticipated consequences of countless choices about means to immediate ends that were taken in myriads of interconnecting and competing markets and bureaucracies. Weber thus wrote of the 'iron cage' of bureaucracy (1930: 181) and speculated that the domination of the official in modern society might become yet more powerful than that of the slave owner.

Following the theories of Marx and Weber, we might therefore describe the development of modern capitalism to be the rise of the rule of offices not men. This is true in two senses. Offices come to run people, rather than the other way around, but at the same time, men become less able to occupy the most powerful or rewarding offices by virtue of their sex. They must start to compete for them with women, on the basis of their competence to fulfil the role. An important aspect of modernity thus appears to be the rise of forces which encourage sexual equality, but also subordinate both men and women to the abstract rule of markets and the iron cage of bureaucracy. This paradox underpins the argument in the rest of this book. I return to it explicitly in Chapter 8.

The essence of modernity has thus been the working through of the realization that people's relations with one another, and thus the societies they inhabited, were their own creations, both conscious and unconscious, willed or inadvertent, for which they were individually and collectively responsible – what Giddens terms reflexivity. Brecht captures the key character of rationalization and disenchantment in modernity in *Life of Galileo*, when he imagines the astronomer talking to his young pupil (Brecht, 1980: 6–8):

> For two thousand years people have believed that the sun and all the stars of heaven rotate around mankind. Pope, cardinals, princes, professors, captains, merchants, fishwives, and schoolkids, thought they were sitting motionless inside this crystal sphere. But now we are breaking out of it, Andrea, and at full speed. Because the old days are over and this is a new time. . . . And the earth is rolling cheerfully around the sun, and the fishwives, merchants, princes, cardinals and even the Pope are rolling with it.
>
> The universe has lost its centre overnight, and woken up to find it has countless centres. So that each one can now be seen as the centre, or none at all. Suddenly there is a lot of room.

A popular way of conceiving of this new reflexivity (which had the advantage that it could be used while continuing to profess piety and due respect for God and the Bible) was to think of society as a series of explicit and implicit *contracts* which its members made with each other, and to define the essence of a just society as one whose members were free to make whatever contracts they wished with each other, as opposed to earlier forms of society in which people inherited or were ascribed a fixed *status* defined by their kinship. This led to the idea that people had an implicit contract with themselves; they owned their selves as property over which they therefore exercised control, and aspects of which they could lend or hire out to others.

One example was the employment contract, where rather than a servant being bound to a master for life, or subordinated to the authority of a master not of their choosing, all persons were, in theory, free to negotiate whatever terms they could best secure for the temporary use of their abilities. Wage labour was formally free, even if in substance, as Marx, Weber and others were to argue, this could mean a still more powerful servitude than ever for the proletariat. Contracts could just as easily be an engine of the reproduction of subordination and substantive inequality bequeathed by status society, as a social relation that constituted equality. Nor did the reign of social contract simply mean unlimited freedom or license, a sort of polymorphous perversity of the polity. Hence Marx could argue that beneath the appearance of free and equal exchange in the labour market lay the essence of the primitive accumulation of capital, which meant that through their monopoly of ownership of the means of production, the purchasers of labour power enjoyed a systematic advantage in the terms of exchange over the sellers. As we shall see Pateman (1988) uses a similar analysis to argue that the primal rape also sets the terms of sexual exchange in universal societies in advance; behind the social contract lay this, hidden, sexual contract that created masculine and feminine individuals. Contracts could therefore still generate social relations of inequality, and also produce results which were unforeseen by the original parties to them.

The social contract theorists were concerned to work out the social preconditions of contracts, which turned upon issues of trust, that made the freedom to make individual contracts possible in the first place, but avoided civil disorder or anarchy. If the social order was not the product of natural or divine laws, then the restraints and contradictions underlying that order needed to be understood by people since they were its authors. Ignorance of how that order operated was to court the danger of swapping the miseries of its imperfections for the much greater miseries of its collapse into a state of nature or anarchy.[5] Thus only if people learned politics might they avoid the chaos and anarchy that the patriarchalists and royalists argued must inevitably result from the attempt to create a society where government and obedience was based only on consciously given consent rather than on what they imagined to be a naturally or supernaturally regulated order. Hobbes aimed to show that submission to the Leviathan of political authority paradoxically increased people's freedom by making society possible. People exchanged their fear of each other (or their fear of God) for the fear of the sovereign state power. Freud's later attempts to argue that sexuality was not simply naturally defined were made possible by the parallel attempt of Hobbes and others to argue that neither were humans 'naturally' a political animal. Like Hobbes, he was to see the sexual order as one that was socially constructed, and which made civilization possible by placing some restraints on human action (the incest taboo) and by demonstrating the limiting and disappointing choices mortals inevitably faced (the Oedipus complex).

Hitherto, all historically existing societies for which we have good evidence, had been characterized by a sexual division of labour, legitimated by what it was imagined to be natural or godly for men and women to do. This division of labour, although it took a vast variety of forms, had systematically privileged men, who characteristically enjoyed superior power, resources and status to women, and who legitimated this by claiming that they were naturally superior to women by virtue of their sex. This can be the only coherent definition of patriarchy or male sex-right, and it took the form of the rule of the father. The term patriarchy has been controversial within feminism, as Pateman argues (1988: 20), because it has been so hard to define, but dropping it would mean that 'feminist political theory would then be without the only concept that refers specifically to the subjection of women, that singles out the form of political right that all men exercise by virtue of being men.' This controversy over patriarchy can be resolved by recognizing that what we face in modern societies is no longer patriarchy itself, but its material and ideological legacy which in turn is systematically undermined by the key social relations of modernity.

Because it inherited the material and ideological legacy of the patriarchal era, modernity presented men (and women) with the novel problem of rationalizing and explaining men's greater power, resources and status without recourse to the straightforward patriarchal assertion that men's *natural* difference to women gave them a *natural* right to rule them. The concept of masculinity (and the corresponding concepts of gender and femininity) was their solution to this problem. Differences between men and women which in a pre-modern patriarchal context could have been defined as naturally determined (the result of sex) had now to be imagined as socially produced – as masculinity and femininity (the result of gender). If gender was imagined to cause the sexual division of labour, the latter could be thought of as something that was socially constructed (the result of contrasting gender identities into which men and women were socialized) and therefore compatible with a modern universalist society. Without gender, the sexual division of labour must either prove that patriarchy was an inevitable aspect of society and that natural differences between men and women *did* determine relations between them, setting limits to their social construction and change; or prove that men's claims that modern society was truly universal were bogus by demonstrating the continued existence of inequality between men and women in modernity because of their sex.

The idea that society comprised a series of contracts was developed by male theorists (such as Locke, Hobbes, Rousseau or Pufendorf) in political struggle with other men, such as Sir Robert Filmer (d. 1653), who championed the theory of 'patriarchalism': an explicit defence of the argument that relations between people could only reflect a 'natural' order which it was illusory and disastrous to attempt to transcend. As I discuss in Chapter 7, Filmer based his arguments on the proposition that generation granted dominion. By this he meant that the authority which a father exercised over an infant, which alone could secure its survival and development, formed the direct basis of the political order, through the obligation that the infant would thus later owe to its father. This was seen not just as an analogy to the relation between a king and his subjects, but its actual original form. This debate was one conducted among patriarchs about the proper social rights of patriarchs, in the sense of male heads of households. The early contract theorists were concerned, as the Declaration of Independence put it, with the rights of *man* and lived in a society, seventeenth and eighteenth-century Britain, where men enjoyed an array of rights and privileges by virtue of their *natural* sex and where status and position in the social division of labour was heavily determined by sex. Indeed the early stages of capitalism probably worsened sexual inequalities, particularly for women in wealthier households who fell victim to the development of the ideology of 'separate spheres' which drove women into the private household from more public work. But these ideas, and the social changes they represented, led to consequences, almost certainly unanticipated, of a historically revolutionary kind, whose significance is even now not appreciated sufficiently. Claims by white male slave owners for equal rights, one with another, rooted in the universalizing forces of modernity (for what else led them to think of the world in this way?) led inexorably in the longer term to the emancipation of slaves, women and people of colour.

The contract theorists faced an insurmountable problem. If social relations were constructed by contract rather than nature, how could the two sexes come to occupy such contrasting positions; why did they make such different contracts? If, in modern societies, men and women were formally equal individuals endowed with the same human rights, and possessed of the same human capacities to develop their skills and powers in different directions, form contracts and allegiances, build institutions and so on; how was it that men and women came always to have such contrasting and unequal life experiences and opportunities? Brennan and Pateman (1979: 183) point to 'a very embarrassing question, namely, why it is that a free and equal female individual should always be assumed to place herself under the authority of a free and equal male individual.' Moreover some of the key relations between them – such as the marriage contract – appeared to be anything but a contract, in that it was permanent, its terms were fixed and the relative positions of the parties to it determined by their sex, not their personal wishes.[6]

The contract theorists appeared to face an insoluble dilemma. If they argued that sexual relations were natural, and that relations between men and women were determined by nature, then they could explain and rationalize the existing sexual division of labour and its associated institutions such as marriage, the domestic authority of husbands and fathers, and the public rule of men; but at the cost of abandoning what was originally the core proposition of their theories and basis of the claim that modernity was something new, the proposition that people made societies. If a man was naturally superior to a woman, then why not also to another man, for example by virtue of being born to a particular rank?

If such superiority was simply natural this undermined the whole basis of social contract and the concept of the individual. If nature governed relations between men and women then such relations could hardly be said to be constituted by contracts made between naturally free individual persons.

On the other hand, if they stuck with their principles and declared sexual relations to be social ones, they faced the prospect of demanding an unprecedented sexual revolution and denouncing all currently existing differences in the status, experience, power or social position of women and men as the legacy of patriarchalist institutions, which it was the business of the social contracts made possible by modernity to sweep away because they were just as much illegitimate feudal relics of the old order as the divine right of kings. If all men were born free and equal, and so too were all women, there ought to be little more difference between them, on average, than the fact of possessing a male or female body. The scope of Hobbes's writings on this subject shows how far the contract theorists' imaginations were prepared to travel. In terms astonishingly reminiscent of Freud over two centuries later, he cheerfully discusses cannibalism, infanticide, contracting 'for the society of bed only' and the matriarchal societies of 'Amazons'.[7] Thus it was not some lack of originality or creativity that stalled this potential social revolution in thought. It was that another solution to the contract theorists' problems was available.

One possible solution would have been to argue that sexual relations were as much socially constructed as other relations, and that the defeat of patriarchalism would therefore eventually lead to the virtual abolition of difference between the sexes, since the contracts persons chose to make, rather than their possession of a male or female body, would henceforth determine their sexual identities or place in the social division of labour. If people in modernity really did own their persons as property, which they could dispose of as they chose, then what difference ought the sex of the body nature gave them make? I argue in the following chapters that individual thinkers such as Hobbes and Freud approached this solution and shied away from its consequences. It still haunts discussions within feminism about equality and difference. This is a solution we refuse ourselves, even today, as we increasingly acknowledge the equal 'rights' of women and men, but cling on to the conviction that the different sexes of our bodies contain the key to other, more fundamental distinctions, distinctions we imagine to be captured by concepts such as masculinity. But it is a solution which the material logic of modernity continually forces upon us 'behind our backs', even at the same time as it provides us with the means to avoid this solution by creating the concept of gender through what I call the fetishism of sexual difference. It is the solution which this book argues is the only possible logically sustainable one, but with one, crucial, qualification that contemporary sociology tends to overlook: we cannot socially construct babies.

I think it is possible to complete, in a sense, the revolution that the social contract theorists started, but which they drew back from completing. We can do so by following to its logical conclusion the proposition that relations of sexual difference too are as much social constructions as the other social 'contracts' which people make. This involves, however, recognizing, that like all other social relations they have a component that is natural, which is not subject to a purely sociological explanation, and which is rooted in the sexual genesis of human beings. It leads to a surprising conclusion: that what Connell has called 'the historical consciousness of gender' (1995: 227) is a consciousness of something that does not exist. Gender is something which we imagine to exist and which is represented to us in a material form through the existence of the two sexes male and female. It is therefore like a religious fetish, whereby an external material object comes to be endowed with powers by those who worship it. The origin of the power of a religious fetish lies in the imaginations of its worshippers, although the consequences of these imaginations can be far reaching and very real. So it is with gender. It might be seen as a fetish, the last vestige of enchantment, an attempt, in a godless and chaotic world to 'worship' sex as an anchor for social relations and thus defend men's privilege against the corrosive logic of modernity.

Seventeenth-century debates about social contracts appear at first to have little obvious relevance to the analysis of contemporary masculinity, but they are crucial for two reasons. First they laid the basis for ways of thinking about society that we find today as sociology and social constructionism. Second, because although the contract theorists hardly used the term itself, they invented the concept of masculinity, and the concept of gender, in the sense of the social construction of sexual difference which accounted for a sexual division of labour. They were forced to do so, in order to explain men's superiority to women without rooting it directly in nature, and thereby falling back upon the arguments of their patriarchalist opponents. They implied that masculinity might describe some fundamental difference between men and women. They implied that all relations between people were socially constructed with one vital exception: sexual difference. These relations, they argued, were *both* natural *and* social. If they could imagine the differences between men and women to be social in some way, as well as natural, and that it was these social differences which explained the vastly different behaviour and experience of men and women, so that they could attribute men's public power to their 'masculinity' rather than their anatomy, then the theoretical circle could be squared, as it were. The apparently patriarchal sexual division of labour could now be seen to be the result of the contrasting gender identities of men and women and, as such, to be socially constructed, not naturally determined. Of course this proposition begged the question: if gender (and masculinity) caused the sexual division of labour, what caused gender?

Like Freud, the social contract theorists found it impossible to combine a coherent theory of how society was based on the consent to the social and sexual order of the individuals comprising it, with an account of how men and women came to occupy such different places and roles in that order. Like Freud, they ultimately resorted to arguments about natural differences between men and women – and thus explanations of the social order which understood it as naturally determined – in order to solve these problems. They too thus ended up covertly accepting what they had set out to challenge: that relations between people were in fact naturally ordered. And they too had to conceal this reliance on the assertion of natural difference behind an account of how such difference was either socially constructed or expressed, in order to avoid admitting that the resort to natural sexual difference in their accounts was to return to a patriarchal explanation of society, and how it was in part still ordered by nature. Hobbes, Locke and Rousseau did not use the concept 'gender' as explicitly as Freud did but no term could describe the structure of their arguments more accurately. They were driven into its paradoxes in order to avoid a conclusion we still try to avoid today: social differences between men and women, including their relative power, status and resources are not the social expression of some natural difference between them, but the (crumbling) material and ideological legacy of a patriarchal order incompatible with modernity and universalism. Hobbes, and those who have followed him sincerely wished to defeat patriarchalism. He continually insisted, for example, that generation gave no right of dominion, because that seemed to him to lead straight to the law of the father and the divine right of kings. But he also wished to avoid what the logic of this argument inexorably led to: the defeat not only of patriarchalism but also of patriarchy and the whole edifice, established over millennia, of men's power and the divine right of men.

It has become a cliché to argue that masculinity is in crisis. But although men's privilege is under unprecedented material and ideological challenge, the briefest historical survey will show that masculinity has always been in one crisis or another (see e.g. Kimmel 1987). This is because the whole idea that men's natures can be understood in terms of their 'masculinity' arose out of a 'crisis' for all men: the fundamental incompatibility between the core principle of modernity that all human beings are essentially equal (regardless of their sex) and the core tenet of patriarchy that men are naturally superior to women and thus destined to rule over them. Insofar as we live in societies that are still marked by the material and ideological legacy of patriarchy, we still struggle (just as much in our daily lives as when we sit down to write abstract sociological theory) to reconcile two opposing and incompatible ideas: that men and women are in principle the same (that they enjoy the same human rights, are as worthy as each other, are equally capable given the appropriate opportunities and conditions of doing anything humans can do, from holding babies to holding up banks) and that they are fundamentally different (that in addition to their complementary reproductive capacities, they have selves, identities or personalities, whether formed by nature or society, which develop in dramatically contrasting ways and which explain the existence of a far reaching sexual division of labour).

We are used to thinking of gender as a radical and progressive concept, because of its emphasis on the *social* construction of masculinity and femininity, which appears to point us towards arguments about how they might be reconstructed or transcended, and the oppression of women thereby challenged, diminished or ended. But we often forget, in doing so, that this progressive result only follows if we swing over to the *natural* dimension of the concept to explain how masculinity contributes to the oppression of women by men, not 'feminines' by 'masculines', were there such things. Thus, for example, it is sometimes argued that men's instrumentalism, a greater commitment to a career in the public sphere and cultivation of the sorts of skills required to pursue that – a certain competitive-ness and ruthlessness perhaps – enables them to dominate public achievement, power and resources, compared to women, who have been socialized into expres-siveness and a commitment to intimacy and the nurturance of infants. Such arguments tell us nothing about men and women, however, unless we can show how only males must become masculine.

Here lies the essence of the problem with the concept of gender, because this swing can be used just as logically and in an equally empirically valid way to argue that claims that women are oppressed are misconceived because gender arrangements merely socially express a sexual difference which is ultimately natural. If all women are expressive, their femininity reflects some fundamental difference to men, such that direct comparisons to them are meaningless. The complementary power, resources and status that women pursue in the private sphere or reproduction may be seen as equal or superior to that found in the production of 'children of the mind' erected by men in the public sphere: men consumed by 'womb envy' (Sayers 1992: 100–106) and privately or uncon-sciously oppressed by the puniness of their public endeavour compared to the reproductive power of women. This is because the concept of gender, in the sense of the social expression of natural difference, does not have its origin in the attempt to challenge and undermine sexual inequality through demonstrating that it is socially constructed, but, on the contrary, was invented to *defend* the fact of sexual inequality on the basis that it *was* socially constructed, through the gender iden-tities of the men and women who made society, and thus was consistent with a modern society which claimed to have left patriarchy behind.

Modernity, mortality and psychic security

Through the processes of bureaucratization, 'the rule of offices not men', the rise of the market and its impersonality, commoditization and rationalization, modern-ity continually confronts members of a society with the recognition that they themselves are responsible for making society. This 'disenchantment' produces a tremendous challenge to what Giddens (1991) has termed 'ontological security', because individuals are more aware of the extent to which they are themselves the authors of the societies they inhabit and the identities they possess. Before modernity individuals could project such psychic insecurity and anxiety about their mortal fate onto God or nature, along with their powers of social construc-tion, or to put it another way, their responsibility for making history. They could imagine God to be the author of their identity, or an expert on how they must live to give their lives meaning in the face of their mortality. They could take this as far as imagining that just as their lives were ultimately only an expression of

God's greater and ultimately unfathomable purpose, so might they also escape the terrors of death and enjoy a life after it.

Members of a modern society can accept the consolations of religion or nature only as a matter of choice, which must to some extent be conscious. They can choose to project the meaning of their lives onto God, or to imagine that their beliefs and behaviour are caused by their natures and their natural differences one with another, but it is less easy to hide this choice from themselves and pretend that they are not in any way the authors of their own destiny. They are forced to be more ingenious with this process of hiding; they must as it were hide from the hiding – forget that they have chosen to forget. They must become neurotic. One side of such awareness is freedom, but its obverse is what Kundera (1984) accurately called 'the unbearable lightness of being' or what Phillips (1995) describes as the realization that there are terrors but no experts. As Weeks puts it (1995: 33) 'We have no choice but to choose' how we live, and take responsibility for it, knowing that there are no experts who can prove to us how we must do so, and knowing too that as mortal beings, our choices are always limited and disappointing, that our awareness of and control over ourselves can never be complete, and that one day our bodies will die. In a sense we are condemned to responsibility without power, together with an increased awareness of the implications of our sexual origins for our mortality. I wish to argue that as sacred forms of escape from this awareness have become less feasible, the fetishism of religion (whereby people projected their existential anxiety onto God and dealt with it through their imagined relationship to Him) has been replaced by the fetishism of sex, whereby existential anxiety is often dealt with by projecting it onto sexual difference, imagined as gender.

In the face of what Weber (1930: 104) called 'unprecedented inner loneliness' we search for some guarantee or anchor of what we truly are, for what we can imagine to be our 'authentic' nature. An obvious candidate for this is our sex as either a male or female. In turn, if we can then imagine our expression of this sex to be something we ourselves construct, as our gender identity, we can imagine that we take control of it again. If we imagine ourselves as persons to be entirely the products of socialization, to be nothing but social constructions, we can imagine that our ability to reconstruct ourselves is limitless. We can imagine that, like societies, we might live forever, or at least, find ways to stay socially 'forever young'. By projecting aspects of our psychic insecurity, rooted in our mortality, on to what we come to imagine are the complimentary characteristics of men and women (understood in terms of instrumentality and expressiveness, or independence and dependence) we can project some of our responsibility for our lives, and our mortality, onto others. This is why sex has become the secular religion of disenchanted modernity, dominating all aspects of its culture, and gender the chief means of hiding from the psychic terrors of mortality. As I hope to show below, this is why claims about the essence of masculinity or femininity often turn into fantasies about immortality. The mysteries of the orgasm have become the antidote to the demands of the increasingly dense and complex social relations of modernity, not only in the pages of lifestyle magazines, but also in classic sociological theory.[8] What this overlooks is our sexual genesis, and that is why we overlook it. What we 'truly are', as the offspring of our parents, are mortal individuals who must ourselves find the meaning of our inexorably finite lives, while also learning to accept that our identity is not something we can ever fully control.

Defining masculinity

> There is only one complete unblushing male in America: a young, married, white, urban, northern, heterosexual Protestant father of college education, fully employed, of good complexion, weight, and height, and recent record in sports.
>
> (Goffman 1963: 128)

Let me illustrate these abstract ideas with a concrete illustration. I have conducted an exercise several times where I invite students, individually or in groups, to set down what they imagine the essence of masculinity to be. This list must describe some aspect of social reality, since it is easy to get students and others to produce such a list, and the degree of consistency in the kind of list that is produced each time is great. Terms such as hard, aggressive, strong, dominant, remote, powerful, fearful of intimacy, rational, unemotional, competitive, sexist and their synonyms crop up regularly. Similarly, Craib (1987: 723–4) surveys literature on masculinity, male roles and identity and concludes:

> The qualities of masculinity, however, seem invariable, and are associated with the male as breadwinner, provider, worker, the active and public half of the species: a man is strong, aggressive, rational, independent, task orientated, invulnerable and successful (O'Neill 1982). Such qualities are listed whether the work is based on attitude surveys or whether it is theoretically derived, whether it is concerned with identifying a cultural stereotype, a sex or gender role or the male identity – a man's sense of himself.

Such a list of qualities seems to be what Bob Connell (1987, 1995) has in mind when he uses the term 'hegemonic masculinity', although significantly, he nowhere attempts an empirical definition. It is not hard to see why, for as my students produce these lists they usually also point out immediately that this list is stereotypical and does not correspond fully to any actually existing man they know. They also concede (and I think it can be easily proved) that none of these qualities can only be possessed by men and that many women have demonstrated them too; discussion usually promptly turns to Margaret Thatcher.

Harry Christian (1994) tries to define hegemonic masculinity by a set of male chauvinist attitudes which boil down to a belief in an innate difference between instrumental, violent men and expressive nurturant women, belief in the natural superiority of the former to run the public world and rule the private one, and a belief that sex is the only non-demeaning way for men to be intimate with women, which in turn implies that sexual intimacy is about power as much as pleasure. He himself comments that his list is 'somewhat stereotypical'. Interestingly Craib (1994a) cites a similar list of features to describe what might have been seen as 'manly' half a century ago, and suggests of analyses of masculinity:

> it is striking this work shares a conception of masculinity with work that pre-dates modern feminism (Carrigan *et al.* 1987). The difference lies in the evaluation. Whereas masculine qualities were once seen as normal and good they are now seen as politically and morally wrong, as perhaps in crisis, and as damaging for all concerned.
>
> (Craib 1987: 724)

We can all recognize such lists of features. We can also recognize that there is a significant difference between such lists and any empirical men we might know. Being a biological male not only does not confer masculinity in this sense, but also cannot do so! The qualities contained in such lists are sufficiently contradictory to make living them out in any consistent way impossible, a point that both Segal and Horrocks make eloquently, discussing the example of one icon of hegemonic masculinity: Ernest Hemingway (Segal 1990: 111–14, Horrocks 1994: 91–5). At best lists of such traits represent tendencies and possibilities that individuals have more or less access to at different points in time, and coexist in an uneasy and messy alliance. Any empirical individual's identity is always complex and contradictory, rather than something that can be defined by any list of qualities no matter how comprehensive or carefully defined. Were it otherwise it would no longer be an identity. It would have lost that element of agency or subjectivity that enables us to think of it as one. Bullies reveal themselves as cowards, Popeye discovers the delights of Swee'pea, the assertively independent crave affection and intimacy. Brain can coexist with brawn and both with compassion, sensitivity and a capacity for emotional intimacy. Nor need they have any direct connection with having a male or female body – which is what a century of 'sex difference' research has been telling us.

Freud famously commented that 'the concepts of "masculine" and "feminine" . . . are amongst the most confused that occur in science' (1986: 355n). We could add the concept of gender as well. There is a good reason why these are confused and difficult concepts. If we use them to describe properties of persons, masculinity, femininity and gender describe something that cannot logically exist. This leads to three interrelated questions, which the rest of this book tries to answer.

1 Why is it that masculinity is an obvious concept which must therefore have a real social existence (so that people can readily produce lists of what it comprises and these lists are remarkably consistent), yet is incapable of any precise empirical definition, such that people will reject these same lists as useful or accurate descriptions of empirically existing men? How is masculinity at once so familiar and yet so obscure? This raises the question of what masculinity is.
2 What is male about masculinity? The category male is a natural or biological one: having a penis or possession of testes which produce sperm, or fertilize

eggs, the potential ability to father a child, rather than possess ovaries or produce eggs, the potential ability to mother one. The category masculine is a social, historical one. Were it not so, masculine would not be a separate category from male. But if this is the case, what association with sex can the social characteristics imagined to define masculinity have? Why should males rather than females monopolize masculinity, or putting the same question another way: how can gender be imagined to be a function of sex?

3 So far as we have available historical evidence, men have always had greater power, resources and status, on average, than women; this remains true in contemporary industrial capitalist society. This has usually been termed 'patriarchy'. But what has been the basis of men's power? If this basis is social it is difficult to explain how only biological males have access to it, and it is used to rule over females. Thus, explanations in terms of masculinity must explain how only men can become masculine, or alternatively, why patriarchy does not take the form of the rule of masculines (regardless of sex) over feminines (regardless of sex) and how, under such circumstances, anyone would choose to be feminine. How is it that a system which does not depend on biological differences nevertheless leads to the oppression of one biological sex by the other? If the basis is not social but biological (for example the argument that men have a biologically determined ability to rape women which is the ultimate basis of their power), so that we can explain why it is men rather than 'masculines' who have benefited from patriarchy, it is difficult to imagine how patriarchy could ever be abolished, and equally difficult to explain how modernity has undermined it to any extent. Yet compared even to 50 years ago, let alone two centuries ago, men in contemporary industrial capitalist societies have few public rights, if any, which they enjoy by virtue of their sex.

We can think of this dilemma in terms of the penis and the phallus. If it is possession of a penis that underpins patriarchy, we have a good explanation of why it has hitherto always been men who have exercised power over women, but little scope for explaining how that power, as an aspect of a natural difference between men and women, could be brought to an end. Penises are 'transhistorical' or natural. But if it is the phallus that underpins patriarchy, as symbolic representative of a socially or historically created structure that gives power to men, we have a good explanation of how it could be brought to an end as a function of a social structure which men and women have created, but little scope for explaining why and how men have hitherto exercised power over women; why could women not get their hands on the phallus; what basis does the phallus have in sex?

Sexual genesis and sexual difference

Modernity thus posed some especially puzzling problems. It drove people towards imagining gender as something that was social, but which corresponded to natural categories. It drove them towards finding a new refuge from ontological insecurity as rationalization undermined that provided by religion. Finally it drove men towards demonstrating what masculinity might comprise that was not natural, yet explained men's monopoly of power, resources and status. These solutions depended upon a systematic confusion of sexual *difference* with sexual *genesis*, such that what are in reality issues of the natural generation of individuals (about the relationship between parents and infants) have been displaced onto issues of social differences between sexes (about the social production of 'masculine' and 'feminine' from male and female). We have come to systematically confuse what results from us all being born *of* a man *and* a woman with what results from us all being born *as* a man *or* a woman, so that the natural limits to our social identities come to appear to be the fact that we are all born of one sex or another, rather than being set by the inexorable fact that we are the products of biological sexual reproduction. We enter the world as helpless, socially incapable infants, utterly dependent on our carers, and having thus entered it, can come to participate in it as conscious individuals only on condition that we become aware that we have no choice but to leave it some day. Given that the legitimation of patriarchy has always depended on claiming that men are more fully human, or more highly developed than women, it is unsurprising that the concept of masculinity should ultimately rest on an equation between the position of women and children. For patriarchal ideology, women must be condemned to eternal infancy. The confusion between sexual difference and sexual genesis has not therefore been an historical error, but has been the necessary product of the conflict between the legacy of patriarchy and the ideological and material forces of universalism. The rest of this chapter thus considers the significance of sexual genesis, because it is systematically overlooked by modern social science, for reasons I explore further in Chapter 2. That chapter also discusses the confusion of sexual difference and sexual genesis as the key to analysing the fetishism of gender in transitional societies, while Chapter 3 examines the inexorable crisis which modernity produces for patriarchy.

Sexual genesis: attachment, individuation and the capacity to be alone

> I think we must start with the recognition that *in the beginning there is the body*. As soon as the body is mentioned the specter of biological determinism raises its head and sociologists draw back in fright. And certainly their view of man is sufficiently disembodied and non-materialistic to satisfy Bishop Berkeley, as well as being de-sexualized enough to please Mrs. Grundy.
>
> (Wrong 1961: 129)

It is all too easy in social theory to think first in terms of production (in the sense of the symbolic and material dimensions of the societies people inhabit) and only second in terms of reproduction (in the sense of where the people who inhabit them come from – both socially and biologically). We find it easier to think about democracy than parenthood in grand terms, to focus on workers' control rather than where babies come from or how to bring them up. This is a perspective that it is often useful to rever_e, however, to ask 'how do societies ensure the reproduction of the kind of persons they require to function?'

The sexual genesis of individuals is the process whereby helpless, dependent infants arrive originally as products of nature, sexually produced by a father and a mother and fused with them, but come to develop into relatively autonomous selves with a distinct identity, capable of forming social relations with others and constructing societies. This process of 'generation' addresses the problem of the natural limits to social construction by analysing how the production of independent selves, persons who comprise societies and can make social relations with one another, is possible in the first place. It centres on the inevitable natural difference between infants and adults. I suggest that it is best understood by the concept of 'attachment', that it forms the basis for distinguishing a 'private' from a 'public' sphere, that such a sphere is what makes societies or politics possible, and that it might best be understood in terms of the fundamental distinction between persons and societies. The identity of any self that emerges from this process can only ever be understood as a combination of contradictory potential capacities (such as love and hate, empathy and independence), whose expression and management comprise the stuff of life, the inevitably anxious biography of a self conscious of its vulnerability and mortality.

Attachment

As Dinnerstein notes, the length of human infancy can be seen as a biological solution to the evolutionary problem of the reproduction of creatures combining a brain large enough to think with a pelvis narrow enough to walk; the solution was for humans to be born at a relatively early stage of their development (1987: 16ff.). This infant need for prolonged physical and emotional nurturance has come to be seen by theorists such as Bowlby (1951, 1971, 1975, 1981) in terms of 'attachment'. By this I understand a need which human infants have for close physical and emotional contact with another human being without which the infant's survival and development of a sense of self is not possible. The nature of this link is perhaps best expressed in its purest form by Winnicott (1975: xxxvii) when he argues that it is not possible to think of a baby except in relation to its carer; a baby on its own could not, by definition, exist. This need has both symbolic and biological dimensions and may be strongest in infancy but it is far from obvious that it is ever completely transcended. If we accept the existence of such a need, for which there seems to be compelling empirical evidence, then I think we must accept that babies do not enter the world as selves ready to be appropriately socialized, that they become so only in relation to their adult carer(s) and that this relation therefore has two characteristics. While it takes a social form, it is inexorably naturally determined; it cannot be transcended. Second, it is unlike other social relations, in so far as one party to it is, in a sense, not social to begin with. On the contrary attachment is about the production of persons who can become capable of social relations, or making societies, in the first place.

We need not be concerned with the precise empirical mechanisms of the attachment process, only with accepting the analytical point that without some such process human development from infancy to maturity is unthinkable. Babies are inevitably dependent on adults, cannot develop without them, and the nature of the relationship between them cannot be imagined in terms of an 'exchange' or two sided contract or conscious relation. It makes sense to see it as in some part 'natural' in the sense that although we might imagine its form changing, it must always exist, in the sense that infants start out as the bio-logical product of their parents. It is impossible to describe the attachment rela-tion between an infant and its carer in terms of social contracts of the kind that Hobbes imagined society to comprise. The definition of an infant is a person who does not yet have a fully formed self that it is possible for them to possess. They have no 'I' that relates to a 'me', and in so far as they develop this, they do so in relation to their carer(s). Babies cannot make contracts. In Hirschmann's (1970) terms they cannot 'exit'. They certainly have 'voice' but they have almost no power to compel their carer(s) to listen. They have no choice but loyalty, and loyalty to a relationship whose terms are almost exclusively determined by their carer(s).

This distinction between the kind of relations that exist on the one hand between infants and carers and on the other hand between adults, defines the distinction between a private and public sphere. The family, as a site for both genesis and attachment, must exist in any imaginable society; it is part of the inevitable social context of reproduction, so inevitable that it is difficult to think of it as social. It is difficult to imagine a society except as a system whereby individuals emerge in a family of origin and proceed to form a family of destiny. This need not determine the form the family must take, however. It is perfectly clear, for example, that men can satisfy attachment needs as well as women, that 'social' parents can satisfy them as well as genitors or genitrices, and that one parent can do the job as well as two. It is far from certain that only the same parent over long periods of time can provide enough security, though we might have many grounds for suspecting this to be the case. It is also clear that attach-ment must have a fundamentally ambivalent character, in that to work properly it must also contain the seeds of its own destruction. Secure attachments have to be a base from which to venture forth, not an alternative to the exigencies of life 'outside'. We might think of such a process as the genesis or the development of individuals conscious of their difference one from another and thus able to relate to each other to form societies – a process of how they come to possess what we might call an identity, self, subjectivity, agency or personality, which at the same time is how they come to be a distinguishable objectivity, something that can be acted upon, or occupy a social structure. The development of a new and separ-ate self out of the infant begotten by two parents is one of the emergence of independence out of dependence, the evolution of what Winnicott (1965a) has described as 'the capacity to be alone'.

The capacity to be alone: individuation, envy and mortality

Paradoxically this capacity can only be produced by faith in the non-intrusive presence of other(s) and some minimal security of the environment made possible by the primary carer(s) for an infant.[9] It is impossible, I suspect, to think of this relationship in terms of self interest. It implies, by definition, some concern or love for the infant on the part of the adult, which cannot be explained by any certain hope of present or future return. Any power we might imagine the infant to have within the attachment relationship (and any parents of young children will testify to the magnitude of this power – particularly at 5 in the morning) is a function of the desire of its parent(s) to have it survive, to prioritize its interests above their own in some way. One way of seeing this is as a gift across generations. The essence of this gift is that, in a democratic society, nothing is expected in return.

Another way of seeing this, paradoxically, is as the fundamental meaning of the incest taboo. Only if such a taboo exists, is the intense attachment ambivalent enough for the infant ultimately to become independent of its family of origin. Without this social independence it is difficult to imagine much psychological independence, or the emergence of a self as we would recognize it. Thus love, if we take this as the essence of attachment, is the basis of the need for the prohibition of its sexual expression (between parents and children) through the incest taboo. Attachment thus expresses some basic connectedness between persons we imagine to be individuals without which society is not possible and which expresses a 'natural' fact about society: not that there is a 'natural' biological connection between carer and infant (though that might also exist) but that infants are born incapable of forming societies or caring for themselves; they must thus be born into societies and acquire this.[10]

This process of attachment and the development of a capacity to be alone could also be seen as at the boundary of the natural and the social, in the sense of describing how infants as natural products of sexual reproduction become social actors. Human society is inexorably a mixture of the cultural and the natural, what Giddens (1991) calls the existential contradiction. It is cultural in that our symbolism is potentially infinite. We can remember persons and societies that no longer exist, and imagine our alternative future possibilities. Civilization, in this sense, has emancipated itself from the brute routine of nature. We can imagine that we take responsibility for what we do. We are conscious of 'time–space distanciation' in societies. We can imagine a time in the past when we have not existed, and foresee a time in the future when society will abandon us. It is natural in that our experience of society is contained within our carnal, mortal bodies and inevitably finite in both time and space. Just as we could not choose whether to be born, so neither can we avoid our death (nor others do this for us), nor can we ever choose our parents or be anyone other than who we are. There is a boundary between our own self and those of others. Being one living individual implies not being another one. Living in any meaningful way requires some consciousness of this boundary, and being conscious of it is synonymous with being conscious of our mortality, though it is doubtful if it is ever possible to become fully or perfectly aware or conscious of it, and much of our pleasure in life may come from imagining that it is not really there, or denying its existence.

Paradoxically this boundary must also be permeable, in so far as our existence is only possible in the presence of others, and predicated on our ability (no matter how impossible in any complete sense) to enter imaginatively into their inner life world. Two phrases of Winnicott's catch the terms of this contradiction well: 'A sign of health in the mind is the ability of one individual to enter imaginatively and accurately into the thoughts and feelings and hopes and fears of another person; also to allow the other person to do the same to us' (quoted in Phillips 1988: 12–13); 'Yet it is a hallmark of madness when adults put too powerful a claim on the credulity of others, forcing them to acknowledge a sharing of illusion that is not their own' (Winnicott 1975: 231). Thus envy of difference, combined with the ability to tolerate it, is an inevitable product of our sexual genesis, developed via attachment, into a capacity to be alone that can never be complete, and can only be developed in the presence of others. Yet only those who have developed such a capacity, or something like it, have the ego-strength to let others alone too. They have the capacity to be alone in the sense of not having to insist neurotically on other people adjusting their identities in order to make their own one bearable. The 'existential contradiction' means that any living being faces a continual struggle to balance the conflicting pull of independence and dependence, knowing that no final 'balance' as such is possible. Phillips (1989) argues that the problems often start when we imagine that life could be anything other than a mess. We get stuck on the fantasies of what a messless life would comprise rather than appreciating its messiness and making real choices. He suggests that we all face a paradox of learning how to organize our lives and plan for the future, even as we know that life and the future is something which ultimately cannot be fully planned for and is valuable and nourishing to the extent that this is the case. We can create meaning for ourselves even knowing that there can be no final meaning to discover. The capacity to be alone thus has another, terrible, paradox: we reach a final state of aloneness only with our deaths.

Sexual genesis and social construction

This process is one that every mortal who has ever existed on the planet has experienced, but each mortal's experience of this process has been unique. Much of its uniqueness, what we might think of as the raw material of identity, is how each individual and its carers negotiate, consciously and unconsciously, the ambivalences of attachment and the incest taboo. These ambivalences are well caught by the contrast between expressiveness and instrumentalism, in so far as they describe the contradictory pull of dependence and independence, aggression and compassion, and the inexorable presence of each side of these antinomies in the other. Each mortal self must find some meaning in its existence and take responsibility for it, in the knowledge that there can be no final meaning and that responsibility here does not confer power, in part because as products of sexual genesis, we must by definition possess an unconscious. Any real, as opposed to imagined, life must be in large part one of limit, lack and disappointment (Craib 1994a). If the positive side of liberty is that I can be myself, its negative side is that that is all I can be, and I can never be totally sure of what that is. Logically, the essence of our identity is that which we cannot identify about ourselves.

If this process can never be complete, the infant's emergence as a social being cannot erase its sexual genesis entirely. To some extent it will only ever be possible for it to be alone in the presence of others. One result of this is that all social relations must have an element of attachment, and therefore of unconscious desire. To some extent, any adult who was once an infant must remain unconscious of the roots of their desires and motivations. They cannot simply choose how to feel, or how to reshape or reinterpret their self or its meaning in the world. They might imagine their self as a powerful self, but it could never actually become one. In other words they will have an identity, or aspect of their self (what Winnicott referred to as the 'true' self) that lies beyond social construction. Winnicott (1965a) expressed this most forcefully when he suggested that the core of the 'true' self is that which lies beyond communication not just of others but ourselves. We might think of it as the part that Winston Smith in *Nineteen Eighty-Four* (Orwell 1949) cannot change by some effort of will, in order to love Big Brother rather than merely obey, no matter how strongly he might desire to. It is the part that Weber described in terms of fate (Gane 1993), which it can only be human to endure, precisely because we are only human, such that we can neither deny our experience of it, nor simply demand some right to act out, nor yet obey some social obligation to experience it only in a socially acceptable way. It is that part of the 'I' of ourselves which were it to be understood and brought within our consciousness, could no longer be the 'I', but would have become part of the 'me'.

It might be thought that this aspect of the self, produced by sexual genesis and lying beyond social construction presents some qualification to the claims of modern society to be socially constructed by the persons who comprise it. On the contrary, it is this which makes it possible in the first place. Were it possible to think of the personal as constructed entirely by the political, persons could be unproblematically subordinated to the demands of society – what Dennis Wrong (1961) criticized as the 'oversocialized conception of man'. The process of rationalization, bureaucratization or the general law of capitalist accumulation, could have no limits. Winston Smith could be taught not only to obey Big Brother, but to love him too. It is because there is an inevitable distance between the personal and the political that the political is possible. The core of our identity, and its only definition, is that it comprises what we cannot, ourselves, identify about it. Dreams might be the royal road to the unconscious, but it is the latter, through the way in which it represents an inevitable distance between the personal and the political that is the royal road to democracy.

However, this recognition has been obscured by the fetishism of gender, which has systematically overlooked the sexual genesis of persons, in order to legitimate the survival of a patriarchal sexual division of labour in modernity, and to avoid the challenge to psychic security that the recognition of sexual genesis implies. It is to the analysis of this process that I now turn.

Notes

1 Quoted by Pateman (1988: 90).
2 This is true both for the men's movement sympathetic to feminism (my impression is that most supporters have feminist partners) and those hostile to it (comprising men angry that feminist achievements have diminished the privileges they previously took for granted).
3 I use the term ideology here in the sense used by Marx (1976).
4 The potential lines of cause and effect between the three developments are complex and controversial, but they have no direct bearing on the argument I wish to pursue here.
5 See the useful discussion in Zvesper (1985: 29–30).
6 Pateman (1988) has an excellent discussion of the marriage contract.
7 Lesbian separatists might enjoy this account from *Leviathan* (1651):

> We find in History that the *Amazons* Contracted with the Men of the neighbouring Countries, to whom they had recourse for issue, that the issue Male should be sent back, but the Female remain with themselves: so that the dominion of the Females was in the Mother.
>
> (Hobbes 1991: 140)

8 See my discussion of Weber and Giddens on pp. 36–8 below.
9 Carol Gilligan (1982: 63) is getting at the same idea, I think, when she argues that 'we know ourselves as separate only in so far as we live in connection with others, and that we experience relationships only in so far as we differentiate other from self.'
10 Thus I think Giddens (1976), for example, is mistaken in *New Rules of Sociological Method* in so far as he assumes that persons are skilled and knowledgeable members of society; this begs the crucial question of how they become so, given that the educator must be educated.

2

The fetishism of sexual difference and its secret

His mind slid away into the labyrinthine world of doublethink. To know and not to know, to be conscious of complete truthfulness while telling carefully constructed lies, to hold simultaneously two opinions which cancelled out, knowing them to be contradictory and believing in both of them; to use logic against logic, to repudiate morality while laying claim to it, to believe that democracy was impossible and that the Party was the guardian of democracy; to forget whatever it was necessary to forget, then to draw it back into memory again at the moment when it was needed, and then promptly to forget it again: and above all, to apply the same process to the process itself. That was the ultimate subtlety: consciously to induce unconsciousness, and then once again, to become unconscious of the act of hypnosis you had just performed. Even to understand the word 'doublethink' involved the use of doublethink.

(Orwell 1949: 31–2)

Gender: Contradictory ideology of a transitional era

My argument, then, is that masculinity, along with the complementary concepts of femininity and gender, can only be understood as ideological mechanisms that are the product of a very specific set of historical circumstances: an era in which men and women attempt to reconcile two quite contradictory views about the significance of their biological sex. These are that all men and women are fundamentally equal (so that, for example, as citizens, consumers or employees they may enjoy formally equal rights and treatment, and have their sex disregarded; or are free to choose to construct their identities and lead their lives in whatever way they may aspire to) and that men and women, as two naturally different sexes, are fundamentally different (so that even in a context of formal equality of rights and opportunities, men and women will end up doing different things, or having contrasting beliefs or feelings, because of their sex; or that their gender identity, their masculinity and femininity will ultimately depend upon their sex).

For masculinity and femininity to have anything to do with sex (rather than simply comprise a list of social capacities which could be associated with either sex) and thus be capable of explaining the sexual division of labour or nature of the marriage contract for example, there had to be something specifically male about masculinity, and female about femininity. There had to be a mechanism, natural or social, which rendered males masculine. In order to maintain the integrity of social contract theory, however, gender had to be something quite distinct from sex – something social rather than natural. Only if both men and women could develop masculinity and femininity, was there any point in making the distinction in the first place. Males had to be allowed their feminine sides, in theory at any rate, or the character of masculinity and femininity had to be historically mutable. Masculinity had, in theory, to be imaginable as lists of empirical characteristics (such as strength, aggression or rationality) that were not inherently connected with sexual difference (such as possession of testes or ovaries) but which nevertheless could be seen as 'expressing' it.

The concept of gender thus implied being able to hold two diametrically opposed beliefs at once: that masculinity (and its counterpart femininity) was socially constructed (and thus in theory constructable by members of either sex) and that it was naturally determined (so that there was a special connection between masculinity and being male). Without both sides of this paradox the concept of masculinity does not work. Without the first masculinity collapses back into maleness, without the second it loses all connection to sex at all. This paradox is routinely expressed in the way most uses of the term casually and unself-consciously slip between discussion of 'masculinity' and analysis of empirically existing men. We can think that men and women are fundamentally similar and therefore enjoy equal social rights and socially construct those relations that exist between them, and that men and women are naturally different (although the nature of this difference remains obscure) which explains the continued existence of a division of labour so strongly marked by sex, and our ability to think of social capacities (of the sort regularly described in terms of masculinity and femininity) as organized in terms of sex.

This created the problem of explaining how this social production of gender identity nevertheless corresponded to natural categories: how males became masculine, and how females became feminine; or what we might think of as the 'origin' of gender. It also created the problem of specifying what the 'content' of gender comprised: of how social capacities could be linked to biological categories. This required a process that linked the 'natural' in the sense of sexual difference (male/female) to the 'social' in the sense of gender identity. Moreover this socialization process had to be both natural in the sense of confronting every boy and girl in the same way on the basis of their sex, yet social and conscious enough to be seen as a product of culture to avoid collapsing masculine and feminine straight back into male and female, to allow gender identity to change historically over time (both for persons and societies) and to allow men and women both their masculine and feminine sides. The essence of gender was that it was *both* social *and* natural, being represented as either as the need arose.

The socially constructed self and the denial of sexual genesis

We do but flatter ourselves, if we hope ever to be governed without an arbit-rary power.
(Sir Robert Filmer, *The Anarchy of a Mixed or Limited Monarchy*, in Sommerville 1991: 132)

Nature hath given to every one a right to all.
(Hobbes 1651/1983: 47)

The revolution in human thought that the seventeenth-century theorists cre-ated faced two further problems concerning sex. The first was that the origins of individual members of society in sexual reproduction appeared to give nature a continuing and important role despite the claims of the contract theorists that relations between people were governed by contract. Men and women might 'contract' with each other to decide to have a child, but the process of sexual reproduction itself was a thoroughly 'natural' one; people might make society, but nature, as it were, made the people. Unless denied, this natural boundary set by sexual genesis to human social relationships appeared to threaten the whole theory of those who argued that society issued from the contracts men and women made. This was because their opponents, the patriarchalists, who argued that social relationships were best seen as a reflection of relations determined by nature and ordained by God, could and did seize on any qualification to the idea that men and women were born free and equal as proof that it was indeed qualities inherent in nature that formed the basis of what were only apparently social relationships. The *natural* relationship between father and son formed the basis for all other social relationships; for example, a subject might owe his sovereign that same obedience, rooted in his dependence on him, that an infant naturally and inevitably owed its father.

The patriarchalists pointed out that it was hard to conceive of relations be-tween infants and parents in the same terms as relations between adults. If men were *born* free and equal, as the social contract theorists claimed, then even the youngest infant ought to enjoy equal political rights with adults. It was useless to argue, as the contract theorists did, that infants could be protected by parents until they matured, because the rationale for such protection implied recogniz-ing the very inequality of abilities and rights in nature that the patriarchalists claimed formed the natural basis of the whole social order in the first place. A second criticism was that in a social order governed by contract and thus the pursuit of self interest, rather than subordination to the laws of God or nature, it was very difficult to explain how it would be in anyone's interest to contract with another to produce a baby. Such production was bound to imply various costs and obligations in order to nurture an infant. Indeed these costs and obligations were likely to be very substantial, and were the infants to become free to pursue their independent interests on reaching maturity, there could be no guarantee of any return to the parents. The contract theorists attempted to escape this problem in various unconvincing ways which all fell foul of the problem that any return to the parents depended on some obligation towards them on the part of their children, which must again form exactly that 'natural' power relation between child and father that the patriarchalists argued was the original basis of the entire social order.

The patriarchalists had identified a crucial weak link in the contract theorists' logic. Because the latter focused on the social construction of society, and thus the natural equality of human beings, imagining them as *tabulae rasae*, they ignored nature, in the sense of the biological sexual reproduction of individual members of the species as infants, which was also central to the making of society through supplying people to inhabit it. They ignored the issue of sexual genesis or generation, the question of the relationship between parent and infant that it posed, and the implications of the natural limits to social processes which the sexual reproduction of members of society as persons suggested. In order to confront the claim that nature was everything, the contract theorists tended to end up arguing that nature was nothing and socialization was all. They threw out the natural origins of babies along with the patriarchal bath water. In doing so they laid the foundations of contemporary social constructionism in modern social science, together with its focus on socialization as the concept which explains the development of identity by infants, and its tendency to deny nature any role, to the extent that the latter can come to be seen as determined or constituted by culture. I argued above that modern psychic insecurity encourages us to imagine our selves as entirely social constructions that we might therefore remodel at will. The social contract theorists thus also provided a model of how to think of the self in this way.

Natural sexual genesis and social sexual difference

The solution of the contract theorists was to root the natural limits to the social order in the existence of sexual difference rather than the fact of sexual genesis, and to use this to suggest that sexual difference formed a natural limit to the scope of social relations governed by contract. They swapped the two dimensions of human sexual dimorphism one with the other, and called the result (although they did not use the word) *gender*. They displaced the issue of the sexual origins of human beings, which appeared to give nature a role in the construction of social relationships, onto the issue of sexual difference – the fact that there were two sexes. Henceforth it would be the existence of two sexes and the (unspecified) differences that existed between them which would be seen as setting natural limits to society, by limiting the kind of social contracts that men and women could make because they were different sexes. Generation was confused with sexual dimorphism. At first sight this might look like escaping the frying pan of sexual genesis for the fire of sexual status. If nature determined the different social positions of men and women by limiting the kinds of contracts they were capable of making this seemed to indicate a retreat back to patriarchalism. This was even more the case if these natural differences essentially concerned male superiority, whether this was expressed in terms of rationality, strength, aggression or capacity for sexual violence.

However, were the essential differences between men and women to be imagined to be *socially* constructed or expressed, even if they *related* to their natural sexual difference, then the idea that society was made by people through contracts could be preserved. The character of the people making these contracts, and the sort of contracts they would seek to make, would not depend on their natural sex itself, but *the social expression of it*. To think in terms of the contracts which males and females could make was to return to the language of patriarchalism. But to think in terms of what it was possible for *masculine* and *feminine* individuals to do was another matter, if this masculinity and femininity could be thought of as something other than a natural, biological or anatomical fixed essence. Thus were born the concepts of masculine, feminine and gender.

If men and women made contracts not as males and females, but as individuals who were masculine and feminine, and this masculinity and femininity were themselves social and historical constructs, themselves products of 'contracts' in some way – for example through the socialization of infants – then the principle of social contract could be reconciled with the facts of sexual inequality and difference. To use the language of Carole Pateman (1988), an invisible *sexual contract* was placed behind the visible social contract. The trick was to make this invisible contract both natural and social, and in so far as it was natural obscure the fact that it was anything but a contract at all. No one can choose or 'contract' to obtain a male or female body, but we are comfortable with the idea that we might 'choose' to develop or renounce our 'masculinity' or 'femininity'. Through this second step in the argument, from sexual difference to gender, the contract theorists established a confusion in thought that has lasted down to the contemporary period, and which, in a sense, the whole of this book explores; *gender* has been systematically confused with *generation*.

This confusion could also provide a defence against the terrors of unprecedented inner loneliness if it were now imagined that natural limits to the self were not set by sexual genesis but by sexual difference. Were this difference imagined as gender, as the antinomies of instrumentalism and expressiveness, this could provide a core for the identity: a naturally determined relief from the unbearable lightness of being. Instead of developing to the full the capacity to be alone, people could imagine themselves to become masculine and feminine, and thus be condemned (or rather chosen) to fashion their identities in a certain way, to find the meaning of their lives in a certain set of scripts providing answers to the terrors of some existential choices. Aspects of the self that must inevitably be experienced because it was mortal, could now be split off and projected onto those of another sex, imagined as a gender. This defence against psychic insecurity depended upon denying the implications of sexual genesis (and therefore mortality). What had appeared as a problem for the social contract theorists could now be presented as a triumph! If the self could be imagined to be socially constructed, it was as if human history could emancipate itself from its carnal and mortal origins by individuals now being able to construct their own identities free of natural constraints. Moreover an explanation for the origin and content of gender could be provided, and thus the existence of a sexual division of labour legitimated in a society that claimed to be no longer patriarchal. This required one final step. What had hitherto been seen as a natural process of generation – sexual genesis – had now to be imagined as a social process of socialization – the construction of gender.

Sexual genesis and gender socialization

The concept of gender could be developed if the process of sexual genesis, focused on the natural difference between parent and infant and producing a social person, could be seen as a process of 'socialization', focused on the natural difference between male and female and producing a gendered person. The process whereby persons emerged from nature into selves with boundaries one from another by virtue of possessing a mortal body, the precipitation of an independent, bounded self, out of an infant originally fused, as it were, to its parents and produced by sexual genesis, could be reimagined as the process whereby genders separate from one another emerged from originally ungendered or polymorphously perverse infants, by virtue of their having differently sexed bodies. Properties of individuals that they possessed by virtue of their sexual genesis (such as their potential for instrumentalism and expressiveness) could be imagined as properties of genders because they were socialized. The boundary between self and other could be imagined as the boundary between male and female. The creation of independent selves could be imagined as the production of masculine and feminine identities, so that the ambivalences of attachment could become the drama of the Oedipus complex. Inexorable envy, disappointment and lack rooted in being a mortal individual could become womb and penis envy. Qualities that were inevitable and one-sided aspects of natural persons because they were the product of a male and a female became the fixed identities of social genders, which might in turn explain the social relations constructed by men and women and the sexual division of labour between them. Because such 'socialization' could thus be imagined to ascribe to men and women on the basis of their sexual difference, capacities which both have by virtue of having a sexual genesis (such as aggression or tenderness) it could solve an otherwise insurmountable problem which any account of gender would face: the absence of any natural difference between men and women (aside from their complementary reproductive capacities) which could form its empirical basis. In turn this association was made possible by the existence of a sexual division of labour that associated each sex with different activities and competencies which could be reimagined in this way.

By imagining the concept of gender, and the socialization process which gives rise to it, men could represent the continued existence of a sexual division of labour as something socially constructed by people with gendered identities rather than as a material legacy of the era of patriarchy. In so far as it was necessary to understand society as something socially constructed, gender could be seen (through the socialization processes that gave rise to it) as a product of that sexual division of labour itself – what I refer to below as theories that emphasize the phallus – and the reform of such gender identities, since they were social products, could be imagined to undermine that sexual division of labour and challenge patriarchy. Gender vertigo might supplant hegemonic masculinity. In so far as it was necessary to understand the natural limits to the social order, why the sexual division of labour should exist in the first place, how men had been able to create patriarchy or why only men could become 'masculine', gender could be seen as expressing natural differences, what I refer to below as theories which emphasise the penis. What I thus call 'swinging between the penis and the phallus' is a continual conceptual slippage, both between the social and the natural, and between masculine and male, without which gender theory cannot operate.

The fetishism of sexual difference as the origin of gender

The social production of gender ideology is thus parallel to the production of commodity fetishism analysed by Marx (1976) and can be seen as another dimension of the unanticipated consequences of market relations. What are in fact social relations between people assume for them the form of relations between things – in this case a fixed identity as masculine or feminine which people with differently sexed bodies are imagined to possess. Just as people in pre-modern societies projected their psychic insecurity, rooted in their sexual genesis and mortality, onto an external object, God, and dealt collectively with their own existential predicament by means of a relationship with Him, investing God with aspects of their own capacities, by means of religion, so do people in modern society project them onto sexual difference, and deal with them by imagining them as gender. They can do so because the sexual division of labour bequeathed by the era of patriarchy makes it appear that men and women are fundamentally different, and because their bodies are *both* mortal products of sexual genesis *and* are of one sex only. People can thus think of the natural limits that their mortality sets to their powers of social construction as the natural limit imposed by the fact that they are of one or other sex.

They can attempt to escape from the anxieties of psychic insecurity, to deny and hide from their mortal limits, by imagining their personal mortal capacities for instrumentalism and expressiveness as social capacities possessed by each gender. They can imagine their capacity for independence and aggression which originally allowed them to become separate from their parent or carer as 'masculinity' while imagining their need for dependence and empathy which originally allowed them to be connected as 'femininity'. By doing this they may exchange their 'unprecedented inner loneliness' for the search for 'true' masculinity and femininity, in the same way as their pre-modern ancestors sought the true God. This explains the question Craib (1987) raises of why gender identity should so often seem to be so much more central than others. Part of the answer is that it is not a question of 'identity' at all, but a recognition of the limit of being of one sex only; however, part is that we use our gender identity as a means to experience (or avoid experiencing) our mortality. Arguments about 'gender' in lifestyle magazines, as much as sociological theory, are usually covert moral arguments about the meaning and purpose of life and how we should live.

Just as the fetishism of commodities arises behind people's backs, and represents their own social but unintentionally or unconsciously created relations to them as the property of objects external to them (commodities with different values, and market forces to which people have no choice but respond) so the fetishism of gender represents people's own existential choices and dilemmas to them as the imagined properties of masculine and feminine, materially represented by male and female, with which they must cope.[1] Just as the classical political economists searched in vain for the origin of the value of a commodity in its characteristics, so too do contemporary sociologists search for the origin of 'gender' in sexual difference. In both cases it is the social relations for which the object comes to stand as the material representative which must be discovered and analysed, not the object itself.

The fetishism of sexual difference, based on the imagination of sexual genesis as gender socialization provided two things. It gave the inhabitants of a transitional society a way to imagine the sexual division of labour created by the preceding era of patriarchy as their own social construction, a product of their gender identities. It replaced religion as a defence against psychic insecurity. It produced an otherwise elusive 'content' for gender, which though it could never be lived out in a pure form by any man or woman, was immediately recognizable to them as (one-sided) aspects of their own experience. Depending on the perspective taken, this could appear either as the *cause* of gender identity (through 'socialization' theories), and be used in practical everyday life as proof of the existence of these gender identities (as breadwinners, men must be more instrumental) or as the *result* of them (because men are instrumental, they avoid infant nurturance).

We can now understand the paradox that I posed in Chapter 1 between the strength of our convictions about what masculinity essentially comprises, and the remarkable consensus about this; and on the other hand, the distance between this model of masculinity and any empirically existing men whom we actually experience. This paradox arises because our model of masculinity has its origin not in the behaviour of empirically existing men, but in our recognition of our own personal genesis and the contradictions of attachment which every mortal self experiences (such as the need for both intimacy *and* distance, love *and* hate), which we split and project outwards as instrumentalism onto males as masculinity, and expressiveness onto females as femininity. This contrast can be elaborated *ad infinitum*, instrumentalism standing for independence, culture, symbolism, rationality and the break from nature, Freud's 'libido'; Adler's (1992) 'masculine' protest; while expressiveness can stand for dependence, passivity, attachment, emotion, the link to nature, primal 'maternal' nurturance. The more absurd generalizations this produces can then be excused by asserting that since it is *gender*, not sex, which is under discussion this refers only to the 'masculine' or 'feminine' *aspects* of men or women. But the generalizations overall can be imagined to be true because of the existence of the sexual division of labour which associates men with the monopoly of public power resources and status.

Gender can be thought of as a category analogous to Orwell's 'doublethink'; it allows us to hold two mutually contradictory views in harmony with each other. At one and the same time we can think of characteristics of individuals as both related and not related to their sex. We are happy to acknowledge, for example, that an instrumental, aggressive and competitive preoccupation with a career in paid work (perhaps invoking a spirit of sacrifice of extreme manual or mental effort in order to support financial dependants) to the exclusion of interest in domestic life, the rearing of infants and the cultivation of intimacy with a partner, represents a 'masculine' orientation. We could not describe it as 'male' because it is clear that we could describe some women in this way too, and there are many men whose experience it does not fit. In this sense we acknowledge that such an orientation has no logical connection with biological sex and cannot account for the sexual division of labour. Yet by describing it as masculine in the first place we suggest simultaneously that just such a connection does exist.

Gender also resembles doublethink in that it allows men and women to hold an awareness of their sexual genesis, for example through the pursuit of an 'authentic' gender identity, while simultaneously being unconscious of it, and hiding from themselves the fact that they have thus hidden it, because of the implications for their psychic security. Of course they do not set out consciously to construct such a process, just as they did not set out to construct the fetishism of commodities. Both are social processes which arise, unintended and unanticipated, behind their modern backs. Of course Orwell had his tongue firmly in his cheek as he wrote; the essence of *Nineteen Eighty-Four* as a radical critique is that it is an ironic parody, as I discuss in Chapter 8.[2] Orwell's point was that it would have been logically and empirically impossible to perfect doublethink, the memory hole and the triumph of Ingsoc. So too for us, the doublethink of gender never works quite well enough; our everyday experience and our most abstract academic speculation are haunted by the tensions between our belief in the formal equality of men and women, and our knowledge of their substantive difference and inequality. What we have to understand however, is how the concepts of masculine and feminine have come to support that inequality and difference, not subvert it.

The legacy of the fetishism of sexual difference: the politics of identity

The confusion of sexual difference and sexual genesis leads to other dramatic effects. Questions that are properly about how infants become persons who as autonomous adults can form social relations come to appear as questions about how, in the social order, men are different from women. Contradictory aspects of personal identity, which must comprise any empirically existing mortal self, come to be seen as descriptions of social gender characteristics that explain the sexual division of labour. Thus as difference gets confused with generation, so too do persons get confused with societies, and the personal with the political.

As we lose sight of generation by denying its significance, and the natural limits to the social order are imagined to be set by sexual difference, the recognition that such differences are socially produced as gender rather than naturally determined by sex then develops into the illusion that there are no natural limits to the identities of individuals. Craib (1994a) has called the idea that we can consciously socially construct our identities as we choose 'the powerful self'. We tend to imagine societies whose inhabitants arrive fully formed at the moment of their birth (as Hobbes was to put it, springing out of the ground like mushrooms) and who from then on are capable of whatever change is necessary to produce the social order they aspire to inhabit. Indeed, persons have to be imagined thus, if they are to be socialized into their gender identities. In turn, just as persons come to be purely socially constructed – the epiphenomena of politics – so too do societies come to appear as nothing more than an effect of the persons, or identities, who comprise them. The distinction between the personal and the political is obscured, and the personal comes to appear to be about sexual difference and gender.

It is not whether we are male or female that sets natural limits to our social capacities or self determination, but the fact that we are all of us of women born and fathered by men. Much as we might like to imagine it, we did not emerge mysteriously into the world as bundles of some infinitely malleable symbolic essence. Because of this, while we can conceive of societies, civilization and our symbolic culture in terms of historical progress, we also know, though we usually find it easier to deny, that our personal careers, be they ever so creative, productive or successful, take us inexorably to the grave. Sociology, other social sciences, and modern democratic thought generally, have a problem coping with our carnal, sexual origins. If we did in fact spring into life ready-formed – like mushrooms – we could avoid all manner of awkward questions about how infants come to be the independent autonomous conscious rational selves which form the building blocks for social and political theory. However, to accept the importance of the brute, inexorable fact of our carnal origins, implies that we must also accept that no person, as opposed to a god, can aspire to some perfect state of autonomy nor to the ability to make themselves in their own ideal image. They are inevitably limited. Paradoxically, this is the only hope for a genuinely liberal, as opposed to totalitarian, society. Not for nothing were the children in *Brave New World* hatched in incubators (Huxley, 1994). For if we can never fully control our own private selves, then neither can any public authority achieve this either.

In so far as the natural limits to human culture were imagined to be rooted in sexual difference rather than sexual genesis, it could come to appear that accepting the existence of such limits meant accepting patriarchy (in the sense of there being natural differences between men and women) and that attacking patriarchy meant insisting that the personal was entirely political, and that it could thus accordingly be modernized or democratized. A false choice was thus created about how the distinction between the private and public spheres of social life might be understood. This was between insisting that such a distinction existed, but accepting that the private sphere was 'naturally' patriarchal, and arguing that no such distinction existed, that, to use a modern phrase, the personal is political and can therefore be analysed using concepts appropriate to the public sphere, such as the 'democratization of personal relationships' discussed by Giddens (1992). If we unwittingly accept this false choice, our analysis of how societies come to have a sexual division of labour and of how we might get rid of it, risks turning into a one-sided politics of identity. Such an approach concentrates on whether the social order contains a private sphere which is separate and therefore patriarchal, producing sexual identities such as 'hegemonic masculinity' which reproduce the wider sexual division of labour, or whether this private sphere has been sufficiently politicized and democratized, so that it produces selves which undermine patriarchy. Material questions of social structure and political and economic power come to be seen as questions of the proper development of the self. Realizing the limits to the politicization of the personal thus means accepting personal responsibility for the politics we construct, rather than trying always to imagine such politics to be a product of a masculinity or femininity which we possess by virtue of our sex.

If we see the natural limits to society as set by sexual genesis, however, then accepting them is quite consistent with attacking patriarchy and supporting the material and ideological equality of the sexes. What it is not consistent with is arguing that relations between infants and adults are purely social, or that adults can emancipate themselves fully from the legacy of attachment in their own relations; they will have an element of the unconscious. If we realize this, then arguing that the personal is *not* political in some important respects is only to argue that relations between infants and adults cannot be understood entirely in terms of social construction or socialization, and that the fact that this is so is in fact fundamental to democracy. Were persons entirely social constructions, they would become mere ciphers or agents of social or political processes. The boundaries to our personal sovereignty over ourselves because we are mortal products of sexual reproduction, because we are merely human, also set the limits to social and political sovereignty over individuals, and make any democratic politics possible. In so far as the personal is about the development of the capacity to be alone it is not political; it is what makes the political possible. In so far as this capacity is produced by the private or personal sphere and that this is the inevitable product of a family or unit in which attachment takes place, defence of personal autonomy is vital to democracy. In so far as this capacity is about the achievement of psychic security without having to defend against anxiety by projecting our own responsibilities and our terror of them onto others, especially those of the 'other' sex, its final development depends upon the defence of the personal from the political. It is only the confusion of sexual genesis and sexual difference that can make such a demand appear as a defence of patriarchy, rather than what it is: the best means to further erode the ideological and material legacy of patriarchy in contemporary society.

On the other hand, it is mistaken to try to politicize or 'democratize' the self and its intimate relations – what we might think of as the private, or personal sphere – and undermine its autonomy in the mistaken belief that we are thus challenging patriarchy because we are challenging sexual difference. This only adds to powerful social forces of rationalization and bureaucratization in modernity which threaten to subordinate the self, weaken its independence and turn it into a loyal servant of the political and economic order. I shall return to the discussion of the politics of identity in the next chapter, but first review some of the other implications of seeing gender as the result of the fetishism of sexual difference.

The legacy of the fetishism of sexual difference: sex as religion

We are often reminded of the countless procedures which Christianity once employed to make us detest the body; but let us ponder all the ruses that were employed for centuries to make us love sex, to make the knowledge of it desirable and everything said about it precious. Let us consider the stratagems by which we were induced to apply all our skills to discovering its secrets, by which we were attached to the obligation to draw out its truth, and made guilty for having failed to recognise it for so long. These devices are what ought to make us wonder today. Moreover, we need to consider the possibility that one day, perhaps in a different economy of bodies and pleasures, people will no longer quite understand how the ruses of sexuality, and the power that sustains its organisation, were able to subject us to that austere monarchy of sex, so that we became dedicated to the endless task of forcing its secret, of exacting the truest of confessions from a shadow.

(Foucault 1984: 159)

If genesis and difference were transposed, sex could, and did, become the new religion. If social relations in modernity increasingly concerned the market, rationalization, and the prospect of the lifeless iron cage of bureaucracy, so then might expressiveness be imagined as an escape from this, focused on the celebration of 'natural' sexual difference as the last route back to the authentic, the final chance to grasp the 'kernel of the truly living' (Weber 1948c: 347). Not for nothing is orgasm called 'le petit mort'.[3] We are thus fascinated by sex in modernity, I suspect, not because we like or loathe it any more or less than before, or because we live in more or less liberated times, but because of the confusion between sexual genesis and sexual difference we imagine that our sex, our sexuality (or what we may think of as our gender identity or talk of as our masculinity or femininity) offers to tell us some elusive truth about our mortality. This is because what we imagine as our masculinity or femininity, are ultimately the ambivalent and contradictory capacities of instrumentalism and expressiveness that we possess and must manage because we are mortal. In the era of the powerful self we have learned to displace our disappointment at our mortality and carnality (our sexual genesis) onto another related disappointment: that we are only one sex or the other (our sexual difference).

But the more we can imagine that the truth of our sex lies in our gender, and that this gender is something we construct and control, we can imagine that we can escape the most crushing of all disappointments. Thus between the endless stream of images of youthful bodies, articles on sex and the adverts for wrinkle cream and plastic surgery in the lifestyle magazines lie the therapy columns offering the spiritual body the prospect of a life free of the dilemmas of mortality, through a succession of 'pure' relationships. Segal (1994) has drawn attention to our modern celebration of and preoccupation with the orgasm. It is perhaps best described in Erica Jong's concept of the 'zipless fuck' (Jong 1974) which seems to me to capture the essence of the pure relationship as well: fleeting, emancipated from the distortion of traditional gender identities, the potential inertial drag of children or the need to be coordinated with other social obligations (family, career) and sustained only so long as it gives both parties pleasure. Gender is the favourite anchor point of the powerful self because it allows it to project its own mortality onto persons of the opposite sex. Thus it turns its greatest defeat (its mortal limits of being of one sex only, of being mortal and of being only itself) into an everlasting victory. Lurking behind the glossy pages of men's and women's lifestyle magazines, and the endless exploration of the self and its potential for 'growth' is our fear of something else: its inevitable carnal decay and death. The inner child only conceals the inner corpse.

This is not entirely a product of modernity; any society has to have enough interest in enough heterosexual procreative sex to reproduce itself over time, and we might expect this to be reflected widely in its culture. Anthony and Cleopatra or the characters of ancient mythology remind us that the Enlightenment did not invent sex. There is something qualitatively different about our modern preoccupation, however. Sex sells. Media baron Rupert Murdoch uses it to sell newspapers. I use it to interest students in the more boring bits of quantitative methodology. In proportion as our lives become increasingly regulated by the abstract rationalization and bureaucratization of modernity; as we spend our time performing the duties of our various offices, or following our prescribed social roles or inhabiting our appropriate identities, sex appears to offer an escape. We can find all this expressed clearly in Weber (1978a: 975):

> Bureaucracy develops the more perfectly the more it is 'dehumanised', the more completely it succeeds in eliminating from official business love, hatred, all purely personal, irrational and emotional elements which escape calculation. This is appraised as its special virtue by capitalism.

In contrast to this remorseless expulsion of expressiveness from the public sphere, Weber counterposes the sexual encounter which is specifically extra marital (and therefore beyond the social) and appears to root any achievable meaning of life in this (Weber 1948c: 346–7):

> The last accentuation of the erotical sphere occurred in terms of intellectualist cultures. It occurred where this sphere collided with the unavoidably ascetic trait of the vocational specialist type of man. Under this tension between the erotic sphere and rational everyday life, specifically extramarital sexual life, which had been removed from everyday affairs, could appear as the only tie which linked man with the natural fountain of all life. For man had now been completely emancipated from the cycle of the old, simple, and organic existence of the peasant . . .
>
> Under these conditions the erotic relation seems to offer the unsurpassable peak of the fulfilment of the request for love in the direct fusion of the souls of the one to the other . . . The lover realizes himself to be rooted in the kernel of the truly living, which is eternally inaccessible to any rational endeavour. He knows himself to be freed from the cold skeleton hands of rational orders, just as completely as from the banality of everyday routine . . . The experience is by no means communicable.

In *Economy and Society*, Weber produces what can only be seen as an astonishing fantasy of Arcadian sex before the 'fall' imposed by the development of social relations and civilization (1978a: 606–60):

> At the level of the peasant, the sexual act is an everyday occurrence; primitive people do not regard this act as containing anything unusual, and they may indeed enact it before the eyes of onlooking travelers [*sic*] without the slightest feeling of shame.

Weber's vision of the remorseless triumph of the iron cage in contrast to blissful peasant sex resembles Freud's opposition of ego, civilization and neurosis to id, instinct and polymorphous perversity. Both contrast civilization to a world beyond the incest taboo, a fantasy world beyond its initial division, in our early experience, into self and other. Freud sees the costs of this in the vicissitudes of the neurotic repression of 'uncivilized' urges, since attachments must be kept in check by contracts – discontent is the inevitable price of civilization – and the best that can be hoped for is routine unhappiness or disappointment compared to neurotic misery. Weber sees the cost in the way rationalization comes to dominate even the most intimate spheres of life, but ironically, given his violent criticism of the 'free love' interpretation of Freud developed by Otto Gross and his circle (Weber 1978b) he sees sex emancipated from any social context as a potential saviour of the true self – the means both to reach it and express it. The pure relationship can be seen as its contemporary sociological child, and one that is less critical of modernity than Weber, just as Weber can be seen, in this respect, as less critical than Freud. Compared to Freud's vision, Weber it seems to me, is naively optimistic about the redeeming capacity of the orgasm as an antidote to the skeletal hand of the iron cage. Compared to Weber's vision, Giddens's (1992) account of the pure relationship (and Beck and Beck-Gernsheim's account of *The Normal Chaos of Love*, 1995) loses the critical vision of the extent and character of the reach of the processes of rationalization into the pianissimo of life. What Weber condemns as the tightening grip of the iron cage, and modernity devouring its own preconditions, Giddens celebrates as the growth of consciousness, 'self reflexivity' and the democratization of personal relationships. The weak, socially subordinated self, its boundaries invaded by the public sphere, dependent on the manuals of personal growth and publicly defined priorities for its development, preoccupied with its self-image, narcissistically imagines itself as its opposite: the powerful self, conscious, reflexive author of its destiny.

It is surely no accident that in a world which imagines itself to comprise a purely instrumental rationalization, people come to imagine their escape in terms of a return to pure expressiveness: a regression to the effortless wish fulfilment of a heavenly cosmic orgasm without disappointment. What is, to say the least, surprising is that sociology would join them in this fantasy. We can see this as a legacy of the fetishism of sexual difference. Because it leads people to project their most fundamental concerns about their identity and psychic security onto sexual difference (through imagining that effects that flow from possession of a mortal body flow from possession of a male or female one) and in turn imagine this difference in terms of gender, the celebration of this sexual identity, through the emancipation of its 'authentic' nature from social constraint, appears to make the orgasm the critical opponent of the disenchanted instrumental rationalization of modernity. But this is merely an appearance thrown up by the fetishism of sexual difference. The key conflict in modernity is not that between love and money, nor between competing definitions of gender identity, but the continuing struggle for genuinely equal public rights.

The symbolic and material body

This conflict helps us understand another paradox created by the fetishism of sexual difference. Men and women in contemporary society appear to treat each other increasingly as *equals* (formally and ultimately substantively) even when they might personally regret this, while becoming increasingly preoccupied with discovering and expressing ('authentically') the symbolic meaning and social significance of their difference, through their sexed bodies. Changes in social relations and developments in technology mean that possession of a male or female body, or for that matter a strong or weak, short or tall body (regardless of its sex), while still significant, almost certainly has much less direct effect on our life experience now than at any other time in human history (Dunning 1986). Yet we seem captivated by images of real or true men and women or 'authentic' masculinity or 'essential' feminism. Modernity is a revolution that has thought of itself as the emancipation of all human relationships from the rule of nature and the realization that it is us mortals who make history and society. Yet in the heat of this revolution we seek to return to the bonds of nature once more and imagine this as escape, as liberation. We come to imagine that only that for which we deny responsibility is genuinely authentic, by projecting our mortal limits, rooted in our sexual genesis, onto the reassuring categories of sexual difference. We are increasingly obsessed with the symbolism of sex, because we imagine that it offers us some truth about ourselves, at the very time at which we are also more prepared than ever before to believe that our sex is no barrier to achieving whatever individual identity or social position we aspire to: whether it is to learn to talk to Mum on the phone, perhaps expressing our innermost feelings to her, or to fight for our country. Thus, as Foucault argued, do we try to force 'the truest of confessions from a shadow'.

Gender and the sexual division of labour

My argument in this chapter has been that gender does not exist as a property of persons, except as a set of assumptions which people hold about each other and themselves in certain contexts, and which in other contexts they simultaneously deny. I have argued that the historical conditions that produce such bizarre beliefs are those of the transition from a patriarchal to universal society which creates the fetishism of sexual difference and 'gender' as a category created to make sense of a contradictory and threatening world. If 'masculinity' can only be seen as an ideological construct arising from these historical conditions, which in turn is rooted in one side only of the inevitably two-sided potential of any individual personal identity, it is misguided to try to make it the subject of empirical analysis. For the same reasons it is also fruitless to develop theories that try to explain how certain types of masculinity, gender identity or personality types inhabited by actual men contribute to the subordination of women. Just as there is no such thing as masculinity, neither are there any such things as masculinities – the increasing recourse to the plural is only a dim recognition of the insoluble theoretical problems offered by the singular term. We cannot understand gender identity to be something which produces or reproduces the sexual division of labour. Rather it is the ideological reflection, created through the fetishism of sexual difference, of men and women's attempts to explain that division of labour to themselves.

This is an argument that we have come to accept when analysing other aspects of identity, and an analogy from there may make my argument clearer. It is clear that national identity is an important feature of modern societies. People imagine themselves to be members of particular national communities, that real differences exist between these national communities and that, in this sense, something called a 'nation' actually exists. Powerful consequences flow from these beliefs. But it would be a naive theorist indeed who assumed that the psychological essence of any national identity could be discovered or that such an essence 'caused' nationalism or could be used to explain the 'differences' between nations or the dynamics of international relations. We wouldn't look for national identity in the personalities of individually existing members of a nation, nor would we dream of trying to define what the essence of a 'true' or 'authentic' national identity or culture might comprise. But we would expect the behaviour and self-image of a nation's members to reflect both their belief that they were a member of a nation, and the material fact of being a citizen of a state. Nations and nation states are so obviously historical constructions that we look for the origins of 'imagined communities' elsewhere, including the way in which the material development of states and economies has encouraged different social groups to develop myths of national identity, which while seldom wholly fictitious, depend on forgetting as much history as is remembered (Nairn 1977; Anderson 1991). We would never search for some primary ethnos as the basis of national identity and its supposed 'character traits', because it could not explain why nations had at one time not existed, nor how modern national sentiment changes over time. But while we would therefore never imagine dissecting a Scotsman to discover the secret of his national identity, we too easily fall into the trap of looking under his kilt to discover the clue to his gender identity, because the natural fact of sexual difference provides a convenient peg on which to hang our definitions.

If we think of race and ethnicity, we might be clear about the existence of a group of people who were defined by others as 'black', or who thought of themselves in this way. But we would, I hope, shudder at explanations of the radically different average wealth, power or status of black people in terms of either some feature of their identity, or some putative 'natural' capacity or characteristic which was thus socially expressed. Similarly, it was quite popular, until the beginning of the twentieth century, to search for explanations of class difference in terms of eugenics, or the quality of human 'stock'. Few would dare to advance such arguments in respectable scientific debate – not because prejudice against the fecklessness of the poor has weakened – but because the argument would be so swiftly rebutted for its lack of basic logic or empirical evidence.

Yet, in part because of the continued power of men, and in part because of the existence of two clearly defined sexes, we continue to make such arguments about sex, usually under the guise of arguing about 'gender'. Explanations of the subordination of women by men usually depend on arguing that men and women come to inhabit actually existing and contrasting 'gender identities' which explain their capacity to behave in different ways under otherwise similar historical conditions. We tend to favour explanations of the different social positions and character of men and women based on their gender identities rather than social mechanisms that allocate otherwise similar people to radically different life experiences, opportunities and positions in the social division of labour. We can do this and not feel that we are falling into arguments about 'natural' differences between the sexes because we imagine that 'gender' is a social rather than a natural process. Unfortunately, in terms of persons, gender makes no logical sense except as a description of sex. We can do this ultimately because behind our modern beliefs in universal human rights lies the conviction, reinforced by what our anatomy reminds us of every day, that men and women are different and that this difference lies beyond any process of social construction. The strength of this conviction arises not from its empirical validity, but in its twin uses to legitimate the existing sexual division of labour, and to shelter from the psychic threat posed by our modern knowledge of the significance of our sexual genesis.

The origins of patriarchy: sexual genesis, the sexual division of labour and the forces of production

If gender is caused by the fetishism of sexual difference in societies transitional between an era of patriarchy and the abolition of the sexual division of labour, we cannot look to gender to explain patriarchy, so that we are still left to explain the origin of patriarchy in premodern societies. If it is caused by sexual difference then patriarchy would just be a part of the natural, biological species character of human beings, untranscendable in any imaginable form of society. Nor do I think we can look for the origins of patriarchy or of the solidarities of sex or of the nature of the phallus or the structures of kinship and culture in the impact *on individuals* of the biological division of labour involved in procreation, pregnancy and lactation. These facts impose a reciprocal dependency on males and females, but cannot tell us much about the social form it can or must take.

At the level of society, however, this biological division of labour in sexual genesis has an effect which we might expect to vary dramatically with the level of development of what we might call the forces of reproduction. Until quite recently in human societies – say within the last three centuries – high fertility rates and levels of infant mortality, combined with relatively unreliable methods of contraception (whether cultural or physical) and no safe alternative to breastfeeding of infants has meant that on average, whatever the fortunes of individual women, most women will have spent perhaps 50 per cent of their adult lives pregnant or breastfeeding infants (either their own or others). In such circumstances, regardless of the social relations within which such forces develop, it is not difficult to imagine solidarities of sex emerging between those who are liable to or do become pregnant or have to feed infants, and those who do not.

It is also highly likely that within such solidarities of sex, men are likely to be able to develop advantages in the public sphere of social relations because they are less directly physically tied to procreation and nurturance, whatever their symbolic association with them. Dinnerstein (1987: 20) describes it as follows.

> Her young are born less mature than those of other mammals; they require more physical care for a relatively longer time; they have much more to learn before they can function without adult supervision. Without contraception, she must spend most of her vigorous adult life pregnant or lactating. Given these handicaps to wide-ranging mobility, she has been the logical keeper of the hearth and doer of domestic tasks and also (usually in collaboration with other females) the logical guardian and educator of the slow-maturing toddler.

These solidarities do not depend at all on any contrast whatsoever in the social capacities of males and females as individuals, but we could well imagine how they might develop ideologies about such a contrast so as to rationalize the existence of a social division of labour between the sexes resting on the biologically determined division of labour in procreation and early feeding.

In arguing this I am not assuming any direct individual connection between pregnancy, lactation and place in the wider division of labour, as in some of the cruder versions of men hunt and women nurse the hearth theories. Anthropological evidence, in so far as it is relevant, shows tremendous variations between societies at a primitive level of productive forces in the extent to which men and women are jointly or exclusively involved in activities that require physical and geographical mobility such as hunting on the one hand and in the nurturance of children on the other. Given the early link between sex and infant feeding, however, is it so surprising that we know of no society in which men take primary responsibility for infant childcare (as opposed to offering assistance) and many where men's involvement is minimal? Men's power therefore, lay not in the penis in an individual sense, but in the relative freedom of their sex from some inevitable species' needs to perform various social tasks associated with reproduction to which women were more closely tied collectively, as opposed to individually. Surely men were able to use this capacity in a great variety of ways to shape social arrangements that have made the most of this freedom, and to develop ideologies that legitimated its ramifications as natural.

From this perspective, it could be argued that it is not surprising that the rise of feminism over the last two and a half centuries has coincided with dramatic changes in the level of the reproductive forces and their implications for the sexual division of labour in reproduction. Modernity has been, in part, about the scientific analysis and technological manipulation of nature, in the attempt to harness or control its forces to human ends. This has included fertility, reproduction and childbirth and infant nurturance. Fertility and infant mortality rates have plummeted in western industrial capitalist societies, so that now a woman might, on average, expect to spend perhaps 3 per cent of her adult life pregnant or breastfeeding (Dinnerstein 1987: 25). Relatively safe and reliable contraception and abortion is available, which makes it technically possible for women to personally take control over their fertility if they have the political power to demand the right to do so. 'Breast' may be 'best' but other feeding options, including expressing milk, are available, liberating women collectively as well as individually from monopoly over this aspect of infant nurturance.

Thus the demographic transition, and the rise in the level of productive forces with which it has been bound up, has fundamentally loosened what must previously have been a much tighter connection, even though it was one whose form and content was not determined, between the sexual division of labour in procreation and the wider social division of labour. There is less infant nurturance to do, and men have the technological potential to do much more of it. In more primitive societies there was simply a much greater proportion of activity necessary to reproduce society *that only females could do.* Just as in contemporary and in any imaginable society, males and females were reciprocally dependent on each other by virtue of the biological division of labour in reproduction. But this reciprocal dependence had very different implications for males and females in terms of material obligations within the overall social division of labour. Men had only to ejaculate. Women had to go through pregnancy, childbirth and lactation. In such circumstances surely, lay the ability of men, through many diverse means, to develop a division of other socially necessary labour according to sex which privileged men. Such a development would not depend on any particular symbolic construction being put on sexual difference and the mechanics of procreation, though we might well imagine symbolic order being developed which emphasized men's fertility and cultural centrality to the process, in contrast to their much smaller material contribution. In this sense, men's power was rooted in the penis; not by virtue of any connection between biology and a capacity for sexual violence or any other individual characteristics, but by virtue of the relative advantage conferred on them in the biological division of labour in reproduction.

Notes

1 In the words of Marx (1976: 165, 166–7):

> In order, therefore, to find an analogy, we must take flight into the misty realm of religion. There the products of the human brain appear as autonomous figures endowed with a life of their own, which enter into relations both with each other and with the human race. So it is in the world of commodities with the products of men's hands. I call this the fetishism which attaches itself to the product of labour as soon as they are produced as commodities, and is therefore inseparable from the production of commodities . . . Men do not therefore bring the products of their labour into relation with each other as values because they see these objects merely as the material integuments of homogeneous human labour.

> The reverse is true: by equating their different products to each other in exchange as values, they equate their different kinds of labour as human labour. They do this without being aware of it.

What Marx describes as 'fetishism', psychodynamic thinkers have described as 'projection': the displacement of a conscious social relation onto external objects or people. Marx emphasizes that fetishism results from rather than causes the system of social relations he is analysing, and sees market relations as central to this process. I am making an exactly parallel argument with respect to gender.

Men and women are born into a society with a sexual division of labour first established in the era of patriarchy. The material and ideological forces of modernity encourage them to treat each other as formal equals, so that they must find some way of representing the legacy of this sexual division of labour to themselves. They find a way to do this by projecting aspects of their personal identities which they possess because they are mortal, onto each sex, imagining that the latter possess them because they have been socialized into a gender identity. But this process results from, rather than establishes, the sexual division of labour.

2 Appropriately, given my subject matter, Orwell's original title for the book was 'the last man in Europe' (Crick 1982).

3 Wouters (1991: 703) draws attention to this expression.

3

The crisis of masculinity and the politics of identity

Man, that plausible creature whose wagging tongue so often hides the despair and darkness in his heart.

(Wrong 1961: 131)

The previous chapter argued that masculinity was an ideology produced by men as a result of the threat posed to the survival of the patriarchal sexual division of labour by the rise of modernity. Their monopoly of power, resources and status which they had previously been able to claim directly by virtue of their sex, they now had to assert was due to their socially constructed gender identity which expressed some undefined natural difference. Since this invention of masculinity was essentially a holding operation, however, it has been in crisis ever since, for three reasons. First, by definition, the essence of masculinity can never be grasped or defined. If it comprises essentially social characteristics or capacities, we have to explain on what grounds women have been incapable of, or prevented from, acquiring them. Masculinity is something for the girls as much as the boys, and over time, it must surely come to have no special connection to either biological sex. If, conversely, it comprises something beyond the social, we are back to arguments about maleness and biology, and traditional premodern arguments about nature determining society and males being innately superior to females.

Second, exactly those concepts of masculinity, femininity and gender originally devised to rationalize male privilege could equally be used to attack it, and have been so used ever since. Although it started out as a conservative concept – an attempt to reconcile a patriarchal reality with claims that both men and women participate in history, as it were – the argument could just as easily be reversed and run the other way. If sexual difference was socially expressed or constructed, then it could be changed. Masculinity and femininity could be made differently, or the social mechanisms imagined to produce them could be challenged. The attempt to defend the legacy of patriarchy in the language of contract, by a neat irony of history, provided the conceptual basis for feminism and the challenge that women made to men from the dawn of modernity onwards on the basis of contract theory itself that if all men were born free then so too must all women be. If masculinity, rather than maleness, explained men's privilege, men could be challenged to reform or abolish their masculinity in the name of equal rights, in a way that they could not be asked to change or abolish their sex. The truth of the next three centuries has been ably summed up by Mann (1994: 186–7):

> from about the time of Locke, there was greater interest in tracing political rights and duties to the qualities of abstract individuals . . . most of the doctrines, when elaborated, made clear that the person and the nation were not universal: servants, almost always, and usually labourers and those without property, were not to be an active part of the political community . . . Women got similar treatment . . . Nevertheless, from the 1680s to the 1980s the same liberal rhetoric has been used by radicals to achieve legal and political equality for all men and even for all women. Feminism, like socialism, built on top of the rhetoric . . . Liberalism . . . could erect no powerful ideological defences against enfranchising either subordinate classes or women.

Third, the constant revolutionizing and innovation of modernity, the material side of the forces of universalism enshrined in the institutions of the market and bureaucracy, increasingly undermined established aspects of the sexual division of labour and encouraged men and women to treat each other as formal equals. This is not because of any attempt on the part of men or women to change men's personal gender identities – either collectively or individually – but as a result of material forces unleashed by the transition to a modern, market based, technological society. The material pressures of the logic of rationalization and development of the impersonal market encourages individuals to treat each other without regard to their sex, even in situations where they would otherwise prefer to do so. The demographic transition and declining fertility and infant mortality rates shrank the proportion of time that adult females spent in pregnancy or lactation. Technological innovation rendered the secondary physical characteristics of possession of a male or female body less relevant.

The ability of men to sustain a coherent public ideology of what masculinity comprises is constantly being undermined by the material progress of modernity (at a personal level a 'coherent' masculine identity has never been sustainable). In this sense we are witnessing the end of masculinity. Given that we have not reached the end of ideology, let alone the end of history, and given the popularity of ill-proven fin de siècle portents of the finality of this, that and the other, let me make it clear that I do not think that the end of masculinity as such is upon us or that an androgynous Utopia is near. The sexed character of human bodies must have social consequences in any imaginable society. In this limited sense there will never be an end of masculinity, but it would under these conditions be just as sensible to talk of maleness. But we are living through the final period, or at least the beginning of the final period, of belief in masculinity as a gender identity specific to men which accounts for their privileged command of power, resources and status. I suspect that in years to come historians will book back upon the last two centuries as those in which whole societies, as opposed to individual philosophers, started to realize that there was no difference between men and women (aside from their complimentary places in biological reproduction and the anatomical and secondary physical characteristics flowing from that) and to work through the fundamentally revolutionary consequences of that realization. In both the real world, and our analysis of it, it is time for the end of masculinity.

A bad time to be a man?

Men are now discriminated against in most aspects of life.
(United Kingdom Men's Movement 1995: v)

It has become something of a cliché to argue that it is now 'a bad time to be a man'. Men's material privileges in the law, economy and politics are under increasing scrutiny and attack. Fifty years ago there were still many institutions that were male bastions where women were either legally barred or totally absent. Although men still monopolize public power, hardly any such institutions survive today, aside from gentlemen's clubs and the Catholic priesthood. Significantly neither has a good reputation. Today's boys cannot assume the privileges their fathers could take for granted or assume to be natural. The public evaluation of masculinity has also undergone a profound shift. What were once claimed to be manly virtues (heroism, independence, courage, strength, rationality, will, backbone, virility) have become masculine vices (abuse, destructive aggression, coldness, emotional inarticulacy, detachment, isolation, an inability to be flexible, to communicate, to empathize, to be soft, supportive or life affirming). A study of the treatment of men as fathers or carers in British newspapers for the month of June 1994 reported the largest single category of stories concerned 'men as monsters', who had bullied, abused or killed their children (Lloyd 1994). In the cinema, television and advertising imagery, the hegemony of the 'male gaze' has been broken. Not only have we seen the rise of the 'female gaze', but the rise of increasingly heterogeneous representations of men, many of which set out explicitly to subvert older images of masculinity. While it is ludicrous to imagine, as some militant men's groups have done, that this attack has brought about anything even approaching substantive equality, let alone a reversal of the balance of power, women have made substantial progress in achieving greater juridical, political and economic equality, especially over the last half century.

It is possible to see such arguments as part of a backlash by men against the impact of feminism: a determination to fight even the smallest gains which women have been able to achieve, in order to preserve male superiority. It is true that there is now a small but vociferous men's movement ready to argue that men are now the oppressed sex (e.g. United Kingdom Men's Movement 1995). It is also true that if it is a bad time to be a man, it is still, in almost every area of life, a worse time to be a woman. What has to be understood, however, alongside the scope of men's continuing privilege, is how far and how fast that privilege has been undermined by the development of modern industrial capitalist society generally, and in particular by its transformations over the last half century.

All premodern societies display a dramatic sexual division of labour. Only a little over three centuries ago we lived in a world where men had always ruled the public sphere and enjoyed virtually arbitrary power in the private sphere, and did so through the universal belief that they were naturally quite different to and superior to women. Mann (1994: 180) is right when he argues that:

> We could write a history of power relations almost up to the eighteenth century and confine it to men, as long as we add the defensive proviso, 'Oh, and by the way, remember that this is a story of the relations between male patriarchs. Underneath them all the time were women (and junior men, and children).'

Fathers could choose husbands for their daughters, who henceforth enjoyed virtually total power over them, including their mutilation or murder.[1] Women's public role, the work they did, or relations they could form, were largely determined by men. There may have been many versions of patriarchy, and many societies where the social division of labour between the sexes was more equal than that found, say, in Britain in the Middle Ages, but we have no evidence of any society where men took primary responsibility for the nurturance of infant children, or women enjoyed any preponderance of public political power over men, or where tasks and social roles were not sex-typed.

The material and ideological legacy of millennia of patriarchy remains in the dramatic material inequality between men and women, the continued dominance of men in the public sphere, especially in politics, in the systematic misogyny of all kinds of mental representations of the sexes and in the ubiquitous physical violence that characterizes sexual relations. In 1996 there were around 350 dollar billionaires in the world; all were men (*The Guardian*, 22 July 1996). Joshi recently estimated that women in the UK lost around half their lifetime earnings potential, compared to men, because of their continued primary responsibility for looking after infants in the home (Davis and Joshi 1990). In a survey conducted in 1994 in Britain less than a fifth of mothers were working full time when they were parents of preschool-age children. The equivalent figure for fathers was more than four-fifths.[2] The same survey in Sweden, a country normally thought of as pioneering advances in sexual equality, produced similar results. Eighty per cent of respondents in Britain who lived as a couple said that it was usually or always the woman's job to do the laundry; a mere 5 per cent reported that it was her job to do 'small repairs'. Again Sweden produced similar responses of 81 per cent and 2 per cent! (ISSP 1994). In the 1990s it was possible for John Major to announce his first cabinet without a single woman member; even 20 years before Edward Heath had felt obliged to include a 'token' woman: Margaret Thatcher. At the 1992 General Election in Britain, Scotland managed to return five women MPs out of 72 – about the same proportion as in the first elections after women secured the vote.[3] In Britain today, less than 3 per cent of men report to supervisors or managers at work who are women.

The 'male gaze' is still strong; 'page 3' pictures of nude women are used to sell newspapers and there is a thriving pornography industry adapting itself to new forms of technology. Jokes about mothers-in-law and women drivers are still common. Cultural associations between women and inferiority, weakness or pollution still abound. A sexual double standard continues to operate. Judges can continue to assume that women wearing 'provocative' clothing in public solicit any sexual violence of which they become victims. Sexual and physical violence by men on women, often their partners or children, is endemic. Scottish police records suggest that wife assault is the second most common violent crime, while estimates of the incidence of rape or sexual abuse range up to one-third or two-fifths of all women in western countries; girls are much more likely to be abused than boys.[4]

Yet there are also strong material and ideological pressures in modern western societies which appear to work against patriarchy. They are forcing or encouraging men to become more involved in childcare and domestic labour and to accept a steadily greater role for women in the public sphere. They are continually undermining traditional ideas about what is 'natural' or appropriate for men and women to do. The force of the constant revolutionizing of the relations of production and the drive towards rationalization is now blowing hard against sexual difference. The solidity of sex is melting into the air, along with other 'fast-frozen relations with their train of ancient and venerable prejudices' (Marx and Engels 1968: 38). This does not mean that women have gained equality, or anything like it, or that these processes are inexorable or irreversible, but it is to argue that change in social relations between the sexes has been dramatic, particularly within a longer historical time scale, and the dynamics behind this change needs to be analysed. There is also some evidence that these processes are speeding up and have become stronger over the last half century.

For example, just over a century ago in Britain, husbands married wives who henceforth had virtually no separate legal existence and whose rights were entirely subordinated to them. A husband not only held his wife's property but could rape, beat and virtually imprison her (within certain limits) without legal sanction. She had no right of divorce but he could and sometimes did *sell* her (Pateman 1988). Women were not quite commodities traded by fathers to husbands, but their status was not far removed from that. It is only just over half a century ago that men conceded the franchise to women on equal terms in Britain. It is not much more than a quarter century ago that proscriptions on the employment of women in certain jobs or on the basis of their marital status were made illegal. The marriage bar in the post office was abolished as recently as

Table 3.1 UK employees in employment, seasonally adjusted, in thousands

	All males and females	Males			Females		
		All	Full time	Part time	All	Full time	Part time
June 1971	22,131	13,735	13,133	602	8,396	5,603	2,793
Proportion of all employees (per cent)	100.0	62.1	59.3	2.7	37.9	25.3	12.6
June 1996	22,205	11,227	9,908	1,319	10,978	5,950	5,028
Proportion of all employees (per cent)	100.0	50.6	44.6	5.9	49.4	26.8	22.6
Absolute change 1971–96	74	-2,508	-3,225	717	2,582	347	2,235
Relative change 1971–96 (per cent)	0.3	-18.3	-24.6	119.1	30.8	6.2	80.0

Source: *Employment Gazette* and *Labour Market Trends* (various issues).

1962. Men in the Federal Republic of Germany only lost the legal right to forbid their wives to take paid employment in 1977 (Ostner 1993); men in Spain did so a year later (Threlfall 1996).

In the last 50 years women's employment has continually expanded in all western industrial capitalist countries. Since the start of the 1970s, when the UK was last thought to enjoy 'full employment', the number of jobs held by women has increased by over two and half million, as Table 3.1 shows. The number of jobs today is almost exactly the same as it was 25 years ago, because roughly the same number of men have left the employed workforce so that its sexual composition has changed dramatically.[5] This has been accompanied by a change in the proportion of full and part time jobs; there are now three million more part time jobs than in 1971. Women's full time employment has risen by one third of a million over the period, while men have lost over three million full time jobs – equivalent to one in every four that existed in 1971.[6] As a result of these changes the proportion of all employment held by men declined from 62 per cent in 1971 to just over half by 1996. If this rate of change continues men will have fewer jobs in the UK than women by the time this book is published.

The dynamics behind this employment change are complex, but four factors stand out. One is the shift away from production industries and from occupations that used skills traditionally associated with men and masculinity such as muscle power. A second factor is the shift towards part time working, but it is far from clear how much this is caused by an increase in employer's *demand* for part time jobs as such, and how far this is caused by the *supply* of female labour, which is relatively cheaper because its access to the labour market is restricted by commitments imposed by the unequal sexual division of labour in the household, combined with low levels of public provision of childcare or subsidies to it. Third is the rise in formal, juridical sexual equality. Men have lost the power to formally exclude women from jobs or education and training simply on the basis of their sex or marital status. A final factor which is often overlooked in these figures is the increase in class inequality that they conceal. The number of households with two adults working has increased, as has the number of single person households. Since the level of employment has not changed, the losers have been the large number of households where there are two adults unemployed. Thus in 1973, both partners were at work in 43 per cent of households comprising couples with dependent children. By 1992 this figure had risen to 60 per cent. In the same year, neither partner was working in 10 per cent of such couples (Condy 1994; General Household Survey 1994).

This feminization of employment (Jensen *et al.* 1988; Yeandle 1995), which is linked to so many other social changes, is not only occurring in the UK. 'Participation rates' measure the proportion of men or women of working age who are in the labour force. As Table 3.2 shows, male participation rates have been falling and female rates rising across all the countries in the Organisation for Economic Cooperation and Development (OECD). The last line of the table shows how much of the change that would be necessary to equalize participation rates

Table 3.2 Working age males and females in the labour force 1960–1990

	All OECD	UK	US	Germany	Sweden
Males					
Labour force as per cent of population aged 15–64 yrs					
Average 1960–67	92.1	97.5	88.2	94.4	93.4
Average 1988–90	83.5	86.9	85.2	81.5	84.9
Change over period	−8.6	−10.6	−3.0	−12.9	−8.5
Females					
Labour force as per cent of population aged 15–64 yrs					
Average 1960–67	45.8	48.1	43.9	48.9	53.5
Average 1988–90	58.7	64.5	67.6	55.9	80.6
Change over period	12.9	16.4	23.7	7.0	27.1
Per cent ratio of female rate to male rate: 1960s	49.7	49.3	49.8	51.8	57.3
Per cent ratio of female rate to male rate: 1988–90	70.3	74.2	79.3	68.6	94.9
Per cent increase in ratio from 1960s to 1988–90	20.6	24.9	29.6	16.8	37.7
Increase in ratio as per cent of increase needed to reach equality in male and female rates	40.9	49.1	58.9	34.8	88.1

Note: Single years have been averaged to remove cyclical effects.
Source: Organisation for Economic Cooperation and Development (OECD) 1996.

between men and women was actually achieved in the quarter century between the mid-1960s and the end of the 1980s. Across the OECD as a whole something over two-fifths of such change occurred; some countries, such as Sweden, achieved double this amount.[7]

While debate over the nature of the 'glass ceiling' remains, women's entry to what were previously male-dominated professions has risen substantially. This has also been supported by state moves to remove some of the formal systems of discrimination in employment. For example in one five-year period, 1978–1983, 62 countries introduced equal pay legislation. Formally equal rights is not the same thing as substantive material equality of opportunity, but it is an important component of the battle to achieve it. These changes have had significant effects in education where the aspirations of young women have moved closer to those of young men, and their performance has come to be better, on average, than that of young men across most subjects at most ages in the UK. This has given rise to concern about the performance of boys which the 'underperformance' of girls rarely produced, an example of ideologies of gender in operation.

There is also clear evidence that such change in women's employment status has had an effect on the domestic division of labour as well. Gershuny *et al.* (1994: 173), in a recent review of time budget evidence from a range of western industrial countries, concluded that the proportion of unpaid domestic labour undertaken by men had risen from around a quarter in the 1960s to around two-fifths a quarter century later. Thus the same survey which I quoted earlier to provide evidence of areas of highly sex-segregated domestic labour in the household found around one half of both male and female respondents in couples claiming to share such tasks as shopping for groceries (ISSP 1994). Again this does not mean that we are approaching an era of equality in the domestic division of labour, or that more than significant but small minorities of men take equal or principal responsibility for childcare. We have not yet reached a situation where there is public concern, for example, about fathers of young children going out to work. On the contrary, a major obstacle to men's greater involvement in childcare in Britain is the *increases* in average working hours of fathers of young children in a context where 10 per cent of men commit 68 hours or more per week to paid work (Marsh 1991). But in the historical context of men's ability, for millennia, to define childcare and domestic labour exclusively as a woman's job, the changes over the last 50 years are surely significant.

The fundamental material social change of expanding women's employment is linked to many others; a decisive one is the gradual death of male breadwinner ideology. Attitudes to women working vary far more according to generation than by sex. Older men and women still subscribe to the ideology of the male breadwinner and the female homemaker but younger men and women do not (Scott *et al.* 1996). There is also a clear relationship to female employment trends, both over time and across countries. In countries where women form a substantial part of the labour force, male breadwinner ideology has all but collapsed in terms of popular support for its core idea, as Figure 3.1 shows. It plots the scale of

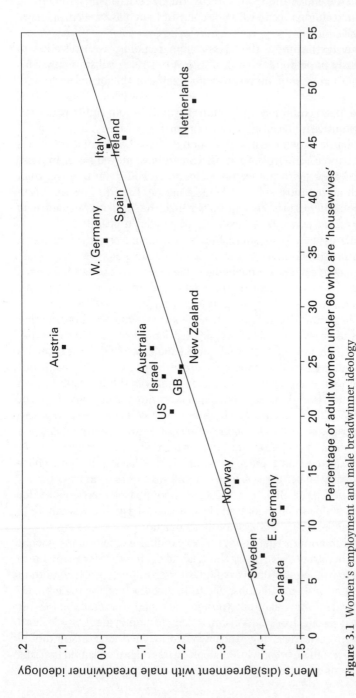

Figure 3.1 Women's employment and male breadwinner ideology

Note: Respondents were asked whether they (strongly) agreed or disagreed with the statement: 'A husband's job is to earn money; a wife's job is to look after the home and family.' A score of −1 was given to respondents who disagreed strongly, −0.5 to those who disagreed, 0 to those who neither agreed nor disagreed, or expressed no opinion, +0.5 to those who agreed and +1 to those who agreed strongly with this statement. Mean scores were then calculated for *male* respondents in each country. For example, a country where all the men agreed strongly with the statement would produce a score of +1. The figure shows these mean scores plotted against the percentage of adult *female* respondents of working age who were neither in the labour force or in training or education in each country. There is a clear relationship, for these industrial capitalist countries, between men's lack of belief in breadwinner ideology, and women's participation in the public sphere.
Source: author's analysis of ISSP 1994.

women's involvement in employment, training or education in several western industrial capitalist countries against the degree of agreement or disagreement reported by men in these countries with the statement, 'A husband's job is to earn money; a wife's job is to look after the home and family'. A clear relationship stands out between the level of *women's* labour market involvement and *men's* loss of faith in breadwinner ideology. There has also been, alongside the survival of what we might call routine popular misogyny, evidence of the partial reversal of the traditional evaluation of stereotypical masculine and feminine traits, which I mentioned above. This is not evidence of the arrival of sexual equality in material or ideological terms, but it is evidence of dramatic change, especially over the period since the Second World War.

This suggests that popular discussion of the 'crisis' in masculinity and changes in the prospects that face men, or the popularity of appeals to rediscover 'the deep masculine' proffered by Robert Bly (1991) are more than an anti-feminist backlash. They are evidence of the material and ideological weakening and collapse of patriarchy. It *is* a bad time to be a man, compared to the supremacy men have enjoyed in the past – and this is a thoroughly good thing. This raises the question of the dynamic behind such change. The answer, which I explore in the rest of this book, is that modern capitalism, and the liberal political philosophy which is central to it, is not only not patriarchal; it systematically undermines patriarchy and creates the conditions for feminist struggle in much the same way as it has created the conditions for class struggle. Men may still monopolize the powerful offices in such a society, but in so far as it is a society characterized by 'the rule of offices, not men' it is one in which for the first time these self-same men come under pressure, despite their own desires, to disregard the sex of the people with whom they deal, treat women as their formal equals and limit their sexual solidarity with their brothers.

The politics of identity and the sociology of masculinity

One result of the erosion of patriarchy by modernity has been a reversal in the popular evaluation of what masculinity is imagined to comprise. What were once male virtues are often now viewed as masculine vices – part of the 'crisis' of masculinity. It is now often argued that a major contribution to further progress in equality between men and women would be for men to consciously reform their misogynist and oppressive gender identities. This message can be found in both popular journalism and the more abstract and philosophical reaches of academic discourse. For example it is possible to read Bob Connell's excellent study *Masculinities* (1995) as an analysis of the relationship between forms of masculine gender identity, especially 'hegemonic masculinity', and social institutions and processes that exploit or oppress women and maintain the power of men as a sex over women. This has a strong intuitive appeal. Many powerful men are obnoxious, homophobic and misogynist, and these qualities appear to be vital to maintaining and reproducing a social order which maintains the sub-ordination and oppression of women.

At a more general level male 'instrumentalism' is increasingly seen as central to the dynamics of modern society, and contrasted with the virtues of feminine expressiveness. It is common to encounter the argument that because of their detachment from (what we imagine ought to be) their true feelings, men are a danger to others, the planet and ultimately to themselves. There is an aston-ishingly broad contemporary consensus which urges men to abandon what is imagined to be traditional masculinity in order to get in touch with their feel-ings and develop their emotional articulacy, for they have nothing to lose but their inhibitions, loneliness, and alienation from intimacy and the source of their humanity. It is argued that this will benefit men themselves, their intimate asso-ciates and wider society. It lies behind the rationale both for progressive men's consciousness-raising groups, and for work with violent male offenders – who are argued to dislike a confrontation with their feelings far more intensely than any varieties of 'short sharp shock' treatment, which from this perspective rein-forces rather than reforms their aggression. It lies behind all those approaches that view masculinity as some kind of exchange of 'outer' social public and political power for 'inner' personal sacrifice and pain, such as that of Kaufman (1994). It is a commonplace of men's and women's lifestyle magazines, the ubi-quitous counselling or therapy columns in newspapers and the raw material of television documentary, sitcom, soap and drama as well as most Hollywood films.

These ideas are reflected in many aspects of sociology: the expansion of inter-est in the 'sociology of emotions', in issues of identity, the self and intimate relations, calls for integration of psychology and sociology (Adorno 1968; Connell 1987) and the whole drive towards 'theorizing subjectivity'. This politics of iden-tity approach to masculinity appears in a radical and theoretically explicit way in academic arguments that masculinity is a form of identity that prioritizes instru-mental aggressive and politically or ecologically aggressive relationships with other human beings and with nature over expressive nurturance of emotional intimacy. It haunts Giddens's arguments in *The Transformation of Intimacy* (1992), although he ably criticizes its more simplistic variants. For example he argues that women have been the 'emotional revolutionaries' of modernity and characterizes dispassionate instrumentalism as male. For some writers, for example Dinnerstein (1987), such emotional inarticulacy is virtually constitutional of masculine iden-tity, or tied into a longstanding division of labour in childrearing which exists across different cultures and would be difficult to undo. For others, such as Seidler (1989, 1990) or Pahl (1995), the development is tied up with the development of modernity and in particular the divisions of labour that emerged in the indus-trial revolution. Other observers have been less restrained. Duncombe and Marsden (1993, 1995) have asked if male emotional inarticulacy is 'the last frontier of gender inequality'. Connell explicitly tries to go beyond a politics of equal pub-lic rights to an analysis of how 'hegemonic masculinity' reproduces patriarchy in modern societies (1995: 231). From this he invites men to embrace 'gender vertigo' in order to undermine patriarchy, although he concedes that, for example, the green pro-feminist activists he considers, who could be taken as living examples of this political strategy, do not themselves believe that by changing their masculinity they are doing much to change the world. Connell agrees with them.

I think that this approach to masculinity is misleading for four reasons. First, it smuggles in the assumption that it is only men who possess masculinity, by collapsing ideology into identity on the basis of biology. The only common feature of the diverse masculinities studied is that it is biological men who possess these gender identities. There are ultimately as many varieties of masculinity as there are men, however, and this is an unhelpful way to theorize gender identity. If we accept that women too can be masculine (as we must do if we take gender to be socially constructed) it becomes difficult to prevent masculinity becoming a general term for anything we don't like. The argument I made in the previous chapter suggests that this is because the fetishism of sexual difference simply reflects back to us as masculinity aspects of our inexorably contradictory personal identities. Thus in much of the literature aspects of modernity which have no intrinsic connection to sex (such as the logic of instrumentalism or the monopolization of the means of violence by the state) come to appear as a product of masculinity. It is not masculinity that creates modernity, however. On the contrary, it is modernity that has created our fetishistic image of masculinity. I pursue this argument further in Chapter 4.

Second it has an unbalanced view of the relationship between the personal and the political. The politics of identity retreats from classical sociology's concern with material social structures and forces to applied psychology.[8] By this I do not mean the concern with feelings and emotion rather than norms or ideologies. I mean the understanding of social structures and processes in terms of the individual behaviour or attitudes of people they comprise. It is unhelpful to see organizations or societies that men control as ultimately an expression of their identities (Young 1984). It is not clear that changing the personal identities of individual powerful men would have much impact on social change. This may be an important part of the truth, but sociology also aims to understand both the unanticipated consequences of individuals' actions and the way in which social structures once created, constrain individuals to act in certain ways regardless of their personalities or predispositions. Modernity is the era of bureaucratization, rationalization, 'the rule of offices, not men'. While Weber may have underestimated the autonomy that more powerful men enjoy, explaining patriarchy in terms of personal misogyny is akin to explaining capitalism in terms of greed. It underestimates the importance of social structures which force men and women to act in certain ways which they might not otherwise choose.[9]

Connell (1987: 57–8), for example, is clear that we cannot posit a 'masculine' predisposition to use physical violence as an explanation of all the social relations of modern violence, including the state and military technology, because these also have other sources and require at least some analysis of how social institutions make use of such a propensity towards violence in a certain way;

how it ends up as nuclear confrontation between states for example rather than interpersonal fisticuffs. Segal (1990: Ch. 9) makes a similar point. If this is the case, however, why theorize patriarchy in terms of a psychological 'hegemonic masculinity'?

In an age of bureaucratization and rationalization it is rarely possible to translate personal values directly into routine public action. Office holders have to maintain the personality associated with their office. This is one way modernity undermines patriarchy. Office holders are required in principle not to discriminate between sexes and genders – to some extent to keep their misogyny, ethnocentrism or homophobia private. It is also possible, so long as they fulfil the duties of the office, to maintain an identity widely at variance with the hegemonic pattern. Here is the positive side of what Baumann has called the 'moral invisibility' of bureaucracy. It need be no concern of employers (although they may try to make it so) whether I am gay, or a transvestite, a passionate feminist or hopeless misogynist. All sorts of powerful men, from politicians to business leaders, live out lives distant from the hegemonic 'ideal', fantasizing, for example, about what Connell (1995: 219) calls 'the receptive pleasures of the anus' (Friday 1980). A vital part of any adequate sociology is thus a sense of the distance between the individual and social structure which modernity makes possible and which provides the material basis for feminism and sex equality in the first place.

The third reason is that it ignores the sexual genesis of human beings, and because of that, falls into the trap of imagining that the personal is purely political, which the confusion of sexual genesis and sexual difference produces, giving us the false choice between the politicization of personal identity and its maintenance in a patriarchal form, which I discussed in Chapter 2. The danger is that attempts to 'reform' the self, in the pursuit of greater sexual equality, may only reinforce a social process whereby all 'selves', whether male or female, become increasingly subordinated to the demands of the universal market and the associated abstract systems and bureaucracies of modernity. This danger is all the greater both because these same social forces have been responsible for undermining patriarchy in the public sphere – and therefore appear progressive, and because this increasing subordination and weakening of the self is always imagined to be its opposite – the development of a liberated and ever more powerful self, a self capable, for example, of a 'pure relationship' or of 'democratizing' its personal life. Meanwhile, little advance in sexual equality may be achieved; indeed the reverse may occur.

Finally, and most fundamental of all, I think such analyses of masculinity confuse the symptom and the cause. Instead of attempting to discover, for example, what sociological and psychological socialization mechanisms within childrearing produce masculinities, as Chodorow (1978), Dinnerstein (1987) and Benjamin (1990) have all attempted and which follows a tradition going back to Parsons and Freud, instead of using such analyses to speculate on how reform of such socialization might produce androgynous gender identities, or how 'gender vertigo' might be encouraged, we could instead ask: what has made people, including sociologists, psychoanalysts and popular journalists, imagine that individuals possess gender? How have they come to see the connection between sex, self and society in this way? The answer to this question takes us towards the analysis of the changing social relations of the sexual division of labour and the changing ideology of gender this throws up in modernity, and towards the ability to see the arena of the private sphere and the personal as something that lies beyond gender, contrary to the socialization theories that are themselves a product of that ideology.

I think that we can best understand the contemporary appeal of this politics of identity, and the other three changes I have outlined, in terms of changing relations between the sexes, which in turn are based upon a fundamental change working itself out in contemporary modernity of the status of the individual in society, perhaps best summed up in the idea of universal human rights. The essence of this change is a world historical shift in the significance of sex difference brought about by the defeat of patriarchy (the rule of men by virtue of their sex) by the four interconnected revolutions of modernity: capitalism, liberalism, rationalization and the demographic transition. This book is therefore about the social relations which characterize the fag-end of patriarchy, about the material and symbolic legacy of millennia of rule by men, about the processes responsible for the collapse of patriarchy, and about the ideologies of gender, masculinity and femininity which women and men use to make sense of the transitional period through which they are now living. Masculinity can be seen as the last ideological defence of male supremacy in a world that has already conceded that men and women are equal. Invented in order to argue that men's power is socially rather than naturally derived, the concept suffers from the patent flaw (from the point of view of defending men's privilege) that what is socially rather than naturally constructed can be socially challenged and changed. I think that we have reached the point where masculinity as a concept obscures the analysis of social relations between the sexes, especially when it is imagined to be something that empirically existing individuals possess, which they might reform.

I would thus like to see the end of masculinity in the sense of turning the focus of the struggle for greater gender equality away from how masculinity is to be abolished or reformed and towards a more thorough pursuit of a politics of equal rights. Such a politics foregrounds questions of which social mechanisms continue to defend men's ability to wield power by virtue of their sex against the corrosive effects of universalism, while also allowing us to resist those aspects of universalism which corrode the independent self rather than patriarchal privilege. Focusing on masculinity has the danger that it leads us into an apparently radical but in practice individualized and conservative cul-de-sac which reinforces the contemporary preoccupation with the self at the expense of its social context. In contrast to the politics of identity I suggest that pursuing a politics of justice and equal rights to its logical conclusion is a more radical option, once we have solved the problems caused by the confusion of sexual genesis and sexual difference. I return to this argument in Chapter 8.

Notes

1 MacFarlane (1986) and others have suggested that fathers' power to do so in Britain was less than elsewhere in Europe.

2 This and other statistics are taken from the author's analyses of the 1994 International Social Survey Program's 1994 survey module *Family and Changing Gender Roles* administered to some 33,000 respondents in 18 countries by national survey research organizations, deposited in the ESRC Data Archive, University of Essex. Those who carried out the original collection and analysis of the data bear no responsibility for the interpretation I have placed on it here. References to this source are referred to below as 'ISSP 1994'.

3 The 1997 General Election changed the position significantly, thanks to the combined effects of the Labour Party's women-only shortlists policy, and the scale of its victory, so that many women were elected in seats which the party might not normally have expected to win. But while the Labour Party had over 100 women MPs in the new parliament, the Conservative Party managed just six.

4 All figures in this paragraph are from Jukes (1993: xv).

5 By 'jobs' I mean employees in employment. The number of self-employed has risen in this period by around 700,000; here too, women's employment has expanded faster than men's but from a smaller base. I have excluded self-employment from the discussion because a breakdown by sex and status was not readily available for June 1996.

6 Of course, this shorthand expression conceals a rather more complex reality. Since employment is really a flow rather than a stock, the actual jobs (and people occupying them) being counted by these levels of employment will have been continually changing across this period.

7 Of course, equal participation rates do not mean labour market equality; it is possible to be in the labour force, but still have a part time, poorly paid, sex-typed job, or indeed, no job at all.

8 Craib (1989) points out that this was essentially Freud's view of the discipline.

9 For a useful critique along these lines see Young (1984).

4

The paradoxes of sex and gender

A typical collection, *Theorising Masculinities*, argues that only by studying men's (socially constructed) *gender* will we be able to analyse men's dominance critically rather than unwittingly reinforce it by placing men in the focus of public and political debate at the expense of women (Brod and Kaufman 1994: 4):[1]

> How does one *really* go about placing men and their institutions at the center of an analysis without replicating the patriarchal biases of previous studies of men? A number of authors here, and many others, have for quite some time now insisted that the difference lay in *how* one theorised men and masculinities, that the new studies we were producing and looking for were about men as *men*, rather than as generic human beings whose gender went unnoticed and untheorized or at least undertheorized.
>
> Such studies . . . incorporate the fundamental feminist insight that gender is a system of power and not just a set of stereotypes or observable differences between men and women.

This begs a major question of what masculinity comprises, which this chapter explores in a variety of ways. The key question is: what is *male* about *masculinity*? At first sight this seems a rather stupid question. But as I suggested in Chapters 1 and 2, addressing it starts to unravel ways we think about sex and gender which currently confuse the relationship between biology and society by slipping, at decisive points, between the conceptual categories of male/female and masculine/feminine, between arguments about what masculinity empirically is (as in a living man's personal experience and acting out of his gender identity) and what ideologies about it imagine it to be (as in ideas about what properly comprises 'true' masculinity) in the search for what Freud (1986: 353) was to call a 'more definite connotation' of it.

Connell argues that it is mistaken to attempt to produce an empirical definition of masculinity:

'Masculinity' to the extent the term can be briefly defined at all, is simultaneously a place in gender relations, the practice through which men and
women engage that place in gender, and the effects of these practices in
bodily experience, personality and culture . . . I emphasize that terms such as
hegemonic masculinity and marginalised masculinities name not fixed character types but configurations of practice generated in particular situations
in a changing structure of relationships.

(1995: 71, 81)

He even suggests that ' "Masculinity" is not a coherent object about which a gen-
eralising science can be produced' (1995: 67). This comes close to my argument
that masculinity as such does not exist, but begs three questions (aside from that
of how Connell can devote an entire book to something that is not a coherent
object of knowledge!). How can we square the impossibility of finding 'a more
definite connotation' with the central role Connell gives to hegemonic masculinity in reproducing patriarchy? If we cannot define it, how are we nevertheless
able to identify it? – which we clearly must be able to do in order to differentiate
between different forms of masculinity. For example he argues that 'The number
of men rigorously practising the hegemonic pattern in its entirety may be quite
small' (1995: 79). We must know what the 'hegemonic pattern' comprises before
we can make such a statement! I suspect there is a more definite model of hegemonic masculinity implicit in Connell's work, and it returns to Freud's (1986:
353) original contrast between activity and passivity, so that at one point he
argues, 'The moment of separation from hegemonic masculinity basically involves
choosing passivity' (1995: 132). Finally, if we cannot define it, how is it that we
nevertheless know it so well that, as I pointed out in Chapter 1, people recognize
it so easily and describe it in lists?

At least Connell argues through the issues of definition of masculinity. As
McMahon (1993: 690) has remarked:

It is remarkable how seldom writers on masculinity explicitly indicate what
kind of concept they take masculinity to be. Michael Kimmel [1986] defines
masculinity as 'what it means to be a man', but this still leaves the matter
rather open.

It is an instructive exercise to check the indexes of recent literature on masculinity. Entries abound on all sorts of aspects of masculinity and the variety of forms
it takes, but very few authors attempt any empirical definition. The best, such as
Segal (1990) emphasize the inevitable contradictoriness and dynamism of masculinity, and some go as far to suggest, as Connell (1995: 44) does at times, that
masculinity can be defined only negatively as that which femininity is not:

Masculinity and femininity are inherently relational concepts, which have
meaning in relation to each other, as a social demarcation and a cultural
opposition. This holds regardless of the changing content of the demarcation
in different societies and periods of history.

This appears to bring the advantage of connecting masculinity to misogyny, examining its roots in the envy and dread of women, but appears to take us back to an opposition between male and female again, and begs the no less intractable question of what the femininity which masculinity is defined in relation to comprises.

One of the best discussions is that by Morgan (1992: 38–44). He considers the problems of 'essentialism, reductionism and reification', looking for

> . . . some essential gender core associated with men and masculinity. . . a set of more or less fixed traits . . . the reduction of social or cultural practices to . . . the sum of individual characteristics and the treatment in turn of these characteristics as things: a sense of something that is external to the observer, that is unchanged by the intervention of the observer and is not dependent on the standpoint of different observers.
>
> (1992: 41–2)

This discussion shows us the core of our problem, however. If masculinity is so variable, what relationship do these varieties have to each other, and in turn to men's dominance over women? We slip between a definition in terms of the range of characteristics empirical men display (male is synonymous with masculine) and one which seeks to keep a theoretical relationship between masculinity and power (masculinity involves the reproduction of patriarchy). Thus Morgan (1992: 46–7) argues, engagingly:

> Men do not routinely remove and replace their sexual organs in everyday encounters. They do, however, sometimes remove their hats or their ties, clench their fists, bare their teeth, smile, weep, relax, straighten up, touch or obviously fail to touch . . . in short we should think of doing masculinities rather than of being masculine.

The key question is what relation this infinite array of men's social behaviour has to the possession of 'their sexual organs'. If it has none, which is one way of reading Morgan's argument, then they are not 'doing masculinities'; they are doing 'humanities'. If it has, then they are being male. I think the resolution of this paradox concerns the nature of the connection, and one which the very terms masculinity and masculinities obscures. Morgan is absolutely correct to focus on reification. For the essential point is that the connection is not one which is made at the level of the individual, as an aspect of the identity of persons, but at the level of society, as an aspect of the ideology produced by the sexual division of labour.

Over the last few years, these problems have led to the tendency to theorize 'masculinities' in the plural as in the works of Mac an Ghaill (1996), Brod and Kaufman (1994) and Connell's (1995) book. This simply begs the question about what it is that these masculin*ities* all share (definitions are just as absent) in these collections, and it is difficult to avoid the conclusion that all they have in common is possession of a penis. Only one author, Jeff Hearn (1996), takes up this issue. He notes that the term is used imprecisely and to cover a wider variety of meanings and describe radically different social phenomena, often slipping, as I have noted above, between masculinity as identity and ideology: 'many descriptions of masculinity are really descriptions of popular ideologies about the actual or ideal characteristics of men' (1996: 207), yet is often used to causally explain other social effects such as describing what males as opposed to females do or the nature of the sexual division of labour. Hearn questions the value of the concept of masculinity, suggests we should define it more carefully and that 'it is generally preferable to move from "masculinities" back to "men"' (1996: 214).

Hearn's points are valuable, but I think a stronger conclusion ought to be drawn: that we cannot see masculinity as a property of persons at all. Since modernity has quite rightly been seen as an era which has made possible a 'historical consciousness of gender', to use Connell's phrase, an era in which gender is seen as something that is made by men and women and that can therefore be remade and reformed by them, and since every sociology course on gender properly starts out from an explanation of the difference between biologically given sex and socially determined or constructed gender, then this must seem a surprising claim, to say the least. But there is something profoundly paradoxical about the historical consciousness of gender. To the extent that we become aware that gender is something that is socially constructed and not naturally ordained, then we must also become aware that it is not determined by sex. At its simplest level this means recognizing that both males and females possess both 'masculine' and 'feminine' attributes, or that there is a difference between the meaning of 'masculine' and 'male'. If we follow through this awareness to its logical conclusions, as I try to do in this chapter, then we must realize that if is not determined by sex, then gender, at least in the sense of properties possessed by men and women *because* of their biological sex, *cannot exist*.

Biological maleness

One source of the confusion lies in seeing gender as a characteristic of persons analogous to their biological sex. This approach is encouraged by much empirical social science which tries to operationalize the study of gender by simply using sex as a face sheet variable then searching for correlations. As Morgan (1986: 37) comments: 'how is it possible to use the labels "feminine" and "masculine" without falling into some kind of essentialism . . . without in some way perpetuating the very stereotypes that a feminist inspired study seeks to undermine?' If I describe someone as male or female I mean that by virtue of having a penis and testicles they may produce sperm and be capable of fertilizing eggs and biologically fathering a child. By possessing ovaries, a vagina and a womb, they may become pregnant and biologically mother a child.

I use the word 'may' for two reasons. Some males or females may be infertile. Second, and more significantly, human reproduction, or sexual genesis, can never be *only* biological, and is hardly thinkable except in a social, cultural and symbolic context that makes it possible and gives it meaning.[2] We cannot, for example, understand it purely in terms of the natural and inevitable operation of some primal 'instinct'. On the contrary, we could view the whole of human history and society as an elaboration of the incest taboo, as the development of increasingly complex ways in which infants come to be socially reproduced as individuals conscious of their difference from others and able to form social relations with them. The key points are that biological reality means that definite membership of one sex precludes me from membership of the other – if I am male, I cannot simultaneously be female, and vice versa – and that two sexes are needed to produce a child.

Thus in contrast to those from an ethnomethodological position who would wish to see this classification of male and female as a product of culture, such as Kessler and McKenna (1978) or Jaggar and Bordo (1989), I would argue that it has a material reality quite independent of any classification system we choose to use to describe it. The proof of this lies in the potential ability of only a combination of male and female to successfully biologically reproduce, whatever I choose to call the two sides in this division of labour. This is not to deny a wide range of what Morgan (1986: 34) has called 'secondary' sexual characteristics such as height, percentage of body fat, distribution of body hair, bone structure or size of chest, which are more variable and which, while they correspond to sex, overlap between the sexes and vary with other factors (for example, as an older, small, man I am aware of my physical vulnerability to more powerful or younger men), but it is to insist that the categories male and female are not exclusively social constructions. I think Craib (1994: 40) sums this up best:

> Sociology... has tended to favour only social explanations. We find arguments not only that what it means to be a man or a woman is different in different types of society (which of course it is) but that what it means to be a man or a woman is entirely a social matter, a matter of the way in which a particular society defines masculinity or femininity. It seems to me that this is plainly not the case: however hard we try, for example, we cannot find a society in which men bear babies or women have penises.

In contrast to defining a person as male or female, and describing the sexual characteristics determined by that biological fact, if I describe a person as possessing a social characteristic, I am defining them as having access to something which has been collectively produced by human beings and cannot simply be seen as a *product* of their bodies even if it uses them, and in that sense, is dependent on them. One example would be language. It is something collectively produced by human interaction. A person's inability to speak might be social; they may not have learned an appropriate language, they may be forbidden to speak or they may have renounced speech. They may even have done so unconsciously or 'hysterically'. It might also be biological, a malfunction of the throat or vocal chords for example. Another instance might be possession of a particular skill: to drive a motor car, throw a punch, dance gracefully, kick a ball, change a nappy or sobbingly convey the full anguish of my inner world to a fellow human being. Each of these skills might *use* my body, but they are essentially learned, social constructions. A throat and larynx is a natural precondition for speech, but it is not sufficient. But possession of a male as opposed to a female body is neither sufficient to produce masculinity (if it is socially constructed), nor a precondition for it (if women can possess it). Were it either, we could simply equate masculinity with male.

Natural difference theories: maleness causes masculinity

Theorists of natural differences between the sexes try to show that there are innate differences between men and women, aside from their complementary reproductive capacities, such as hormone levels or brain physiology, which have directly social manifestations and perhaps replicate 'natural' behaviour differences between the sexes found in other animal species. These differences in turn explain 'gender' arrangements; being masculine is a direct result of being male and is not, in any meaningful sense, socially constructed. At best it may add to or build upon nature's essential base. Such theories have been widely criticized (see for example Fausto-Sterling 1985; Connell 1987: Ch. 4 and *passim*; Fuchs Epstein 1988) chiefly because the impact of what differences that can be determined is far from clear, the line of cause and effect obscure (does aggression lead to higher levels of particular hormones, or vice versa?) and average differences in measurements of these characteristics *between* sexes are typically swamped by differences *within* them.

As Segal (1987), Connell (1987: 170), Fuchs Epstein (1988) and others have noted, sex *difference* research has consistently proved to be sex *similarity* research: 'In tests of cognitive skills and personality traits, experimental subjects stubbornly reveal greater differences within a sex than between them' (Segal 1993: 626–7). This is all the more surprising given the difficulty in such research of controlling for social context. Given the existence of a social division of labour which leads to vastly different life experiences for men and women, given the failure of many researchers to take adequate account of them (Fairweather 1976; Sayers 1986) and given their tendency to privilege nature over nurture in accounts of whatever differences do crop up, it is surprising that some evidence of the sort of psychological traits which people routinely associate with masculinity do not show up more strongly than they do.[3]

The discovery and interpretation of 'natural' differences seems to reflect culture rather than the differences themselves explaining social behaviour. For example brain lateralization research has sometimes been used to argue either that there is a difference in the brains of men and women or in the way in which they operate. The interpretation of such evidence is controversial, particularly the significance and understanding of what 'differences' are measured for any aspect of social behaviour. In such circumstances it is not surprising to find, as Fuchs Epstein points out, that some feminists of difference have now claimed that such findings demonstrate the 'natural' superiority of the female brain, while at least one Japanese theorist has described the way in which brain lateralization works distinctively among the Japanese – of both sexes (1988: 52–6).

Drawing inferences from animal behaviour for human behaviour has two basic flaws. First, it ignores the qualitative difference between other animals and humans which lies in the conscious and self-reflexive character of societies which humans build and which they can build differently tomorrow from how they have been able to construct them today. Animals are more heavily dominated by instincts which they cannot reconstruct. It ignores the decisive intervention of human agency, meaning and symbolism. This need not mean that humans are devoid of instinct, nor 'that both the body and the psyche are postnatally passive *tabulae rasae* . . . a blank slate on which are inscribed various social "lessons"' (Gatens 1996: 4). Second, the descriptions of animal behaviour which tend to be offered are described in the language and concepts of these human societies and symbolism. We can, of course, find examples in nature of female infant nurturance and male aggression, but we can also find the reverse. My favourite is the seahorse – the only male who becomes pregnant and delivers his offspring fully formed for the outside environment. This search for a 'natural' basis to human behaviour is ultimately a search for reassurance and psychic security through the romance of authenticity in a disenchanted world. This, I think is the main reason for what Fuchs Epstein (1988: 3) calls 'the compelling appeal of simplistic biological explanations, especially those that support cultural stereotypes.'

It is quite possible that there are some key biological differences between the sexes that have some implications for the ability to develop particular skills, but given the range of social activities which individual men and women have accomplished that transgress normal sex-typed behaviour, it is difficult to argue that they either explain any aspects of the existing sexual division of labour, or that they set limits to possible future ones. Moreover, even if we *did* discover some such characteristic, it would still be a social and political choice to either amplify its effects, let it take its course or to use social arrangements to assert sexual equality in the face of 'nature'. After discussing biological differences Goffman (1977: 301) concludes, 'For these physical facts of life to have no appreciable social consequences would take a little organising, but at least by modern standards, not much.' I agree with Connell's evaluation (1987: 71):

> It is possible that there are some innate differences in temperament or ability
> between women and men. The hypothesis cannot be ruled out entirely. But
> if they exist, we can say quite confidently that they are not the basis of major
> social institutions.

If this is the case, we are effectively arguing that access to skills or capacities which are social constructions are rarely, if ever, determined directly by biological sex, and that any such capacities as might exist are likely to have few consequences of note. In other words, we *cannot* reduce masculinity to maleness.

It is no accident that sex difference research got underway at about the same time that Freud was proposing that masculinity and femininity were cultural constructions, since both investigations represent different forms of the development of a historical consciousness of gender. While Freud saw men and women as themselves authors of whatever 'sex differences' they might create through their unconscious repression of their original polymorphous perversity, sex difference research took the opposite view. It looked for an explanation and justification for the sexual division of labour between men and women in differences in their psychological or social capacities linked to biological sexual differences. Perhaps men could think or reason better than women, or develop stronger minds as well as stronger muscles.

As we know, however, a century of such 'sex similarity' research has neither convinced people that men and women are fundamentally the same, nor diminished their ability to produce immediately recognizable lists of what the essence of masculinity comprises. We are so convinced that the sexual division of labour *must* be related to the individual personalities of men and women that we hang onto the concepts of masculine and feminine. Books such as *Men Are From Mars, Women Are From Venus* (Gray 1992) are testament to our desire to believe in this, as is Robert Bly's bestseller *Iron John* (1991) which explores 'the deep masculine'. It is difficult to think of a single example of modern popular culture which does not trade, in part, on the prospects and pitfalls of gender difference and confusion. Lifestyle magazines, defined by a male or female audience, and focusing on sex in their copy, are one illustration of the increasing strength of this obsession. Some of this material, such as Bly's, contains some useful analysis along the way, some of it uses humour to yield real insights into the vulnerabilities of our gender identities, but much of it is depressing, dire, stereotyping and misogynistic. Gray's is a paperback bestseller and example of the latter. 'Venusians love to shop' he tells us, and urges Martians 'When listening to her, reassure her that you are interested by making little noises like ah ha, uh-huh, oh, mmhuh, and hmmmmm'.

Unfortunately it is not just the general public who are convinced, deep down, that sex is the true secret of their core identity, but sociologists of gender too. Thus, for example, within a few pages of the quotation on sex difference research, which I noted above, we find Segal (1993: 635) presenting a global opposition between the nature of masculinity and femininity which presupposes just such a fundamental difference:

> A 'pure' masculinity cannot be displayed except in relation to what is defined as its opposite: first and foremost in relation to 'femininity'. But no one can be masculine through and through without constantly, and in the end rather obviously, doing violence to one of the most basic human attributes: the capacity for sensitivity to oneself and others, the expression of fear, the admission of weakness, the wisdom of cooperation, the satisfaction in servicing, the pleasures of passivity, the need to be needed – all quintessentially 'feminine'.

At one level Segal's argument is consistent. The second quotation can be read as an argument about the essential bisexuality underlying the appearance of 'real' masculinity. It makes the point I have just made about the internal inconsistency of definitions of the essence of masculinity. It suggests that there are little frightened boys inside powerful violent men. What this doesn't explain however is why we see *either* set of attributes as connected to sex in the first place, nor why we can identify 'masculine' attributes with men in the absence of evidence from sex difference research that would allow us to do so, nor why what we might call the reparative side of 'basic human attributes' get labelled feminine and the aggressive ones 'masculine'. For if we do make this connection, then the second quotation from Segal can be read in a plainly essentialist way. Men are masculine (rather than bisexual in gender terms), women are feminine and we can identify what this masculinity or femininity comprises. Women represent basic human attributes, men represent a threat to them. We are back to the language of essentialism: the future is female after all. This is all the more ironic an implication given that Segal's aim has been to criticize essentialist theories of sex differences.

For analysts from the 'difference' school of gender relations, there are fewer checks on this line of argument and masculinity appears more clearly as that which it really is in such analyses: the incarnation of evil. The alienation of masculinity (and by implication men) from nature and the physical is condemned, in contrast to the natural ecofeminism of women. 'Life is delivered and nurtured by woman then disappears back into the womb of Mother Earth', argues Pietila (1990: 239) while for men, 'Life is a problem . . . A constant fight to conquer, exploit and mould nature'.[4] Since men have traditionally assumed godliness, it is unsurprising that women should mount a counter-claim, but arguing which sexual organ grants us immortality will do little to advance sexual equality. Masculinity becomes a conceptual dustbin into which everything we dislike is emptied:

> I am developing the thesis that phallocracy is the most basic, radical and universal societal manifestation of evil, underlying not only gynocide but genocide, not only rapism, but also racism, not only nuclear and chemical contamination but also spiritual pollution.
>
> (Daly 1984: 164)

Such an approach is both politically and personally harmful. Politically it leads to Utopian prescriptions about what institutions emancipated from their 'masculine' character might be like (and since masculinity can be associated with almost any aspect of social order, hierarchy or organization we end up with the fantasy of organizations and whole societies which function effectively without constraining their members in any way at all). Personally it invites a monstrous form of denial where aspects of ourselves, such as aggression, are split off and projected onto others once they have been labelled as 'masculine', as Jane Temperley has explored (1984; see also Segal 1990: 266–7). As I suggested in Chapter 2, inexorably contradictory tendencies of any personal identity which could ever exist (aggressive, empathetic or good and bad) have here become transformed into the empirical qualities of one or other gender, and ultimately of actually existing men or women. Such analysis recycles the fetishism of sexual difference, rather than analysing it.

Theories of socially constructed difference: male is determined by masculine

If I describe a person as gendered rather than sexed, as possessing masculine or feminine traits, or displaying a masculine identity, or some variety of *masculinity* rather than being biologically *male*, what does that mean? It is usually taken to mean that I am describing social characteristics, which are nevertheless related to biological sex, or the way biological sexual characteristics are socially expressed. Either way, it is argued that the social characteristics are related to sex, but not determined by it. Masculinity could be seen to describe the way males socially construct their identity in a particular historical form of society. A good example is Connell (1987: 79) again: 'The social practices that construct gender relations do not express natural patterns, nor do they ignore natural patterns; rather they negate them in a practical transformation.' Connell is aware that this brings him close to an 'additive' conception of social gender basing itself on biological sexual dimorphism which would take us back to 'natural difference' theory, so he immediately quotes Rubin's famous article (1975: 180): 'Far from being an expression of natural differences, exclusive gender identity is the suppression of natural similarities.' Connell argues that gender is socially imposed on children, so as to construct the categories of man and woman and 'the solidarity of the sex' (1987: 81) *because of* the absence of any difference of social or physical capacities of boys and girls. He suggests that socially defined gender categories sustain patriarchal power and men's dominance. In contrast to expressing any natural sexual differences, it is gender which socially constructs these differences in the first place.

> Girls in early adolescence are on average bigger and stronger than the boys in their own school classes; yet it is just at this age that enormous pressure is applied to make them dependent and fearful in relation to males. To sustain patriarchal power on the large scale requires the construction of a hypermasculine ideal of toughness and dominance; the physical image of masculinity this produces is grotesquely unlike the actual physique of most men . . . My male body does not confer my masculinity on me; it receives masculinity (or some fragment thereof) as its social definition.
>
> (Connell 1987: 80, 83)

Connell's approach, like that of Goffman (1977), is an argument that takes us beyond biological determinism, but it contains two crucial weaknesses. The first concerns *why* gender should exist. If it is not a social expression of biological dimorphism what is it an expression of? What social relations and structures give rise to it? The second concerns why 'gender' categories (whatever the answer to the first question) should be imposed onto sex categories, rather than onto other characteristics? These two questions are modern variants of the problems that the social contract theorists faced, which I discussed in Chapters 1 and 2.

Merely to ask these questions, and ponder the possible answers, is a rather bizarre process, and to the extent that gender *must* be connected to sex (otherwise the use of the term gender would seem rather odd), it is an absurd exercise in counterfactuals. It is, I hope, a revealing one however. There are two plausible answers to the first question and Connell implicitly cites both of them. The first, best expressed by Gayle Rubin, is that gender is a way of institutionalizing heterosexuality and thus maintaining the reproduction of the species in the absence of 'natural' instincts which could otherwise be expected to perform such a function: 'individuals are engendered so that marriage can be guaranteed' (1975: 180). This connects gender to sexual reproduction, but as Connell himself notes in his critique of the way Parsons (Parsons and Bales 1956) uses such arguments to 'explain' traditional gender roles in the American nuclear family of the 1950s and 60s (1987: 72), 'an enormous range of social arrangements are consistent with the occurrence of enough heterosexual intercourse to reproduce the species.' In other words, Connell argues that gender is a functional requirement of society, but could take a wide variety of forms, leaving us the problem of explaining the origins of the particular form we have in contemporary modern societies, such as 'hegemonic masculinity'. Below, I discuss Freud's theories about the social construction of human sexuality, and his concept of the 'polymorphous perversity' of infants before they learn to adopt appropriate gender roles. Connell's argument here corresponds to Freud's account, and I think both face essentially the same problem: if sexual difference is simply socially constructed through gender, it is difficult to explain how an adult polymorphous perversity would not *also* be consistent with 'enough heterosexual intercourse to reproduce the species'. Gender would not be a functional requirement of societies. If this is the case we have to look elsewhere for the explanation of gender and why it is mapped onto sex categories. We would also have to explain whether such polymorphous perversity resulting from the abolition of gender would threaten the incest taboo. As will become clear when I discuss Freud, what we face here is a confusion between socialization as the production of gender in the sense of masculine and feminine identities, and generation in the sense of the production of identity itself, of selves that are conscious of their separate existence, and capable of taking responsibility for their actions on this basis.

Rubin's (1975) argument has been popular and widely cited because it appears to offer a progressive way out of our dilemma. It appears to resolve the paradoxes of sex and gender by suggesting that there is no essential difference between men and women as sexes, that the appearance of this difference is a social construction, which we can label gender, and that this social construction has a historically functionalist rationale – the survival of the species. The drawback with Rubin's account, apart from its implicit functionalist approach which some would query, is that it is not clear what historical conditions have changed so that what was once a functional imperative for the survival of the species no longer applies. In short, if the polymorphous perversity implied by abandoning gender is now consistent with 'enough heterosexual intercourse' why was this not the case in the past?

There are two further problems with this approach. It assumes that cathexis, or desire, is necessarily founded on difference rather than similarity, otherwise it is not clear why the mapping of gender differences onto sex in order to create the solidarities of sex should promote rather than undermine heterosexuality.[5] Indeed we know from feminist research on sexual violence that the elaboration of gender differences has also meant the elaboration of misogyny, contempt, physical assault, rape and murder. Why should men and women prefer to 'sleep with the enemy'? If Rubin's basic premise is correct – that there is likely to be some social mechanism which promotes 'enough heterosexual intercourse' – could we not expect it to emphasize natural similarities and suppress social differences, in order to maximize all forms of intercourse, social and sexual, between biological males and females? Rubin's attractive argument thus seems to take us back too close to natural difference theory again: gender is a social expression of biological sexual dimorphism.[6]

A final problem, which really lies beyond the scope of sociology, is to account for the genesis of humanity in a social institution. While we might be wary, for good reasons, of making the reproduction of the species a purely biologically determined affair, it seems equally problematic to make it a social construction: did *Homo sapiens* have to culturally 'invent' gender in order to guarantee their species reproduction? To say the least, this looks a bit like putting the cultural cart before the evolutionary horse.

Patriarchy: swinging between the penis and the phallus

The problems inherent in Connell's first answer to the question, 'why does gender exist?' leads to the second answer: that gender sustains patriarchy and the social dominance of men. 'Compulsory heterosexuality' to use Rich's term (1984), is not about the reproduction of the species but the reproduction of men's social power over women. This answer immediately begs another question however: if gender sustains the dominance of biological males (rather than human beings who choose to or are able to become masculine) on what basis were biological men able to organize collectively to develop patriarchal power? Their collective organization in the first place again looks rather like a social 'expression' of biological difference. There are two alternative answers to this question. The first is to root patriarchy in the penis and appeal to biology for an explanation of the power of men – for example by arguing that men have an innately greater capacity for sexual violence. The second is to root patriarchy in the phallus – to see the penis as a socially constructed symbol of the public structures of men's power.

Susan Griffin (1971) and Susan Brownmiller (1976) are two clear examples of theorists who base their accounts on men's innately superior capacity for sexual violence and their approach forms the basis for much radical feminist 'politics of difference'. However I argue below that it also underpins more apparently sociological approaches, such as that of Carole Pateman through the use of terms such as 'sexual contract' and 'male sex-right' (1988) which connect the sociological analysis of rights to biological categories. It is important to be clear here, that such a capacity for violence *has* to be 'biological' for the theory to make sense. Were the theory to be recast in terms of the development of a *social* capacity to exert sexual violence we could not explain why only biological males developed it. If females could also develop it, so that sexual violence was not monopolized by one sex, then we could expect it to have been used to develop other forms of social solidarity and stratification – of one clan over another or whatever. And in other contexts, such as the analysis of the development of state forms and imperialism, or class conflict, for example, this is just what we do accept: that both sexes have a capacity for violence. In other words it has to be the penis rather than the phallus that is used to explain dominance, because otherwise we cannot explain why women cannot get their hands on the phallus, or indeed why anyone would choose not to possess one, or to become 'feminine'.

If sexual violence is ultimately explained biologically, and sexual violence is the key to patriarchy, then patriarchy is produced by natural sexual difference; women's oppression, patriarchy and gender will all be ended only with the abolition of biological sex. As long as heterosexual reproduction remains the basis of human society men will oppress women. This is a profoundly depressing conclusion, which although it has been adopted in part by some radical feminist theorists, has led feminists such as Michele Barrett and Sheila Rowbotham to reject the concept of patriarchy altogether (Rowbotham 1979; Barrett 1980). It appears to give us two choices. One is to develop alternative means of biological reproduction. This was a line taken by some early feminist theorists, such as Shulamith Firestone (1971), and led to a fascinating feminist science fiction novel which imagined a society no longer characterized by fixed sexual dimorphism (Le Guin 1969). It still finds echoes in the writing of some who are Utopian about the prospects for using technology, to overcome the biological differences between men and women. The other is to accept that men will always subordinate women, and that the best 'solution' to this is to minimize all contact between them, or as far as possible, to keep all men 'in their place'.

Both arguments are curiously reminiscent of the profoundly conservative arguments which they appear to oppose. We could rephrase the second argument in the language of traditional patriarchal misogyny: men are inherently superior to women and will always be that way, and the best way to maintain this is to have as little as possible to do with women, who should be kept in their place. Conservatives themselves have not advocated the first argument, but some of the most popular dystopian novels of the modern age have used this theme. For example in Huxley's *Brave New World* the mass production of babies and the abolition of pregnancy plays a key part in the suppression of individual identity and maintenance of social control. A similar theme emerges in Orwell's *Nineteen Eighty-Four* although here the argument centres not on the elimination of biological reproduction itself, but of the sexual feelings associated with it, through the Anti-Sex League:

> Children will be taken from their mothers at birth as one takes eggs from a hen. The sex instinct will be eradicated. Procreation will be an annual formality like the renewal of a ration card. We shall abolish the orgasm. Our neurologists are at work upon it now.
>
> (1949: 214–5)

This suggests that, as I argued in Chapter 2, the natural limits to the social construction of identity implied by the sexual genesis of humans may actually be a positive thing, at least compared to the scenarios summoned up by abolishing these limits in the imagination. These limits set the distance between the personal and political that makes a democratic society possible by creating aspects of our personal identity which lie beyond both our own control and that of others. As Orwell knew well, his diligent neurologist faced a hopeless task. The dystopian novelists have shown more awareness of something sociologists of gender have too often overlooked because the latter have conceptualized the family as an arena of gender socialization rather than generation. We could see this as yet another example of the 'false choice' presented by gender theory of viewing the private sphere as either political or patriarchal. This false choice unwittingly accepts patriarchal ideology, because it assumes that sexual genesis creates men's power and the social relations of gender, rather than mortal individuals. Patriarchs have always claimed that their biological paternity naturally creates their social power.

Finally, arguments which root patriarchy in the penis, or in a sexual contract whose terms are determined by the sex of the parties to it are hard pressed to explain the historical evidence that I surveyed briefly in Chapter 3 which suggested that despite the continuing reality of sexual inequality, women's power relative to that of men has changed dramatically in recent decades in countries such as Britain. It would be difficult to correlate this with either the number of penises around, or what they were doing for the men who possessed them.

The alternative answer has been to root patriarchy in the phallus – the symbolic representative of the penis – and to see the *concept* of 'innate' differences between males and females, rather than any innate difference itself, as the symbolic basis of men's organization. But this is to answer the question by restating it, and takes us into circular forms of argument of the kind that plague discussion of patriarchy. It is very difficult to explain why, if the phallus is *symbolic*, women's lack of a *penis* prevents them possessing it. We cannot escape this riddle by arguing that only men have access to the phallus. If only men have access to it, then it effectively becomes part of the penis; culture merges back into nature. Instead of an explanation of the solidarities of sex or why solidarities become constructed on the basis of sex as opposed to some other criteria, we get what is ultimately a redescription of them. This leads us into socialization theories, of the kind which Duindam has criticized (1995), which typically explain the reproduction of patriarchy though the social construction of gender, but only once we allow the assumption that patriarchy already exists, in order to explain how gender is constructed in this way. The phallus presupposes itself. The problem with such explanations becomes identifying the conditions under which such a logic of patriarchy might come to an end, if we are unable to specify what originally brings it into being. Instead what usually happens is that one link in the logical chain is singled out for attention, and it is argued that removing it will undermine patriarchy. A favourite candidate has been the division of labour in childrearing (explicitly in the work of Chodorow (1978) and Dinnerstein (1976), and implicitly, I would argue, in Freud and most psychoanalytic writing). Craib (1987) and Young (1984) provide trenchant critiques of such an approach. They suggest that even if it were possible to show that the sexual division of labour in childrearing produced complementary gender psychologies which predisposed men to domination (something which they, and I, doubt) we would still need to account for how men were able to turn such a predisposition into successful material practice. The *will* to power is not synonymous with actual world domination – a lesson every infant learns repeatedly in childhood. Now the emphasis has shifted onto *masculinity* from the division of labour in childcare, but the logic remains the same.

This is another form of the circularity of argument surrounding the concepts of male power and patriarchy which Middleton has criticized (1988: 43n):

> Briefly, the hidden structure of reasoning is as follows:
> (a) Men have power which they enjoy and derive benefit from.
> (b) Why do men have power?
> (c) Because men have organised to obtain and retain power.
> (d) Why have men so organised, and why have they succeeded?
> (e) Because men have power which they enjoy and derive benefit from.

Bell and Newby (1991: 25) have made a similar point: 'At best an explanation of inequality in terms of attributes is tautologous – women are subordinate because they are women – at worst it is false.' They add to this the observation that the metaphor of family relationship behind the term patriarchy is thus a substitute for analysis rather than a starting point.

The answer that is usually given to my second question – why should gender categories be mapped onto sex categories? – is another version of this tautology. It is the simple assertion that they would not otherwise be *gender* categories. There are indeed other aspects of the human body which are socially categorized: skin pigmentation, physical age, genealogy, but we do not describe these in gender terms but in terms of race, ethnicity, kinship and life cycle. This takes us back, of course, to natural difference theory again; gender, it appears, has to have a connection to sex in order to begin to explain why no such determination in fact exists!

It is clear that gender is a very slippery concept. It both asserts a connection to biological sex, and denies it at the same time. This slipperiness has been used constructively in an illuminating way by many writers on gender, but now it is a concept which I think threatens to obscure more processes than it clarifies because it always operates by conflating sexual and social characteristics. For example, in Connell's *Masculinities* (1995) the concept of masculine is used in three different ways: to describe the socially constructed gender of males, to describe only those aspects of this socially constructed gender in males that reproduces patriarchy, and to describe such socially constructed characteristics as they are found in either males or females. We slip between treating individuals in our analysis as members of one or other sex, and possessors of certain kinds of social characteristics.

In recent years academics have become steadily more interested in studying masculinity, or masculinities, in order to understand men as gendered beings and the power that they wield by virtue of their gender, rather than as occupiers of particular social positions (e.g. member of the ruling class, an employer, trade union official, parent) whose sex goes unnoticed. Were we able to specify a definite relationship between biological sex (maleness) and specific collections of social characteristics in a particular form of society which served to reproduce systematic inequalities between men and women then this would be a useful exercise. For example this is Bob Connell's aim in his attempt to describe and analyse what comprises 'hegemonic masculinity' in contemporary capitalist societies and to see such hegemonic masculinity as the basis of the logic of patriarchy. Without such a basis, he argues, patriarchy gets reduced to some kind of historical accident with little rationale:

> to focus *only* on dismantling men's advantages over women through a politics of equal rights would be to abandon our knowledge of how these advantages are reproduced and defended. It would, indeed, abandon our knowledge of masculinity as practice; presuming there has been some cosmic accident in which bodies-with-penises happened to land in positions of power and proceeded to recruit their friends-with-penises to replace them ever after.
>
> (1995: 231)

Even in this case, however, we would have to see that the 'masculinity' we were describing and analysing was a function of the society we were examining, not a property of the male individuals within it. However, the attempt to locate any such definite relationship between biological sex and collections of social characteristics at the level of individuals takes us back to a familiar paradox; for 'cosmic accident' read 'appearance of the phallus' in explaining the 'solidarities of sex'. If we wish to get beyond the lack of connection between sex and gender implied by 'accident' we seem to have no alternative but to explain gender by sex; we swing back from the phallus to the penis. From Connell's social constructionist perspective it is difficult to explain how the penises got lucky, as it were. But what we face here is the same problem from a different angle: what can be the origin of gender?

The concepts of gender and masculinity are problematic because they originated in the struggle to defend patriarchy, not demolish it. The modern debates I have discussed in this chapter replicate the earlier problems faced by the social contract theorists of the seventeenth and eighteenth centuries, and social scientists and philosophers since. If the self is seen as entirely socially constructed it is difficult to account for gender, why men have a monopoly on masculinity, or why anyone would choose, or could be forced, to be feminine. Conversely, once we swing back to the penis, and focus on sex differences, we discover little that is significant, and if we find a way to make it significant (by attributing to men a natural capacity for sexual violence for example) we face the problem of how the significance of this might ever be reduced. These debates do this because they still attempt to produce a theory of gender which could either legitimate a sexual division of labour in modern terms, or show how such a division of labour gets produced, which focuses on the gender or sex characteristics of persons. As I hope I have demonstrated, no such theory is possible.

Much of the masculinity literature and the scholarship and research which sustains it is a profoundly misleading exercise, because it continues to try to identify the way in which actually existing men come to live out their masculinity. It fails to grasp that masculinity cannot exist as the property of a person; it can only be a social ideology. What can be more usefully studied is the specific historical conditions under which men and women ever come to believe that such a thing as masculinity exists in the first place, the different forms such beliefs take and the consequence that they have within such historical conditions. What we need to understand, in short, is how men and women come to maintain a passionate conviction of their fundamental dissimilarity and its roots in nature, in the face of overwhelming evidence at every level of experience, from the everyday, routine and mundane, to the further reaches of abstract academic scientific research and philosophical speculation, that, genitals and biological reproductive capacities aside, men and women are not different, and in the face of modern ideologies of equal rights, and the material forces of universalism which sustain them.

The paradoxes of equality and difference

> The secondary status of women in society is one of the true universals, a pan cultural fact. Yet within that universal fact, the specific cultural conceptions and symbolizations of woman are extraordinarily diverse and even mutually contradictory. Further, the actual treatment of women and their relative power and contribution vary enormously from culture to culture, and over different periods in the history of particular cultural traditions. Both these points – the universal fact and the cultural variation – constitute problems to be explained.
>
> (Ortner 1974: 67)

The passage from Segal (1993) which I quoted above (p. 68) suggests that the slippage between sex and gender connects to a parallel conceptual slippage between the sex-typing of gender identity or psychological traits (masculine/

feminine) and their evaluation as positive or negative – life affirming or life threatening. This takes us back to our starting point: the ubiquitous everyday experience of inequality between men and women. Given that the whole point of gender theory is to understand how men oppress women, we are driven to look for ways in which biological men have historically and socially created an oppressive masculinity that achieves this, and for evidence of this 'masculinity' in empirical historically existing men. To explain men's dominance we need to connect up masculinity with maleness and thus emphasize the difference between men and women. To imagine and anticipate a society free of inequality, however, we need to deny that there is such a connection. We want to refute such evidence, if we find it, in that the whole project of gender equality depends on realizing our belief in the fundamental equivalence of men and women in the first place. We are caught in a catch-22. A theory of patriarchy requires us to see masculinity as male, so that it can explain the social dominance of males. A theory of patriarchy as historically constructed and therefore potentially deconstructable requires us to see masculinity as an expression of power relations that are not ultimately rooted in sex – which makes explaining the social dominance of males difficult, to say the least. We are left swinging from penis to phallus.

At two crucial points the arguments of Dinnerstein (1987), Chodorow (1978) about childcare and socialization seem to slip between the phallus and the penis, or to put it another way, smuggle biologically determinist arguments into their overall social constructionist stance. The first concerns how boys and girls learn appropriate gender personalities from their parents. At one level the argument is cast in terms of the phallus: boys learning masculinity and girls learning femininity, whether this is understood in terms of rigidity of ego boundaries, separateness of sense of self or the working through of the awe of maternal omnipotence. It is not an argument about the direct impact of the penis or the breast, but about the gender identities and place in the gender division of labour of the parents. If it were an argument about the penis, changing the division of labour in child-rearing would have no effect, as it would not alter parental biology. But if the whole point of distinguishing masculinity from maleness is to take account of the inherent bisexuality of gender identity – that both males and females are both masculine and feminine – then how do we explain that girls learn their femininity only from their mother and boys learn their masculinity only from their father? In other words how do boys and girls 'identify' with the correct gender identity corresponding to the sex of their bisexually gender identitied parent? It is here that we swing back to the penis from the phallus. Boys recognize their common possession of a penis with their fathers and girls their lack of one with their mothers and this, somehow – we are not told how, guides them to the appropriate aspects of gender identity.

The second concerns the mechanics of abolishing the gender division of labour in parenting. As Young comments, 'Many [feminists] wonder whether men with their present masculine personalities, complete with their insecurities and hatred of women, should be anywhere near children' (1984: 142). Implicit in Chodorow's and Dinnerstein's approach is the idea that abolishing the gender division of labour in childrearing through shared parenting would also abolish the contrast between masculinity and femininity as such, again presupposing the result we hope to obtain. This is because, in the sense of the contribution of masculinity and femininity, parenting already is 'shared'; it is the absences and hostilities and public power of the father that constitutes masculinity and its reproduction, just as much as the private presence of the mother. In the first case the man is absent, but his 'masculinity' is present. To move to emancipatory shared parenting (rather than misogynist abuse) we want the man present, but his masculinity, at least in the form theorized by Chodorow and Dinnerstein, absent.

This takes us to the heart of a controversy within feminist theory and strategy concerning 'equality' and 'difference'. The case for equality depends upon accepting that biological sex (in the sense of bodily differences centred around sexual reproduction such as the capacity to become pregnant or breast feed) is not associated with any other fundamental differences between men and women. It is in this context that the inability of sex difference research to provide any empirical support for traditional assumptions about the naturally superior mental, emotional or moral capacities of men has been a significant contribution to undermining traditional patriarchal or misogynist ideology. But the need for the case for *equality* in the first place depends upon recognizing fundamental and thoroughgoing *differences* in every aspect of social life between men and women, recognizing that, at least in a patriarchal society, anatomy *is* destiny. Indeed, this is what the concept of gender has usually been deployed to explain, and the concept, as we have seen, depends on arguing that there are systematic differences between men and women, which are related to their sex but which express social rather than biological differences.

If the first two dimensions of this paradox concern the positive and negative evaluation of masculinity and femininity and equality versus difference, a third, historical, dimension becomes evident if we consider the use of the term patriarchy. While second wave feminism has as its goal the abolition of inequality between men and women, it faces the fact that in all hitherto existing societies for which we have good evidence, biological sex has been a major determinant of the social division of labour, in the sense of the social positions or roles men and women occupy and the command of resources or power associated with them. While there has been discussion amongst anthropologists about whether every known division of labour between men and women also represents a systematic power inequality between them, there are no known societies where, for example, men assume prime responsibility for infant childcare, let alone any where the gender division of labour we have been familiar with in the West has been reversed (that is to say where men take responsibility for the private sphere, while women command the public sphere and the bulk of social and economic resources). The massive weight of this historical evidence suggests a fundamental difference between men and women that it has been the *raison d'être* of feminism to challenge and erase.

It seems as if we face an insoluble dilemma. If we emphasize equality, we can explain how men and women can throw off the burden of patriarchy and create an era of truly universal human rights. But it becomes difficult to explain the existence of gender, and why patriarchy has ever existed in the first place. What rationale underlay the creation of the solidarities of sex? Alternatively, if we emphasize difference, it is easier to explain the patriarchal gender division of labour, but also difficult not to rationalize it in doing so. We can develop theories which show how biological males are socialized into masculinity, and how in turn this masculinity sustains and reproduces a social order that privileges men and exploits women. We can explain patriarchy, but, if it is ultimately rooted in the penis, not how it began or might end. What we need to understand is how we come to have such deep convictions that men and women as social beings are different, which is to say that biological males and females must also become socially masculine and feminine, in the face of our parallel knowledge that there can be no fundamental differences between men and women, and that as social capacities, masculinity and femininity are qualities which any human being can acquire, regardless of their biological sex.

Some theorists, such as Cockburn (1991: 10–11), have suggested that the best strategy is to see relations between men and women as comprising both equality and difference simultaneously, and refuse to get drawn into what promises to become a fruitless, sectarian and debilitating argument. While this position has a lot of merit, it depends on resolving this paradox the 'right' way, and it is not clear why this should happen. We might also assert, with as much logic, that men and women being both equal and different means that although men and women have different positions in the division of labour, in society as it currently exists they are ultimately equal because we cannot make any simple equation between the public and private spheres. Women's command over the rearing of children or of expressive aspects of emotional life in fact balances men's more visible public power and command of resources. This intensely conservative argument has been an attractive one for various branches of the men's movement, which survives in the multitude of approaches to masculinity that contrast men's public power with their private pain. Indeed all we have done here is to return to the original terms of the social contract theorists' legitimation of the sexual division of labour; it is their socially constructed gender, which expresses but is not determined by their natural sex, that leads men to form contrasting, but complementary, social contracts to those of women.

The way around these paradoxes *appears* to hinge on identifying a social mechanism whereby biological males are socialized into masculinity only within patriarchal societies, a social mechanism which brings sex and gender together, but which because it is a social mechanism, can be abolished, and thus break the link between sex and gender, and so usher in the demise of patriarchy. This approach can be seen in the works of such writers as Connell, Dinnerstein, Chodorow and many others and is based ultimately on the ides of Freud, whom I discuss in the next chapter. I hope that the paradoxes I have outlined in this chapter, however, make it clear that it is by definition logically impossible to identify such a mechanism. Only by choosing the penis can we explain the solidarities of sex and the dominance of men, only by choosing the phallus can we explain how all this might be socially constructed and therefore change. In the search for such a mechanism we inevitably swing between the penis and the phallus.

Notes

1 Segal (1990: 66) credits Stoller (1968) with introducing the term gender, and Morgan's key article (Morgan 1986) cites Oakley (1972), but I think arguments about the social origins of what are imagined to be natural sexual differences predate the actual use of the term itself. As I suggested in Chapter 1 and discuss in Chapter 7, I think it makes sense to see it as originating in the contract theorists and developed by Freud.

2 As Rubin (1975: 165) argues:

> A human group must also reproduce itself from generation to generation. The needs of sexuality and procreation must be satisfied as much as the need to eat, and one of the most obvious deductions which can be made from the data of anthropology is that these needs are hardly ever satisfied in any 'natural' form . . . the biological raw material of human sex and procreation is shaped by human, social intervention and satisfied in a conventional manner, no matter how bizarre some of the conventions may be.

3 As important as these substantive issues of analysis, there is an important procedural feature of such research that is often overlooked. Many rely on statistical tests of the 'significance' of a finding of a difference in measurement between male and female subjects. It is all too easily forgotten that such tests estimate the degree of probability that such a finding could occur because of a difference between the distribution of characteristics in the sample and in the population from which the sample is drawn, rather than accurately describing a relation between sex and some other characteristic in that population. Conventionally a probability of less than one in 20 or one in 100 is accepted as reliable evidence that a relationship found in the sample (say between sex and 'aggressiveness') also exists in the general population. It is too easy to forget that such a procedure implies that roughly either one in 20 or one in 100 experiments will conclude that a relationship exists in the population when it is in fact due to the distribution of characteristics found in the subjects in that sample only. Given the battery of sex difference experiments conducted over the years, we would expect many such spurious 'findings'.

4 I am grateful to Cecile Jackson for alerting me to this article.

5 Freud falls into this trap too. In a section of *Three Essays on Sexuality* entitled 'Prevention of inversion' Freud suggests that 'No doubt the strongest force working against a permanent inversion of the sexual object is the attraction which the opposing sexual characters exercise upon one another.' The rest of the section is a rather unconvincing sociological explanation of the different relations girls and boys have towards their mothers and fathers: 'in the case of men a childhood recollection of the affection shown them by their mothers and others of the female sex who looked after them while they were children contributes powerfully to directing their choice towards women' (1986:

363–4). His attempt to prevent this account becoming a theory of why women should also take a female object choice is weak. We could see this as paving the way for the more rigorous way socialization theorists such as Chodorow (1978) and Dinnerstein (1987) have developed this argument.

6 At times Rubin's argument appears to fall into suggesting that there is no natural difference at all between men and women, a common error in social constructionist accounts. Rubin at first suggests that sex is *both* natural and social, analogous to the production and consumption of food – the social satisfaction of an ultimately biological need (1975: 165):

> A human group must also reproduce itself from generation to generation. The needs of sexuality and procreation must be satisfied as much as the need to eat, and one of the most obvious deductions which can be made from the data of anthropology is that these needs are hardly ever satisfied in any 'natural' from, any more than are the needs for food. Hunger is hunger, but what counts as food is culturally determined and obtained. Every society has some form of organised economic activity. Sex is sex, but what counts as sex is equally culturally determined and obtained. Every society also has a sex/gender system – a set of arrangements by which the biological raw material of human sex and procreation is shaped by human, social intervention and satisfied in a conventional manner, no matter how bizarre some of the conventions may be.

The positive point in Rubin's argument is her insistence that the biological basis of procreation cannot itself determine the social form of sexual relations, any more than other needs determine economic relations. The drawback is how Rubin develops this point. She tends to reverse the direction of cause and effect and argue that sex is determined by gender relations. But babies cannot be produced by conventions – any more than hunger can be satisfied by culturally deciding that something which is not nourishing constitutes food. She argues (1975: 179–80): 'But the idea that men and women are two mutually exclusive categories must arise out of something other than a non-existent "natural" opposition.' It seems to me that the existence of such a natural opposition is clear, in the sense of the existence of a division of labour in procreation which is entirely natural. It can only exist within a social context, but this cannot mean that it is only this social context that *creates* such a division of labour in the first place. Rubin's social constructionism has its origins in Lévi-Strauss's (1969), whose theories Rubin engages to form the basis of her argument: 'the sexual division of labour is nothing else than a device to institute a reciprocal state of dependency between the sexes' (1971: 348, quoted in Rubin 1975: 178). But such a reciprocal state of dependency already exists in nature because of sexual genesis. Each sex is utterly dependent on the other to make children. We can acknowledge the existence of 'natural difference' in this sense without concluding that it explains patriarchy or using it to rationalize social inequality between the sexes.

5

Gender as socialization theory: Freud's *Three Essays*

It is useful to trace our modern confusion between sexual difference and sexual genesis in a work which has been an important intellectual ancestor of our contemporary ways of thinking about these concepts, which has been actively taken up by both second wave feminism and contemporary social science, and which can be seen as the most coherent attempt to solve the problems raised by the social constructionism of the social contract theorists two centuries earlier. Freud's *Three Essays on Sexuality* first appeared in 1905, arousing instant and almost universal indignation and vilification. Freud's revolutionary argument was that human sexuality was not a biological product of complementary 'natural' drives invested in male and female bodies, but was essentially cultural and symbolic and therefore learned and social. Sexuality was a product of gender socialization, rather than biological sex.

He argued that as infants develop they assemble the various 'components' of sexuality in a stage of 'polymorphous perversity' where they are open to a wide range of sexual aims and objects, based on various parts of the body, focusing in turn on the mouth, anus and genitals. These components bear no relation to their own sex, or the sex of the object, including parents or siblings, to which their aim is directed. As they grow they become aware of their biological sex, principally through recognizing that they either possess or lack a penis, become aware of the biological sex of their parents, and aware that their sexual desire for either parent exposes them to the competition and hostility of the other, who is also, frighteningly, much more powerful than they. Babies then learn to repress inappropriate aspects of this polymorphous capacity into a more limited range of sexual desires comprising a more limited set of activities, set in the context of the achievement of a predominantly but not exclusively masculine or feminine identity and usually, but not necessarily, focused on genital arousal with those of the opposite sex beyond their immediate kin.[1] This drama is what Freud called the Oedipus complex.

What Freud attempted at the level of psychology, the social contract theorists had earlier attempted at the level of sociology – a theory of how relations between people were socially constructed rather than naturally determined. In a sense Freud's approach was only made possible by the work of the Enlightenment in general and the social contract theorists in particular. Only if we see people as authors of their own destiny, and not the products of deities or devils does it make sense to investigate scientifically the 'causes' of hysteria, the work which led Freud to his theories. Only if we can imagine sexuality as socially constructed does it make sense to embark on a 'talking cure' rather than search for the organically normal or pathological in something whose development is a natural process. The obverse of social construction was individual and social responsibility. If sexual relations were understood to be originally polymorphously perverse, rather than based on any natural order, then society was only possible when limits were imposed on that polymorphism. Through the incest taboo, produced by the working through of the Oedipus complex, parents and offspring renounced their desire for each other and thus made possible sexual and social relations with all others. Civilization presupposed discontents and disappointments, but its imperfections were preferable to what might be imagined as a state of nature beyond the incest taboo, or some primal realm of the id out of which an ego had yet to precipitate.

Freud's theories provoked outrage because they suggested a direct connection between adult sexuality and the parent–child bond, between physical sexuality and love and most outrageously of all, between civilization and perversion. One way of interpreting Freud's account was to see it as a manual of 'normal' or 'natural' as opposed to pathological sexual and psychological development, and thus offer a 'cure' to deviants from this path. This was the main approach taken by conservative psychoanalysis in the 1950s and 60s, for example in its definition of homosexuality as a disorder. The other interpretation, which Freud's critics perhaps sensed more acutely than his followers, was to see the essence of humanity in its ability to escape from the constraints of a purely naturally or biologically driven sexuality. If biology provided only the components, and left humans as social and cultural beings to assemble them, use them and invest them with meaning, then this implied that what might otherwise be thought of as natural sexual drives or activities were socially and culturally constructed. It also implied an intimate connection between the construction of these drives (including their repression or sublimation) and the whole edifice of human civilization, including its most divine creations. Another way of saying this was that if men and women made their own sexualities, just as they made other aspects of their social relations and did not inherit them from God or nature, then capacity for perversion, the capacity to transcend nature, was the essence of humanity. Freud dropped God in the shit. If sexuality was not naturally determined and defined, people had no choice but to be perverts, what they chose to define as perverse and pathological or natural and normal was only that, a choice, and worst of all, this was a choice, if the existence of the unconscious was accepted, over which they could never be entirely in control.

For our argument here, the most important aspect of Freud's thesis was that boys and girls *shared* the essential components of sexuality that they were to assemble, except for their different sexual organs. If sexuality was essentially social, cultural and symbolic, however, slightly different physical possibilities in sex were not likely to be decisive. Freud's work is therefore central to the development of modernity's 'historical consciousness of gender'; by providing a socialization theory of how boys and girls socially construct masculinity and femininity through their interaction with their parents, through the working out, for example, of the Oedipus complex. Freud offered an account of what Hobbes had only implied, an account of how social relations between the sexes could be seen as the social construction of individuals, rather than a product of their biological natures, but an account too of how the terms of this construction were set by sex. He offered, in other words, an explicit theory of gender.

Here was a theory which accepted that infants had originally similar natures so that relations between males and females could not be explained by their biology or natural difference and could therefore be seen as socially constructed. It was also a theory, however, which offered to explain how, despite this original similarity, boys must usually become masculine, and girls feminine. If it was this socially constructed masculinity and femininity that in turn produced the sexual division of labour – for example, producing girls who desired to mother children, and boys who desired to rule the public world – then sexual inequality between men and women could be seen not as a natural state of affairs (as it had been seen in the era of patriarchy) but as a socially constructed one. But like the incest taboo, with which this process was intimately connected, it could be seen as a necessary and inevitable cost of civilization. The alternative to the social construction of masculinity and femininity (and the unequal sexual division of labour, as well as neuroses or hysteria it implied as its occasional by-products) might be the greater miseries of sexual anarchy or disorder – a sort of sexual 'state of nature'.

The initial attempt to explain sexuality as cultural and symbolic thus coexists uneasily in Freud's work with an emphasis on the way in which this process of social construction of sexuality is seen to have a fairly definite result: ultimately the production of masculine men out of male infants and the production of feminine women out of female ones. It is this aspect of Freud's theory that appeals to Connell, who comments on the Oedipus complex: 'Here was the germ of a theory of the patriarchal organisation of culture, transmitted between generations through the construction of masculinity' (1995: 10). Indeed Freud's theory can be read this way, as a sophisticated socialization theory which explains the reproduction of patriarchy by explaining how males *must* become masculine. Tempting as it is to read it this way, however, this is a reading I think we should reject, because it ultimately represents a retreat from Freud's own greatest insights and a failure to follow those insights through to their logical conclusion.

Freud took forward our understanding of sexual difference by arguing that masculinity and femininity were social constructions rather than biological givens. His limitation was to continue to assume that such a thing as masculinity actually existed as an empirical property of individuals. This implied that the limits to the self and the nature of its structures were still set by its sex in terms of its sexual difference to other selves. In this sense, Freud can be seen as a socialization theorist. But Freud's work frequently gestures towards another conclusion, that the limits to the self are imposed by its sexual genesis from other selves, and the relation of the infant to its parents. Two readings of Freud's work are therefore possible. From one perspective it can be seen as the most eloquent articulation of the fetishism of gender in its purest form. It is the most systematic possible imagination of the existence of masculinity and femininity. Its contradictions are only evidence of its status as fetishism, by which I mean an ideology by which people imagine that social relations they themselves construct are in fact produced by an external object. In this case the 'external object' is the existence of two biological sexes. Alternatively it can be seen as the starting point of a theory which points beyond this fetishism by asking the question 'What is the origin of selves?' rather than 'What is the origin of masculinity and femininity?' Freud's work can be seen as the first attempt to explain how it is sexual genesis that establishes the limits and structures of the self (such as its unconscious), not whether it is a male or female one. What we might call a theory of generation coexists uneasily in his work with a socialization theory.

In the course of his discussion of the different development of boys and girls, Freud (1986: 355) comments that, 'So far as the autoerotic and masturbatory manifestations of sexuality are concerned, we might lay it down that the sexuality of little girls is of a wholly masculine character.' This raises the question of how the behaviour of females can logically be described as masculine – a specific case of the paradox raised by the 'historical consciousness of gender'. If gender was not biological, what connection could it logically be said to have to biological sex in the sense of possession of male or female genitalia? Conversely, if it had no such logical connection, in what sense was it about sex at all?

Freud's answers are illuminating, and I think that variations on them can be found in most writing on gender for the rest of the twentieth century. It is worth quoting him at length. He continues:

> Indeed if we were able to give a more definite connotation to the concepts of 'masculine' and 'feminine', it would even be possible to maintain that libido is invariably and necessarily of a masculine nature, whether it occurs in men or in women and whether its object is a man or a woman.
>
> (1986: 355)

Here Freud seems to suggest that the essence of masculinity is libido, which we might in turn associate with sexual energy, initiative, drive and aggression, what Freud sometimes refers to as 'activity' as opposed to 'passivity'. We can recognize here a concept not unlike that of 'instrumentalism' as used by later theorists, or Connell's 'hegemonic masculinity'. He also suggests that this libido has no intrinsic connection to biological sex categories. It can occur in either sex, and have either sex as its object. However the wording 'a more definite connotation' implies at the very least some caution on Freud's part. It is not hard to see why, for what 'more definite connotation' to the concept of 'masculine' would allow us to call it such, while simultaneously asserting that it has no logical or empirical connection to the nature or behaviour of men as opposed to women? As the masculinity literature demonstrates, however, this has not stopped the search for such 'a more definite connotation' of the essence of masculinity ever since. Freud amplifies his caution in a footnote added to the 1915 edition, which repays careful study:

> It is essential to understand clearly that the concepts of 'masculine' and 'feminine', whose meaning seems so unambiguous to ordinary people, are among the most confused that occur in science. It is possible to distinguish at least three uses. 'Masculine' and 'feminine' are used sometimes in the sense of activity and passivity, sometimes in a biological and sometimes, again, in a sociological sense. The first of these three meanings is the essential one and the most serviceable in psychoanalysis. When, for instance, libido was described in the text above as being 'masculine', the word was being used in this sense for an instinct is always active even when it has a passive aim in view. The second, or biological, meaning of 'masculine' and 'feminine' is one whose applicability can be determined most easily. Here 'masculine' and 'feminine' are characterised by the presence of spermatozoa or ova respectively and by the functions proceeding from them. Activity and its concomitant phenomena (more powerful muscular development, aggressiveness, greater intensity of libido) are as a rule linked with biological masculinity; but they are not necessarily so, for there are animal species in which these qualities are on the contrary assigned to the female. The third, or sociological, meaning receives its connotation from the observation of actually existing masculine and feminine individuals. Such observation shows that in human beings pure masculinity or femininity is not to be found either in a psychological or biological sense. Every individual on the contrary displays a mixture of the character-traits belonging to his own and to the opposite sex; and he shows a combination of activity and passivity whether or not these last character-traits tally with his biological ones.
>
> (1986: 355n1)

The first of Freud's three uses *has* to be 'the essential' one, since it is the only one that gives a meaning to masculinity which does not root it in biological maleness, and which would therefore confound the essence of Freud's theories about the symbolic and social rather than biological essence of human sexuality. But even here Freud appears to undermine his own argument as soon as he makes it. If all 'instincts' or components of sexuality such as libido are active 'even when it has a passive aim in view' then what does activity comprise? It is difficult to see it as anything more than an assertion of the fact of human agency, the constitutional independence of the self, the essence of its individual existence, even if this is lived out willingly as submission to the domination of others. Why should we see this life force as masculine, however, unless as the result of some barely conscious envy that the capacity to give birth to new life appears to rest more immediately with women – what we might call, following the lead of Karen Horney (1967), 'womb envy'? Somehow capacities that any actual man or woman must possess in order to survive – what could be called species capacities – have become capacities that are imagined to be the social or biological prerogative of only one sex or the other to develop. If 'activity' is to be the basis of the 'essential' distinction between masculine and feminine, it appears to rest on remarkably weak and suspiciously biologically determinist theoretical grounds. Freud has fallen foul of the confusion between sexual genesis and sexual difference, attempting to associate with one or other sex, a property which both sexes must possess, in order to arrive at an account of the origin of gender.

The second usage is simply what we would now see as the misuse of the terms masculine and feminine for the terms male and female. The essence of Freud's work was to establish the distance between the two. But what is the role of the curious sentence about 'activity' which follows the conventional definition of male and female in terms of sperms and eggs? It looks suspiciously like another attempt to establish that there are grounds for linking the logically sexless characteristic of 'activity' and other characteristics which Freud associates with this (aggressiveness, greater muscular development) with maleness, even though this link is now presented as a purely empirical rather than a logical one, and by virtue of that, associate activity and masculinity in order to establish his first usage.[2] This leaves Freud with two possibilities. If he emphasizes the empirical nature of this rule, is it to be found at the level of individuals within species, or at the level of species? If it is the former, then he must renounce, again, any logical connection between activity and either maleness or masculinity. As we noted in discussing Connell's rejection of arguments that gender merely expresses biology, we cannot confuse differences between the average characteristics of all males and all females with the contention that all individual males are more muscular than all individual females, for example. If it is the latter, what is the empirical connection to be found in the human species? It cannot be the assignation of aggressiveness and intensity of libido to the male, for this would be to deny the force of the logic which the *Three Essays* was all about: that *biological* sex precisely does not *assign* gender in human beings, which was why Freud could describe the sexuality of infant girls as *masculine* to begin with. This was precisely the avenue that a century of sex-difference research set out, without success, to explore and try to establish.

The third usage is the most confused. Freud thought of sociology very much in terms of the generalization of psychology rather than in terms of social facts or structures that might operate beyond the individual (Craib 1989: 1ff.). Indeed one problem, as Connell (1987) has noted, was that Freud lacked a sense of sociology at all. We can therefore conclude that he refers here to social action in a Weberian sense rather than, for example, to a more Durkheimian sense of ideology as social fact. By 'actually existing masculine and feminine individuals' he means males and females who can actually be observed empirically in social relations. Males and females display a mixture of 'character traits' which belong to both their own and the other sex. By character traits we could understand aspects of identity that we might term 'gender' and which would include symbolic aspects of human sexuality that Freud wished to explain. Freud is therefore suggesting that when we look at male and female members of society, we find that both have and display both masculine and feminine characteristics. If this is the case, however, how do we know which character traits are which? How do we associate any particular character trait with one or other biological sex? If all humans are psychologically bisexual, how have we, or they, ever come to believe that their symbolic sexuality is a function of their biological sex in the first place? We are back into another circle: the sexual division of labour creates and allows us to empirically associate gender identity with sex, which association in turn explains . . . the sexual division of labour. We are at the crux of the problem here, for we might also read this question as: why should males or females ever choose to abandon their 'polymorphous perversity' and establish their gender in the first place? What appears from one angle as the definition of gender appears from the other as its origin. Two answers are implied in Freud's footnote; neither is logically consistent, and both smuggle in the very biological determinism from which Freud had originally sought to escape.

The first solution, hinted at in the phrase 'either in a biological or psychological sense' is to argue that psychological bisexuality is a reflection of biological bisexuality. The advantage of this argument is that it maintains the connection between gender and sex. The disadvantage is that it does so by reducing gender to sex. Variability in gender then becomes a question of identifying variability in sex, as in the arguments that sex does not exist in a purely dimorphic form, but on a range from male to female with the majority of people clustered at one or other pole. It returns people to being functions of their biology, but suggests that this biology itself is more variable. Such an account faces three problems. First, how does this variation express itself over time, whether it is a matter of social and historical change or of individual biography? If I become less hegemonically masculine, 'discover' that I am gay, for example, or after attending my men's group or, taking up a job as a crèche worker, get in touch with my feminine side, does this represent the eruption of my 'true' sexed self through the veneer of 'false' social conditioning that had previously determined my apparently more masculine gender identity? Similarly, does the 'liberation' of sexuality in modern society from its earlier more restrictive definitions of what is normal represent the emancipation of 'natural' sexuality from oppressive social conventions? The language we can use here is testament to the powerful attraction we have, rooted in our modern psychic insecurity, to represent desirable individual or social developments as 'natural' to ourselves and others. It resembles what might be represented as the discovery of a revelation or a calling to a religious vocation in less secular societies. Such arguments take on particular force in a modernity which imagines that it likes to cherish 'authenticity' in proportion as it reveals to itself that there can be no such thing. But sociologists, of all people, would be mistaken to let ourselves delude ourselves in this way. Having wrested responsibility for our individual and social development from 'nature' we cannot just give it back, no matter how much we might want to pretend to; disenchantment is a one way street.

The second problem concerns how we define sex, and operationalize it in terms of 'actually existing masculine and feminine individuals'. No matter how much we might want to define sex as other than dimorphic, and focus on exceptions to this rule, it remains the case that the majority of individuals are unambiguously male or female in the sense of having the capacity to biologically reproduce children with another individual of the opposite sex. No matter how elaborate our analyses of secondary sexual characteristics become, of how, for example, criteria of eligibility for women's athletics events get decided, we cannot escape this fact, and the fact that we observe the vast majority of men and women as unambiguously and dimorphously sexed individuals. We simply swap the problem of how to get from sex to gender for the problem of how to get from male and female to whatever variable aspects of biological sex we propose to define.

Modern versions of such arguments range from biologically determinist forms such as research which looks for 'gay genes' to explain homosexuality to social constructionist and ethnomethodological theories that question dichotomous definitions of biological sex. Any of these arguments may be politically or psychologically progressive or regressive depending on their social context. 'Gay gene' theories, for example, can be used to assert that homosexuality is natural, normal and that therefore discrimination against homosexuals denies self-evident human rights. Unfortunately they can equally well be used to promote eugenics.

The third problem with this first solution is both simpler and more comprehensive than the first two. If psychological sexuality reflects biological sexuality in any simple way at all then the whole point of Freud's work collapses. Why bother with the complex symbolic processes Freud struggled to analyse if they can ultimately be seen as the direct expression of biology? We could simply describe this more varied biology, accept that anatomy is destiny and save ourselves a lot of bother.

Freud's second answer to the problem of the origin and definition of masculinity, femininity and gender was simply to sex-type character traits by loosely associating 'activity' with maleness, slipping between the categories of male and masculine as the occasion demanded and suggesting that 'a more definite connotation' of the concept would ultimately solve the problem. This is clearly the solution which Freud favoured; it is a theme that runs through much of his other writing and in a sense has been the rationale for most subsequent writing on masculinity, especially more recent work inspired by the concept of 'hegemonic masculinity'. His wording, however, suggests a reluctance to accept this solution. It is not difficult to see why.

Freud accepts there is no *logical* connection between activity and biological maleness. Were there to be one, then masculinity collapses into maleness again. In a crucial sense male infants have to be socialized into relatively greater activity than female ones if Freud's theories are to make any sense. Were this not the case then it is difficult to see how anyone would ever become 'passive' in any relevant way, no matter what the social conditions into which they were born. If we accept there is *no* logical connection though, we are still left with the problem: why is *masculinity* active? How is this the sense in which the term can be used within psychoanalysis?

There are two apparent solutions to this problem, neither of which are satisfactory. The first is to resort to a tautological and empirical argument, which Freud hints at in his discussion of 'sociological usage'. Here masculinity is whatever, empirically, males do rather than females. The problem is how we abstract 'masculinity' from the vast range of activities that males and females share. It is clearly the case that only females get pregnant and only males fertilize females, but once we examine the symbolic aspects of sexuality, including the symbolic aspects of reproductive heterosexuality, there is little that is exclusively male or female – that is the point of Freud's argument. We might therefore define masculinity in terms of norms or averages which we would also have to accept were socially relative and would probably change over time. Since Freud's original intention is to show that such norms and averages are socially constructed in the first place, through the abandonment of polymorphous perversity, we end up with a clearly circular argument. Like other 'socialization' arguments, it might serve as an explanation of the social *reproduction* of masculinity and femininity once we had established their origins elsewhere, but it cannot make the decisive link between male and masculine in the first place.

The logic of Freud's three meanings is still to be found in contemporary work; a particularly lucid example is Craib's piece 'Masculinity and male dominance'. He argues that gender must be more fundamental than other aspects of identity. It cannot be the case that 'I learn to be a man in the same way that I learn to be a teacher. It seems to me quite obvious that something more powerful is at work' (1987: 726). This implies the existence of something like masculinity, and Craib notes a surprising amount of agreement across observers and over time about what such masculinity is seen to comprise. This raises the question of how it is socially produced and Craib discusses the 'object relations' accounts of Chodorow (1978) and others, emphasizing how masculinity and femininity diverge from an ideal typical account of how any human individual, regardless of sex, evolves into an independent person with their own separate ego. Craib, like Freud, is acute enough a theorist to ask how boys rather than girls pursue a masculine model, and in his conclusions rejects any straightforward connection between sex typing in the social division of labour on the one hand, whether in the private sphere of childrearing or the public sphere of work, and the production of gender identity on the other, by refusing to make the male body an automatic symbol of social male dominance and masculinity for the growing infant (to do so would be to assume the very identity between penis and phallus, maleness and masculinity we are trying to explain). He is also prepared to see the split between biology and gender identity taken to its logical conclusions in the way he accepts evidence from clinical work of the complexity of the individual personality, involving various cross-sex and cross-gender identifications which undermine any attempt to draw out neat contrasts between masculinity and femininity. . . . There is no reason to doubt that the same 'surface' masculine behaviour may be underpinned by a variety of cross-identifications as numerous in their individuality as there are family backgrounds from which people emerge.

(Craib 1987: 734)

Rather than going on to draw the conclusion that no such thing as masculinity exists at the empirical level and that it is better seen as an ideology or projection – a conclusion implicit in his later work (1994, see especially Ch. 7 and p. 156) Craib focuses on Freud's 'sociological' meaning:

Whilst this individuality is important for the practising psychoanalyst, the common features of masculinity are important for the sociologist, and the existence of these common features is attested to by the persistent recurrence of the same qualities in studies of masculinity.

(1987: 734)

'Observable' men are masculine, at least on average, and with this 'finding' the whole original question of how masculinity is something distinct from maleness, something socially constructed, and as such not reducible to neat contrasts informed by sexual dimorphism, disappears from view.

Womb and penis as metaphors of power

In practice, much of Freud's work, and much theorizing about gender ever since, has solved this problem in another way – by recourse to a metaphor. Male is to activity as female is to passivity because in the act of reproductive sexual intercourse the erect penis penetrates the vagina. It is clear that as a biological fact, this cannot logically explain how or why masculinity is 'active'. On the contrary, the vagina could just as easily be seen as actively engulfing the exposed, and by virtue of that, more vulnerable, penis – a view that clinical evidence suggests plenty, if not all, men and women harbour in their conscious or unconscious. Or the vagina could be seen as actively having the passive aim of receiving the penis. Recent 'sperm wars' research has suggested that far from sperm actively fertilizing the egg, their movements are actively controlled by the woman, whose eggs effectively choose which sperm to accept. As with brain lateralization theories, this tells us a lot more about the way in which culture influences the concepts which 'natural' scientists use than it tells us about any connection between maleness and masculinity. It is surely no accident that at precisely that point at which it has become more socially possible for women to take the initiative sexually, or to actively pursue public power and resources in the way men traditionally have done, that some biologists discover that women are 'biologically' active too.

Why should the penis, rather than the breast, vagina or the clitoris be a symbol of power?[3] One kind of answer emphasizes the social position, power and authority of those who possess them. This takes us directly to a tautological argument: we are trying to understand how men came to occupy such a social position in the first place. The second kind relies on an analogy between the physiology of the erection and the concept of power as penetration. This suffers two problems. The first, as Morgan (1993), amongst others, has pointed out, is that penises are only infrequently erect, and that such erections are as frequently occasions for embarrassment or mortification as demonstrations of male dominance. When flaccid, shrivelled and wrinkly, as some feminist critics have reminded us, the penis is hardly a symbol of anything. And whether erect or not, physiologically, the penis and testicles are as much a site of vulnerability as dominance; a blow or electric shock to the testicles is excruciatingly painful. The second problem is the equation of penetration with power. If we are to reduce this to physiology rather than analogy we have to argue that the erection gives men the *naturally based* power to rape women which the latter cannot have because they lack a penis. This argument lies behind Ziboorg's (1944) reinterpretation of Freud's primal scene as a primal rape. Many theorists since, for example Pateman (1988) have tried to discover the basis of patriarchy in this.

This argument has some force in the limited sense that it is physiologically easier for men to force non-consensual penetrative anal or vaginal intercourse with men or women than it is for women to coerce men into such sex. Women can indeed anally rape men with a fist, bottle or other instrument, but it would be more difficult to maintain that his 'no' meant yes. I suspect that this physiological fact may have some psychological repercussions in relation to inevitable sexual envy rooted in our disappointment at being born with a body of one sex only. It is a poor explanation of patriarchy however. There are many critiques of reducing patriarchy to rape which I need not repeat here (Segal 1990), but the most relevant critique is that rape need not, and often does not, comprise penetration by an erect penis. In this sense men and women have similar physiological capacities for sexual violence. What we need to explain is the social conditions under which some men have come to wield much higher levels of sexual violence than most women despite the relatively similar capacities of both sexes to do so. Moreover the rising level of technology accelerated by modernity has reduced the significance of average physiological differences in weight or musculature which may once have given men on average, slightly greater capacity to use violence. Short, skinny, clumsy, weak people can easily develop greater skills in using weapons than others with stronger bodies, whether they are male or female. We cannot, on the contrary, explain these social conditions as an emanation of an ultimately different natural capacity (and ironically to do so would be to embrace a profoundly patriarchal idea – that men are *naturally* more powerful than women). Once again we are forced back to trying to explain why social characteristics we think of as masculine have any connection to maleness.

Womb envy and penis envy

The masculinist metaphor of the procreative, fertile and therefore powerful prick stands comparison with a parallel feminist metaphor of the potent womb. If we see penis envy as basic then men's public power becomes more important than women's private power. If we see penis envy as a natural thing, as in some conservative interpretations of Freud, then this can become a rationalization of patriarchy; men are more civilized or more 'active' by nature. Alternatively if we see it as a *product* of patriarchy, reproduced through the phallus, then undermining men's public power becomes a prerequisite of undermining penis envy, and vice versa. In turn, we can evaluate the relationship between power and pain in different ways. Men's pain can be seen as the inevitable sacrifice they must make to sustain public progress. This message is at the heart of many ideologies of masculinity. Alternatively men's pain can be seen as the neurotic cost of their public power, which gives them an interest in supporting feminist struggles to undermine that power. This is an argument which Dinnerstein (1987), Segal (1990), Giddens (1992), Kaufman (1994) and Connell (1995) have advanced in a basically similar form. Conversely, if we emphasize womb envy over penis envy, we focus on the private sphere of reproduction. If we see this envy as natural, then we condemn men to an eternal and infantile drive for glory – a vain attempt to measure up to the goddesses who brought them into the world and who have the satisfaction of knowing, despite their public humiliations, that theirs is the fundamental connection to liveliness and human creativity. Conversely if we see it as social, then abolishing its conditions of production (through abolishing the sexual division of labour in childcare for example) is seen as crucial. In so far as men embrace the feminine in the private sphere, the possibility of an androgynous future beckons – a feminine rather than female one.

A theme recurrent in the feminist appropriation of psychoanalytic thought from Karen Horney (1967) onwards has been that of men's envy of women's pregnancy and capacity to give birth; as women lack a penis, so men lack a womb. Mary O'Brien (1981), Dorothy Dinnerstein (1976), Nancy Chodorow (1978), Jessica Benjamin (1990), Jane Flax (1990) and Nancy Hartsock (1985) have all argued that men's domination of the public sphere and their irrational instrumental commitment to the pursuit of public glory in work or politics – to social production – is rooted in their envy of women's power in the private sphere: the capacity to reproduce and nurture human life and to wield infinite power over the suckling infant. O'Brien (1981: 29) contrasts women's direct, bodily and conscious experience of procreation and childbirth to the 'abstract idea' of paternity, while Chodorow (1978) emphasizes men's denial of the intensity of the love, need and attachment in the mother–infant bond, Dinnerstein (1976) emphasizes their fear and hatred of the mother's early domination. For Chodorow 'being mothered by a woman generated in men conflicts over masculinity, a psychology of male dominance, and a need to be superior to women' (1978: 241). Pateman (1988: 102) points out that 'Men give birth to an "artificial" body, the body politic of civil society. . . an act of reason rather than an analogue to a bodily act of procreation'. Hartsock (1985: 253) argues that men create 'immortal children of the mind' through their public endeavour. Or as Dinnerstein puts it, men's 'dominion over what we think of as the world rests on a terror we all feel: the terror of sinking back wholly into the helplessness of infancy' (1976: 161).[4]

Much the same logic that men have used to argue that the penis produces their superiority is used in this approach to explain their ultimate inferiority, in the sense of alienation from the more fundamental species power of the mother. From this perspective the whole history of civilization as we have known it becomes a sort of monstrous collective couvade. The problem, at which the critiques of both Sydie (1987) and Rubin (1975) hint, is that it is difficult to see how this neurotic drive for glory might be abolished without taking either civilization, or at least the incest taboo, with it. If we treat the metaphor as literal, if we root our explanation in the biological fact of having a penis or a womb, then we condemn ourselves to arguing about what must be transhistorical truths about men and women. It seems reasonable to speculate that there are some such transhistorical truths, for example in some of the more unconscious fantasies that men and women will have about each other based on what we might call their constitutional reciprocal envy.[5] An inevitable and insurmountable fact about myself as a man, for example is that I will never directly experience menstruation, childbirth, an infant feeding from my breasts or a sexual partner bringing me to orgasm by stimulating my clitoris or entering my vagina. But it also seems highly problematic to link either men or women to a specific connection to social power by virtue of these biological facts. The womb would seem to have as good a claim as the penis – except that we know from empirical history that men have overwhelmingly monopolized public power. Chodorow, for example, concludes that 'the basic feminine sense of self is connected to the world, the basic masculine sense of self is separate' (1978: 169).

Nancy Hartsock (1983) develops this idea into the concept of 'abstract masculinity', which through establishing a dualism and opposition between the self and the other is argued to underline all forms of hierarchy and domination. Something similar is conveyed, I think, by Dworkin's claim (1981: 13), which fits more obviously into an essentialist analysis of sex-difference that:

> the power of men is first a metaphysical assertion of self, an *I am* that exists
> *a priori*, bedrock, absolute, no embellishment or apology required, indifferent
> to denial or challenge. It expresses intrinsic authority. It never ceases to exist.

It is not difficult to perceive here a return to Freud's contrast of activity with passivity, and the whole tradition of thought that attempts to contrast the instrumental with the expressive. It is possible to see yet again how choices inexorably faced by any individual, regardless of sex, species issues of mortality and carnality, have somehow become gender issues of the sexual division of labour. We are back to the confusion between sexual genesis and sexual difference once more.

Penis and womb envy, or masculinity and femininity here describe single aspects of an ambivalence that confronts every human being as both a member of a culture and a maturing organism originally produced by his or her parents. The paradoxes of dependence and independence, creativity and attachment may be created by our sexual genesis, but they have no relation to the fact of our sexual difference; least of all can they be divided up as qualities and apportioned to one or the other sex. Just as there is no simple 'pain' that is the common experience of all men (or all women) nor is there any direct connection between such private pain and the achievement of public power. The *ideology* of such associations is a different matter, however. Finding a link between men and culture, especially if it could be expressed in the language of gender, was important to defend men's privilege in the new era of social contract. Conversely, when attacking the survival of that privilege, feminism has not been slow to reverse the evaluation and argue that it is because of their remoteness from nature that men have produced an alienated, life-threatening and neurotic culture. While superficially attractive, such arguments are ultimately extremely conservative. They invite us to turn our backs on modernity and rediscover 'natural' social relations once more. They offer us a return to enchantment.

Any mortal self, male or female, is about managing the ways in which we are inevitably separate from *and* connected to others, is about how we exist *a priori* from the time the umbilical cord is cut to the point at which we achieve our final separation and 'indifference to denial or challenge' in death. In so far as any self is separate from others, and has boundaries, its capacities to enter imaginatively into the inner worlds of other selves will be finite. I can never actually become anyone else, let alone become someone who is a different sex in the sense in which I have defined it. In this sense envy in its own right, devoid of any connection to sex, is constitutional. It is an inevitable aspect of any mortal self who has attained some degree of autonomy. What we therefore have to analyse is why this aspect of human development has come to be understood in terms of sexual difference.

There is also a confusion here between aspirations we might possess in fantasy, and less grandiose capacities we may be able to fulfil in reality. No living being, as opposed to a divinity, is 'indifferent to denial or challenge', though we may dearly wish to be, and though we may harbour the desire of never ceasing to exist, and may even predicate our ability to get on with our lives on this assumption, even Dworkin would admit that real men die.

Chodorow and Dworkin's contrast is in fact used to smuggle in another idea: that masculinity is ultimately alienating (connected to death) while femininity is ultimately life-affirming (connected to birth). This idea can then be used to connect masculinity up to patriarchy and other negative aspects of the current social order, and assert that feminine values hold out the prospect of social progress; the future is, if not female, at least feminine. This is a superficial and misleading contrast based on evaluating 'connection' as positive and 'detachment' or 'independence' as negative and in turn associating them either with one or other sex or gender. Although this contrast is popular, however, and fundamental to much contemporary criticism of men, it just doesn't work, because of its roots in the confusion of sexual genesis and difference. Is there anything less life-affirming than a 'connection' with wider society or kin that is strong enough to suffocate individuality or closes down the space to transgress the conventional, 'natural' or expected? Should we envisage a society where individuals' selves no longer possessed definite boundaries? Chodorow and Dworkin are ensnared in the fetishism of sexual difference. Personal issues of psychic security – our inexorable mortal predicament of managing our connectedness to and independence from others – have come to appear as the fantastic properties of social genders.

This contrast also sends us back to the choice between the penis and the phallus for its underlying explanation, even if it *were* the case that we could characterize currently existing relations between men and women in the terms of this contrast – which empirically it clearly is not possible to do. This metaphor has been used in other ways than to assert a biological (and therefore biologically determinist) basis for activity and passivity. In so far as the phallus is substituted for the penis in the argument, or women's power in her relationship with infants is substituted for the womb, vagina, clitoris or breast, the connection between masculinity and activity is established through the way in which the penis serves as a symbol of the wider system of men's dominance over women, through their monopoly of public power. Thus in the story of the Oedipus complex, for example, we can see the boy and girl as being impressed not by the size of their father's penis, and his potential to exert sexual authority through his physical capacity for sexual violence, but by the authority of his public power. Or, in Melanie Klein's (1957) account of the good breast and the bad breast, as developed by Dinnerstein (1976), the infant is less concerned with its consumption of milk than its general helpless dependence on its primary female carer.

We can recognize here the circularity of socialization arguments, for how are we to explain men's monopoly of such public power, or women's monopoly of infant childcare in the first place? As I suggested above in a slightly different context, we would have to show why women cannot get their hands on the phallus, or why men haven't, as Dinnerstein puts it, 'stormed the world's nurseries' (1987: 214) to secure the power of the good and bad breast. Thus when Sandra Harding (1981: 140) argues that Chodorow and Dinnerstein have analysed 'the historical and material conditions under which psychological interests in domination in general are reproduced', I have two disagreements. The first is that these material and historical conditions appear as causes of what they have to explain. The second is that Harding's argument can be restated, once stripped of its gender components as 'childbirth produces power relations' or 'civilisation has discontents'. This is true though the lines of cause and effect work in both directions. Another way of saying this is that parenting, in the sense of the social direction of the infant's behaviour, is an inevitable part of civilization. Without the incest taboo or other restraints on polymorphous perversity, consciously or unconsciously exercised, it is difficult to see how we would bother to struggle out of the womb and proceed to construct civilization as an always second-best alternative. Dinnerstein (1976: 60) puts it well:

> As Freud pointed out, the fact that human infants receive such nearly perfect
> care seduces them into fantasies which are inevitably crushed, fantasies of a
> world that automatically obeys, even anticipates, their wishes. The loss of the
> infant illusion of omnipotence – the discovery that circumstance is incom
> pletely controllable, and that there exist centers of subjectivity, of desire and
> will, opposed or indifferent to one's own – is an original and basic human
> grief . . . We manage in part to console ourselves for it indirectly, through
> mastery, competence, enterprise: the new joy of successful activity is some
> compensation for the old joy of passive, effortless wish-fulfilment.

I believe the solution to these problems lies not in rejecting Freud's work, but by ceasing to treat it, as most social scientists have done, as a socialization theory which offers to yield 'a more definite connotation' to masculinity and instead treat it, once it is stripped of its attempts to account for sexual differences, as a theory of how the natural sexual genesis of human beings nevertheless produces independent selves capable of (re)producing societies. Freud's theory offers a theory of the nature of the disenchanted self, the terrors with which certain knowledge of its own mortality confronts it and the paradoxical way in which the unconscious keeps us free by limiting our capacity to rationalize ourselves. It is this self, whether male or female, that has the capacities we imagine as 'gender', in both its masculine and feminine aspects. This is just what is done by the theories of Bowlby and Winnicott, which I summarized in Chapter 1.

The only escape from the paradoxes of socialization theory is to see that gender comprises public ideologies about sex differences which are required by societies which can no longer imagine that 'natural' sex differences lead directly to differences in social capacities and rights, together with the personal sense individuals make of these ideologies for the experience of their self as a man or a woman at a conscious and unconscious level, *not* the 'social' form biological sex difference takes for members of a given society. Neither these ideologies, nor the way individuals square them with their identities, need be consistent, nor based on direct experience, nor testable, in any normal sense of the word.

The alternative to a return to enchantment is to recognize that masculinity and femininity are ideologies about aspects of identity which we all share as mortal beings, which we project as social capacities onto the sexed bodies of others, which we in turn imagine them to possess and govern their social behaviour, and which we then seek to account for (at the level of social theory, and increasingly in popular discourse) by descriptions of gender socialization. Analysing this process, let alone challenging it, will never be achieved by searching for a more perfect definition of the nature of masculinity, or theory of how 'it' is socialized into males, for that is to remain trapped in the fetishism of the very ideology itself; it is to wrestle with shadows. The alternative is to distinguish sexual genesis and sexual difference, reinstate the significance of the former to its proper place in social theory, and reflect further on the development of the capacity to be alone as an alternative to neurotic gender projections, while returning from the politics of identity and the misguided attempt to politicize the purely personal to a more vigorous pursuit of a classic material politics of equal rights.

Notes

1 Segal (1990: 70–82) is a good short introduction to Freud's theories, as is Sydie (1987). A more comprehensive survey is provided by Frosh (1987). Craib (1989, 1994) places psychoanalysis more generally in the context of modernity and discusses its relationship with sociology.
2 This is also the procedure Parsons (Parsons and Bales 1956) adopts in explaining why biological males adopt instrumental roles in the social division of labour: it is simply what the historical evidence shows has hitherto been the case. In this, as I discuss in the next chapter, he followed in the footsteps of Hobbes.
3 Pateman (1988) for example depends on Zilboorg's equation of the primal scene with a rape. It is utterly unclear, however, unless we invest the penis with power, what produces this equation. We could equally fantasize about the huge and powerful clitoris, as Angela Carter's (1990) Eskimo fairy tale does.
4 See Pateman (1988: 89) for other examples in this tradition of feminist thought. We shall return (p. 108) to the importance of the concept that women have a more direct physical or natural relation to reproduction. As we shall see, it is not automatically a feminist argument, lending itself to the conclusion that as the 'natural' reproducers, women and men occupy their respective domains of the public and the private spheres by dint of their natural capacities.
5 Craib (1994a) suggests that there may be some clinical evidence for reciprocal primitive images which men and women have of each sex – man as tyrant, woman as engulfer – that relate ultimately to biology and surface in times of intense insecurity or conflict.

6

The collapse of patriarchy and the origins of gender: kinship and the traffic in women

The last chapter suggested that gender always rests on a theory of socialization whereby males become masculine. The key to abolishing the oppression of women appears to lie in locating and destroying this mechanism. This mechanism, however, must have properties that are magical. Socialization must simultaneously be and not be natural, and be and not be social; it must swing between the penis and the phallus. It must be rooted in natural sex differences, but it cannot be a product of them, for then it would simply collapse masculinity into maleness. It must comprise a set of social and therefore historically changeable capacities and yet it must be more than this, for it must always express a connection back to sex. The magic here is that in order to use it as a concept people must be able to keep these two diametrically opposed conceptions in their heads at once. This is not difficult – simply reread the quotation from Connell cited on p. 70 as a particularly clear example of this magic at work. We employ it every time we use the words masculinity and femininity as properties of persons; the whole point of this usage can only be to represent these properties as *at one and the same time* purely and exclusively natural but also purely and exclusively social. The magical character of gender arises out of the fetishism of sexual difference, which I outlined in Chapter 2, and we are experts at its practice, not because we are gymnasts of social theory, but because we inhabit transitional societies.

The key to understanding this is to disentangle the knot of sexual genesis and sexual difference established by the social contract theorists of the seventeenth and eighteenth centuries, in particular Thomas Hobbes. I want to do this by discussing the work of Gayle Rubin (1975) on 'the traffic in women' and Carole Pateman (1988) on 'the sexual contract', and by examining the way we understand the contrast between traditional societies ordered by status, ascription and kinship, and modern 'universalist' societies characterized by the dominance of exchange, contract and the market. I will argue that a key to a better understanding of this contrast is to avoid models of understanding, in which modern sociology is fully implicated, that present this contrast as a leap from societies determined by natural relations to ones in which there are no longer any limits set by nature at all.

From Hobbes to Freud

The previous chapter examined gender primarily from a psychological viewpoint and considered Freud's attempts to see the relationship between the sexes as one which was socially constructed rather than naturally determined at the level of the person through the construction of their gender identity as a result of the working through of the Oedipus complex. At times I considered society and social processes in this argument, chiefly through discussing theories in which the essence of natural difference becomes the way in which the penis comes to stand for the phallus – the symbolic representation of men's power. The power of the phallus is seen to come from the social power of men which is sustained by a social division of labour in which men and women come to occupy very different positions. I now want to focus on society and these social processes, and thus on the concept of patriarchy that has been used to describe them.

In a political, or social, context, we have been able to draw a distinction between imagining that nature lays down the rules, and the absence of any rules at all. The essence of Hobbes, and political theorists ever since, has been to discuss the contradictions of diverse rules or constraints and their unanticipated consequences, so as to propose what might best minimize miseries and maximize liberties, all the while recognizing that such rules and constraints are social constructions. This is a distinction which has been less easy to make in sexual relations. The major reason for this has been the confusion of sexual genesis and sexual difference, such that men have been able to present us with a false choice arguing that abolishing rules that established a different status for men and women would also mean abolishing rules which established a different status between parents and offspring. They were able to argue that the incest taboo and patriarchy were synonymous, because independent adult selves capable of making societies could only come from the precipitation of masculine and feminine identities out of an original polymorphous perversity, through the working out of the Oedipus complex. At the same time, this has led to a further confusion in how the relationship between nature and society is grasped, which underpins what I described in Chapter 1 as the politics of identity, and whose consequences I explore in Chapter 8. Modernity comes to appear as an era where not only does generation not imply dominion, but also all relations between parents and infants come to be seen as socially constructed in the same way as all others. The self comes to imagine that it can emancipate itself from its carnal origins, or at least come to understand these origins in such a thoroughly sociological way as to make their reconstruction possible and reform the self. This appears to be a thoroughly progressive development, for example in the prospect of the spread of 'pure' relationships as opposed to those marked by traditional ideologies about what age, gender or sexual orientation imply. It is a development anticipated even in the writings of Hobbes. In contrast to this I argue this is a pernicious confusion, which conflates sexual equality with the hollowing out of the self. Just as patriarchy is not necessary to sustain the incest taboo, so too is the politicization and rationalization of the self unnecessary to secure the abolition of patriarchy and the achievement of sexual equality.

Gayle Rubin: women as the gift which establishes the incest taboo and kinship

As the quotation from Rubin (1975: 165) cited above (p. 82) suggested, the human sexual division of labour in procreation must always exist within a social context. We could take the simplest and universal form of this social context as being the incest taboo. If societies, as well as individual persons, are to be reproduced then libido, created and formed in the family of origin, must somehow be directed outward to a family of destiny, repressed desires must be sublimated towards the task of social enterprise. In this sense the incest taboo, and its elaboration into kinship rules, is the fundamental basis of society:

> No doubt the simplest course for the child would be to choose as his sexual objects the same persons whom, since his childhood, he has loved with what may be described as damped-down libido . . . Respect for this barrier [against incest] is essentially a cultural demand made by society. Society must defend itself against the danger that the interests which it needs for the establishment of higher social units may be swallowed up by the family.
>
> (Freud 1986: 360)

It may appear that 'society' here demands the conditions that make its own constitution possible in the first place, but this need not represent tautological or teleological thinking. We could simply understand the incest taboo as something without which in theory it is difficult to imagine the emergence of a society, and which is empirically confirmed in practice by its universality. Freud saw it as universal because it had its origins in the Oedipus complex, which he also believed to be universal: 'Every new arrival on this planet is faced by the task of mastering the Oedipus complex' (1986: 361). Since the end product of the successful working through of the Oedipus complex is the creation of appropriately masculine and feminine gender identities, one implication of his argument is that these, or something like them, must be universal too.[1]

Rubin's argument is an attempt to challenge Freud's assumption about the universality of the Oedipus complex, and by way of a critique of the theories of Lévi-Strauss (1969) about the origins of kinship, to see it as the product of particular kinds of kinship rules which have also been the foundation of patriarchy through creating 'the traffic in women'. Kinship is vital, because until a relatively very recent period of human history, in traditional societies, kinship was the basis of the social division of labour and political organization through the way in which it ascribed social status to their members on the basis of their sex and kin relations established by their birth. 'The social relations of production are organized in terms of lineages, households, and networks of obligation defined by kinship and marriage' (Keesing 1981: 215). As Rubin (1975: 170) puts it, 'the exchange of goods and services, production and distribution, hostility and solidarity, ritual and ceremony, all take place within the organizational structures of kinship.'

Following Lévi-Strauss (1969) and Mauss (1970), Rubin sees the 'gift' as the fundamental element of social relations because it 'expresses, affirms or creates a social link between partners of an exchange' (1975: 172). In traditional societies the most important gift, one which expresses, affirms or creates the rules of kinship, is the 'gift' of women as marriage partners between groups of men. Patriarchy was founded on the status of women as gifts, and in so far as this gift is based on the compulsory expulsion of daughters from their family of origin and the acceptance of women as marriage partners for its sons, it is also the basic form of the incest taboo. Since one cannot be both gift and giver, 'as long as the relations specify that men exchange women, it is men who are the beneficiaries of the product of such exchanges – social organization' (Rubin 1975: 174). Thus

> 'Exchange of women' is a shorthand for expressing that the social relations of a kinship system specify that men have certain rights in their female kin, and that women do not have the same rights either to themselves or to their male kin. In this sense, the exchange of women is a profound perception of a system in which women do not have full rights to themselves.
>
> (Rubin 1975: 177)

This leads Rubin to a pessimistic provisional conclusion, for if the origin of culture and society lies in the application of the incest taboo, as developed into kinship rules, onto the original polymorphous perversity of infants, 'it can be deduced that the world historical defeat of women occurred with the origin of culture, and is a prerequisite of culture' (Rubin 1975: 176). Culture depends on status, which in turn depends on kinship, which in turn depends on patriarchy which gives rise to the production of gender alongside sex. The 'traffic in women', which forms the basis of kinship, is prepared by the specific form which the incest taboo takes through the moulding of polymorphously perverse infants into masculine boys and feminine girls socialized into taking the appropriate part in this traffic. 'If a girl is promised in infancy, her refusal to participate as an adult would disrupt the flow of debts and promises' (Rubin 1975: 182). The penis is central in assigning girls and boys the respective positions of exchanger and exchanged. Thus

> psychoanalysis provides a description of the mechanisms by which the sexes are divided and deformed, of how bisexual, androgynous infants are transformed into boys and girls . . .

> Psychoanalysis describes the residue left within individuals by their con-
> frontation with the rules and regulations of sexuality of the societies to which
> they are born . . .
>
> The presence or absence of the phallus carries the differences between the
> two sexual statuses, 'man' and 'woman' . . . Since these are not equal, the
> phallus also carries a meaning of the dominance of men over women, and it
> may be inferred that 'penis envy' is a recognition thereof. Moreover, as long
> as men have rights in women which women do not have in themselves, the
> phallus also carries the meaning of the difference between the 'exchanger'
> and the 'exchanged,' gift and giver.
>
> > (Rubin 1975: 185, 183, 191)

Thus the Oedipus complex can now be seen as the origin *both* of the original
pair of gifts or exchanges which establish society and culture, *and* of what we
might call 'male sex-right', patriarchy or the sexual division of labour, the status
for men of giver as opposed to gift.[2] It is the simultaneous origin, to use the
language Pateman (1988) later deploys, of both the *sexual* and *social* contracts:

> In exchange for the boy's affirmation of his father's right to his mother, the
> father affirms the phallus in his son (does not castrate him). The boy ex-
> changes his mother for the phallus, the symbolic token which can later be
> exchanged for a woman.
>
> > (Rubin 1975: 193)

Rubin's analysis may seem pessimistic at first; male sex-right and the whole
edifice of patriarchy seems bound up with the constitution of society, the origin
of culture and the maintenance of heterosexual reproduction. The essence of her
interpretation of Freud and Lévi-Strauss is that the traffic in women as gifts from
fathers to sons beyond the family of origin is the basis of the original sexual
contract, which also establishes the incest taboo. It is sexual difference that pre-
cipitates culture out of the natural clutches of sexual genesis. She draws an
optimistic conclusion, however, by sticking to Freud's insistence on the social
construction of gender identity more tenaciously than he himself did.

Rubin points out that kinship is no longer the basis of social organization,
because the social relations of production have emancipated themselves from
this particularistic base and instead have developed to the stage in modern demo-
cracies where people treat themselves as formally equal possessors of property in
their own persons, rather than as persons with social rights and obligations
which flow from their kin status.[3] Status, patriarchy and tradition have given
way to contract and modernity. Since the social contract no longer depends on
kinship, it need no longer depend on the sexual contract either; we can get rid
of the phallus if we choose, and in doing so women can become givers of themselves as gifts, as it were, as indeed can men.

> The kinds of relationships of sexuality established in the dim human past still
> dominate our sexual lives, our ideas about men and women, and the ways we
> raise our children. But they lack the functional load they once carried. One

of the most conspicuous features of kinship is that it has been systematically stripped of its functions – political, economic, educational, and organizational. It has been reduced to its barest bones – *sex and gender.*

Human sexual life will always be subject to convention and human intervention . . . The confrontation between immature and helpless infants and the developed social life of their elders will probably always leave some residue of disturbance. But the mechanism and aims of this process need not be largely independent of conscious choice. Cultural evolution provides us with the opportunity to seize control of the means of sexuality, reproduction, and socialization . . . a thoroughgoing feminist revolution . . . would liberate human personality from the straitjacket of gender.

(Rubin 1975: 199–200)

Rubin's theory at first sight seems to give us what we are looking for: an explanation of the historical roots of patriarchy and gender, an account of their historical universality hitherto, and an explanation of how they might now be transcended. Because the shift from status to contract has undermined the role of kinship, it has also undermined the traffic in women, so that the psychological mechanisms which prepared for it, such as the Oedipus complex, are redundant. Gender is no longer necessary for the generation of adults from children – either as its precondition or its result. The incest taboo might define the difference between a private sphere (where the 'confrontation' between infant and elder can occur) and a public sphere, but doesn't associate either sphere with a particular sex. I agree too with her final conclusion: that the end of patriarchy would leave personality unconstrained by gender stereotypes. And I think that Rubin's argument does contain a vital and useful proposition: that while hitherto the sexual contract has set the terms for the social contract this relationship has now been reversed.

The problem with Rubin's account is twofold: this relationship between the sexual and social contracts is traced through at the level of persons rather than societies. As a result of this, she presents a particular case of swing between the penis and the phallus, which becomes projected onto history. Briefly, her historical account of premodern societies depends on the inevitable superiority of the penis, while her account of modernity and universalism imagines that, since it is socially constructed, men and women have equal access to the phallus. One result of this is that in her account of what a non-patriarchal future could be like, sex all but disappears. Thus an article that starts out with a functionalist explanation of gender as a means of ensuring sexual reproduction, finishes by contemplating the abolition of gender without explaining how 'enough heterosexual intercourse to reproduce the species' would be maintained. In this respect Rubin is reminiscent of Hobbes, who ended up arguing, to the scornful amusement of his patriarchalist opponents, that we could 'consider men as if but even now sprung out of the earth, and suddainly (like Mushromes) come to full maturity without all kind of engagement to each other' (Hobbes 1651/1983: 117). The problem for both of them lies with their social constructionist account of the

genesis of the self, which overlooks sexual genesis. If there is a 'gift' that is fundamental to human culture, I will suggest it is not one exchanged between sexes
but across generations as 'the capacity to be alone'.

In the end Rubin's analysis of the end of patriarchy is also a manifesto of the
liberation of personality from *any* constraints, an analysis of the end of the incest
taboo. It is not clear, for example, how the enjoyment of polymorphous perversity
would be restricted to adults. It is reminiscent, for example, of Connell's (1995)
appeal for 'gender vertigo', a voluntarist disavowal by men of their masculinity
which, if masculinity is central to the reproduction of patriarchy – would undermine it. The roots of such an approach, which we can trace to Hobbes, and down
to contemporary sociology, lies in the characterization of the move from traditional patriarchy to modernity in terms of a shift from an actually naturally
determined order to one that is (potentially) entirely socially constructed.

There are three questions which arise from Rubin's theory of patriarchy. The
first is why the traffic has always been in women: why, hitherto, have women
never been empowered to give men as gifts? What is the origin of this male sex-
right, and therefore of patriarchy? The second concerns the status of women as
gifts. As Pateman (1988) points out in her discussion of the social contract theorists, if women are simply the *objects* of exchange how do men come to marry
them – which implies that the women are a *party* to it? Why don't fathers simply
contract with (or marry) husbands, keeping women as property? This question
is particularly acute in modern society, within which the marriage contract, like
all others, has to be seen as jointly authored by the parties to it. The third concerns the erosion of kinship. It may have been stripped of many of its functions,
but it is still centrally and inexorably involved in one: the procreation and reproduction of children. No one on this earth has not possessed both a biological
father and mother; here, not in the Oedipus complex, lies what is truly universal.
In terms of the logic of Rubin's argument, does this inevitable survival of the last
vestige of kinship not also provide a continuing basis for the survival of status,
and thus patriarchy, in the face of the rise of the universal market? Indeed the
thrust of Pateman's (1988) argument is that behind the appearance of the spread
of the social contract lies the essence of the continued dominance of the sexual
contract embodying the continued rule of male sex right through the continued
construction, through reproduction, of masculine and feminine individuals, whose
apparently free exchanges with each other conceal the continued dominance of
men originally established by the primal rape.

Womb envy and the incest taboo

> In a strange way he [the father] may secretly envy his wife her creativity,
> although perhaps he would be the first to admit it. *His part was so quick and
> unnoticed.*
>
> (Mitchell 1962: 3, my emphasis)

Historically it certainly appears that the traffic has always been in women. Most societies appear to have based exogamy on the expulsion of women, and even in those societies which are matrilineal, such as some Native American ones, where it is the men who leave the family of origin, men have still enjoyed greater political power, and effective control of the 'descent corporations' (Keesing 1981). 'There is not a single society known where women-as-a-group have decision making power *over* men or where they define the rules of sexual conduct or control marriage exchanges' (Lerner 1986: 30). There is nothing in Rubin's account, or indeed that of Lévi-Strauss (1969) which explains why this should be so, however. They are more convincing as accounts of *why* there must be such 'traffic', than why one biological sex must correspond to those who organize the traffic, and the other to those who are its objects.

This may be illustrated by reversing the positions of the sexes in Rubin's account of the exchange of gifts underlying the Oedipus complex, and prioritizing womb rather than penis envy:

> In exchange for the girl's affirmation of her mother's right to her father, the mother affirms the womb in her daughter (does not force a penis on her). The girl exchanges her father for the womb, the symbolic token which can later be exchanged for a man.

This is just as coherent an account of the origin of kinship and the erection of an incest taboo – except that it doesn't fit with any society that we know of historically. We also face the problem that the reason for the traffic being in women *has* to focus on biological or anatomical difference, otherwise it cannot, logically, be used to explain the solidarities of sex, as I argued in the previous chapter. This means that explaining men's capacity to organize the traffic faces the same problem as analyses that start out from men's capacity for sexual violence which I considered in Chapter 2. If the capacity is socially constructed it is hard to explain why women can never possess it; alternatively, if it is naturally given, it is difficult to see how men could ever lose it. We seem to be forced into an account of what turns men into traffickers and women into objects of that traffic at the level of the person. I suggest in the final part of this chapter, it is not to be found there, but I wish first to follow through the way in which the search for such explanation in modernity leads inexorably towards a concept of gender.

Sexual explanations of patriarchy

One tempting answer, adopted both by Hobbes and by contemporary anthropologists, has been to suggest a direct relationship between the biological facts of procreation and childbirth and their cultural interpretation. The existence of such a link could provide us with an explanation of how women might be tied more closely to nature than men, and in turn, a transhistorical and transcultural definition of the nature of the private sphere and women's centrality in it and how men might thus be associated with the public sphere beyond it. In other words sexual genesis could create sexual difference through the natural association of women to the genesis of infants. Thus Pateman (1988: 35) argues

> maternity is a natural and a social fact. But a considerable gap in time separates any act of coitus from the birth of a child; what then is the role of the man in sexual intercourse and childbirth? . . . paternity is merely a social fact, a human invention.

According to this argument, biological motherhood is patently obvious, but biological fatherhood is uncertain and depends on elaborate cultural knowledge of the facts of reproduction. Engels (1968) and O'Brien (1981) see patriarchy emerging, at least in part, as the result of men trying to guarantee paternity. Barnes (1973: 71) has suggested that while motherhood is more natural and less socially determined, fatherhood is more variable symbolically because of the essentially cultural nature of the connection established. Hobbes puts the same argument when he suggests that in a 'state of nature', before society has emerged, there would be a link between mother and infant:

> If there be no Contract, the Dominion is in the Mother. For in the condition of meer Nature, where there are no Matrimonial lawes, it cannot be known who is the Father, unlesse it be declared by the Mother: and therefore the right of Dominion over the Child dependeth on her will, and is consequently hers.
>
> (Hobbes 1651/1991: 140)

As Keesing (1981: 234), a contemporary anthropologist, puts it:

> Physically, women have the more obvious and compelling role in the creation of life. Through pregnancy, the umbilical bond between mother and infant, the drama of birth, and suckling, women literally and visibly create new lives. Male ideologists may portray women as passive containers and nurturers of life created by male seed, but it is a rather shallow denial of the world as humans experience it.

This rather contradicts Keesing's own earlier analysis of the meaning of kinship (1981: 217):

> How can we talk about blood relationships between father and child or mother and child, in cultures that have quite different theories or metaphors about the connection between parent and child? In some the mother is thought to contribute no substance to the child, but only to provide a container for its growth. The Lakher of Burma, for example, believe that two children with the same mother and different fathers are not related at all.
>   Moreover the Trobriand islanders and some Australian Aborigines staunchly deny that copulation between father and mother is the cause of pregnancy – hence seemingly denying the father a physical connection to the child.

I think we can conclude from examples like this that the physical obviousness of biological motherhood can have no direct impact on how it is understood symbolically, and thus explain, through the different processes involved in the construction of fatherhood and motherhood, why the original traffic is in women, and a sexual division of labour is established. Even if such a relationship did exist empirically – if we could show, for example, that in most societies, social and biological motherhood coincided, while social and biological fatherhood was more diverse – we would have a basis for the elaboration of the solidarities of sex perhaps, but one in which we might expect matriarchy rather than patriarchy to develop, to the extent that the construction of gender difference depended on women's fertility being more obvious than men's. Indeed this is just what Hobbes speculated. This, in turn, means that we cannot use the biological aspects of reproduction as a basis for the symbolic or social gender order, or the contrast between masculinity and femininity. As we shall see, however, this argument is still central to understanding patriarchy and its demise, as it was not just exotic tribes who viewed women as mere 'containers'. Such a view was also fundamental to the patriarchalists' account of sex difference and their explanation of the 'natural' character of patriarchy. This, in turn, was an account that Hobbes, and those who followed him, rewrote in the language of masculinity and gender.

The private sphere and the elementary unit of kinship

We could express the argument so far in the language of a related debate in anthropology over what constitutes the most elementary unit of kinship. As Moore (1988) points out, Malinowski argued that the family must be the basic and universal unit of kinship because of human infants' need for prolonged nurturance and care by adults who are bonded to them emotionally, what I described above (p. 18) in terms of Bowlby's concept of attachment. Later anthropologists redefined the family in terms of the mother–child unit. Now feminist anthropologists have emphasized how this confuses natural and social mothering and conflates being a (biological) genetrix with being a (social) parent. There may be close links between the two, but it is again an empirical rather than logical question. Mothers may pass on some or all of the tasks of care and nurturance to other women, or to men. Moore cites Boon's study of the English aristocracy:

> In post-eighteenth century upper class Britain genitrices briefly suckled, nannies did the rest; in pre-eighteenth century aristocratic Britain genitrices did the rest and wet nurses suckled.
>
> (Boon 1974: 138, quoted in Moore 1988: 27)

I think we can see this debate, rather like Freud's theory of the Oedipus complex, as a search for biological or natural limits to the infinite fluidity of human culture. Freud focused on the precipitation of heterosexuality out of the original fluidity of sexual desires, via the symbolic order of the possession or lack by each parent of a penis. Malinowski and the ensuing debate over the universality of the family focused on the limits to social order imposed by infants' needs for prolonged maternal nurturance. O'Brien (1981) and others have tried to locate the origins of gender in the biologically determined sexual division of labour in procreation and childbirth. But this seems to me to be mistaken.

Sexual genesis does logically entail the existence of infant dependence and a 'private sphere' which emerges on the basis of that dependence, as I argue below, but it does not logically entail a division of labour, at the level of individuals, either between giver and gift, provider and nurturer or masculine and feminine. Mothers always give birth, but neither they individually nor women collectively, need nurture; as Hobbes recognized, either sex could do so.[4] A sexual division of labour, and its psychological ramifications, may well exist, but we must search for its origins elsewhere. Sexual genesis implies the existence of 'traffic', to use Rubin's terminology, and also implies, which is less clear in Rubin's argument, that traffic will always exist, in that without some form of incest taboo, society could not exist. What it doesn't do is tell us the precise social form of organization of this traffic, and under what conditions males have been able to control it; in other words, why it should be based on sexual difference between men and women rather than the sexual genesis of infants from parents. To the extent that Rubin's argument runs together the existence of kinship with the existence of traffic and the fact of that traffic being in women, it implies that the end of patriarchy would be dependent on the abolition of kinship. But as she herself recognizes, kinship, at least in the sense of the incest taboo and the existence of a nurturant relationship between parent and child, seems to be a transhistorical fact about human society. As we shall see, the proposition that modernity erodes kinship posed problems for the social contract theorists whom Pateman considers; they also were unable to resolve the contradictory position of women as both the mere objects of traffic and parties to its organization. They too were unable to describe how the abolition of all status relations would be consistent with the continued reproduction of infants. They too could ultimately explain patriarchy only in terms of an original natural superiority of males. It is therefore to an examination of these theorists that I now turn, in order to answer the three questions arising from Rubin's theory. In doing so, I hope to expose the origins of the false choice we appear to face between the abolition of patriarchy on the one hand and the preservation of kinship, the reproduction of children, the incest taboo and the whole edifice of human culture on the other.

Notes

1 We can see here an example of the structure of 'gender' arguments. The Oedipus complex is described by Freud in social terms. Were this not so we could not think in terms of the 'construction' of masculinity or femininity, or different possible resolutions. But if its outcome, particularly if it is seen as a 'universal' process, is always the production of masculinity and femininity, it is far from clear what the qualitative difference

is between such a process and one we might describe in terms of biology, male and female. Thus Freud substitutes a socialization theory for one of generation.

2 Rich (1984) uses the phrase 'law of male sex-right' and Pateman (1988: 2) takes it up.

3 C. B. Macpherson (1962) explores the dimensions of 'possessive individualism'.

4 This is not strictly true, as I pointed out in Chapter 2. Until modernity, technology had not developed far enough to allow men to feed infants.

7

Thomas Hobbes: social contract and the rise of universalism

We hold these truths to be self-evident, that all men are created equal, that they are endowed by their creator with certain inalienable rights, that among these are life, liberty, and the pursuit of happiness.

(Jefferson (1776), Declaration of Independence)

every Man has a Property in his own Person. This no body has any right to but himself.

(Locke (1690/1924) *Of Civil Government: Two Treatises*)

since no man has any natural authority over his fellows, and since force alone bestows no right, all legitimate authority among men must be based on covenants.

(Rousseau (1762/1968) *The Social Contract*)

In order to understand the origins of masculinity in the fetishism of sexual difference, we can finally look in greater depth at the original debates between the social contract theorists and patriarchalists over the nature of men's power. It is here that we can see the origins of the systematic denial by modern social constructionist sociology of the significance of sexual genesis.

As Pateman argues, 'The idea that individuals own property in their persons has been central to the struggle against class and patriarchal domination' (1988: 13). Macpherson (1962) has shown that the theory of 'possessive individualism' of Hobbes, Locke, Rousseau and others was at the centre of the shift from traditional to modern societies, from status to contract and from kinship to universalism. As Pateman quotes Maine's (1982) *Ancient Law*: 'the tie between man and man which replaces by degrees those forms of reciprocity in rights and duties which have their origin in the Family... is Contract' (1988: 27).

We can think of the social contracts of the theorists which Pateman discusses as the modern equivalent of the 'gift' and the theory of the origins and nature of such contracts as the modern equivalent of the 'traffic' that Rubin analysed, because the most important subjects of these contracts are people, and because the way they think of themselves as authors and parties to these contracts is absolutely fundamental to our whole conception of modernity. Contracts are

> a principle of social association and one of the most important means of creating social relationships, such as relation between husband and wife or capitalist and worker... The subject of all the contracts with which I am concerned is a very special kind of property, the property that individuals are held to own in their own persons.
>
> (Pateman 1988: 5)

We can reformulate Rubin's question of gift and giver into: why should property in women's bodies rest with men rather than with themselves, or indeed property in men's bodies rest with women? What for Lévi-Strauss (1969) is the conundrum of the original gift, becomes here 'the story of the original contract' (Pateman 1988: 12). In turn, what these early theorists discussed in terms of contracts, contemporary sociologists analyse in terms of the social construction of relations and institutions, the regulation of behaviour through formal rules and informal norms, and so on.

The idea that societies comprised a series of contracts was thoroughly revolutionary because it suggested that to be legitimate, the entire social order ultimately had to rest on the consent of those in it, because it was ultimately their own creation, through the contracts they arrived at with each other. In so far as *everyone* had the right to make such bonds, and only to be governed by them, contract implied *universal* human rights, equality and the rule of personal responsibility. It meant the collapse of the idea, fundamental to traditional societies, that the social order was created by God's will, or the order of the natural universe, or magic, and that individuals occupied their ascribed and particular place in that order, and the rights to exercise authority or submit to it that went with that place, by virtue of their birth including the kin bonds and obligations that were established by virtue of their sex. If, in contrast to this, individuals were 'naturally' free, then only their consent could form the basis of authority and the exercise of power, rather than God's will, custom, brute force or the purported 'natural' superiority of any class of person by virtue of their ascribed characteristics, including their birth rank or kin relations. In this sense universalism and contract theory posed a straightforward challenge to patriarchy, for its central idea was that fatherhood – a natural, kin relation – was the basis of both domestic and political authority. The patriarchalists argued that interfering with such authority must inevitably lead to chaos and disorder by attempting, hopelessly, to go against the limits of nature. For them it made as much sense to give women the right to determine their future as it would to us to leave a baby to its own devices; both were naturally incapable of exercising either autonomy or authority.

Social preconditions and social consequences
of contract

Much discussion focused on the limits to the kind of contract that could be entered into without undermining the principle of contract itself, and on whether there were other social conditions necessary for the system as a whole to exist. The latter comprised ideological or political mechanisms to ensure that contract would be honoured: trust, appropriate 'moral sentiments' (Smith 1976) and the existence of law and the state. The former concentrated on the nature of contract. If it were possible to contract away one's right to make contracts, then the whole system could be in danger. There must therefore be some limit to the duration of a contract. A permanent one implied that one party to it was reduced to the status of a slave or a thing. There must also be a limit to what the possessive individual 'sells' of their self. While they can sell their labour power – their ability to labour – they ought not to be obliged to sell it in such a way that this impairs their ability to sell it in the future, through exhaustion, injury, denial of bodily integrity or death.

Works such as Mill's *On Liberty* explored some of the potential contradictions involved. Contracts implied the ability of both parties to them to negotiate in some meaningful way, rather than simply dictate terms. The distinction between free and forced agreement was a fine one. A worker may well be free to choose between competing offers of a contract, but forced to choose one of them. A useful restatement of some of these arguments can be found in Hirschman's influential work *Exit, Voice and Loyalty* (1970). Any contract has in principle to imagine the possibility of exit – that one of the parties to it will choose to leave and form another relationship elsewhere. Any contract implies the existence of 'voice', both when it is originally negotiated and as it is fulfilled, in the sense of negotiation over its terms. Finally, its successful conclusion depends ultimately on at least some minimal degree of loyalty to each other by the parties.

In a sense the part of the self which 'possesses' the parts, aspects or capacities of the self which are sold must remain the organizer of contracts, rather than become the object of them. The continued autonomous existence of this 'I', in distinction to the various aspects of 'me' that could be temporarily alienated, was fundamental. Indeed, this has been the thrust of my argument about the limits to the social construction of the self, and the autonomy of the personal from the political, the possibility of existence of a private sphere distinct from a public one, and the distinction drawn by Winnicott (1965a) between the 'true' and false' self. It meant for example that an employer might have use of a worker's faculties, but not their whole person – the kind of distinction which Marx sought to draw in distinguishing between labour and labour-power. For contract society to continue to be able to claim that it was based on the consent of those who comprised it, each 'I' had to remain free of contractual entanglements which could prevent it deliberating over the terms of the contracts it wished to arrange. In this lay the essence of individual freedom within the network of social obligations which contracts built up. This implied the existence of some kind of sphere of social life beyond the reach of contract, or what amounted to the same thing, beyond social construction, what we might call a private or personal as opposed to a public sphere. If the 'I' lies beyond the entanglement of contract, so too must it lie beyond social construction. If this is the case, we must answer a question that the contract theorists, and social science since, have been reluctant to ask: how are such 'I's, or this private sphere produced? The only answer is that it arises from sexual genesis.

The inevitability of parenting and the limits of contract

As Mann (1994) points out (cited on p. 46 above), the universalism of social contract theory in principle was usually qualified theoretically in practice. Servants, labourers and others without independent means were often excluded on the grounds that their economic subordination compromised their political independence. This was a patently weak argument, and moreover, one that was easy for radical critics to reverse: did not universalism imply the need for industrial as well as political democracy, they argued? The case of women however, was more complex, and flowed from the fundamental problem of reconciling the contrasting social position and political rights of men and women which had been created by traditional patriarchal society with the claim that a purely social contract (arrived at freely and equally between men and women) was the basis of men's authority rather than any natural order established by natural sexual differences.

The social contract theorists had to argue that nature did not establish any fundamental difference between the sexes. Thus Pufendorf argued (quoted in Shanley 1982: 89):

> We presuppose at the outset that by nature all individuals have equal rights, and no one enjoys authority over another, unless it has been secured by an act of himself or the other. For although, as a general thing, the male surpasses the female in the strength of body and mind, yet that superiority is of itself far from being capable of giving the former authority over the latter. Therefore, whatever right a man has over a woman, inasmuch as she is his equal, will have to be secured by her consent, or by a just war.

Hobbes, like the other theorists of contract, sought to produce a 'conjectural history' of how the origin of contract could come about. This was not an empirical history of social institutions, but rather a theoretical exercise, a social and political manifesto designed to demonstrate that whatever people might imagine, the social order was politically constructed by themselves. The conservative patriarchalists produced alternative histories, trying to demonstrate the natural basis of the social order. Hobbes therefore started out from a hypothetical 'state of nature' where no social institutions were assumed to exist (rather like Freud's id before the development of an ego) and sought to explain how it would nevertheless be in the individual and collective interests of all the human beings in that 'state of nature' to form a social contract, and to submit to such forms of social regulation as that required. This contract would work best if it need not rely directly on the philanthropy of the parties to it, but found ways to bind them even when they might imagine it was to their personal advantage to dodge its obligations. The social order was thus a way of collectivizing each individual's mistrust and fear of all others into submission to the authority of the laws and political order of society or the 'commonwealth'.

> The force of Words, being (as I have formerly noted) too weak to hold men to the performance of their Covenants; there are in mans nature, but two imaginable helps to strengthen it. And those are either a Feare of the consequence of breaking their word; or a Glory, or Pride in appearing not to need to breake it. This latter is a Generousity too rarely found to be presumed on, especially in the pursuers of Wealth, Command or sensuall Pleasure; which are the greatest part of mankind. The Passion to be reckoned upon, is Fear.
> (Hobbes 1651/1991: 99)

Hobbes's model of the erection of commonwealths through social contract out of an original state of nature is a process not unlike the idea of the precipitation of an incest taboo out of an original state of polymorphous perversity, or of the ego from the id which Freud posited at a psychological level. Like Freud, Hobbes refused to locate women's social inferiority in the state of nature:

> And whereas some have attributed the Dominion to the Man onely, as being of the more excellent Sex; they misreckon in it. For there is not alwayes that difference of strength, or prudence between the man and the woman, as that the right can be determined without War.
> (1651/1991: 139)

Hobbes therefore had to argue that male conjugal rights and the right of the father, which appeared to the patriarchalists as natural and the basis of patriarchy, were a political construction: 'Paternall Dominion ariseth not from generation' (1651/1983: 121) because it took two parents to produce a child. In the 'state of nature' such dominion over children as could exist would be more likely to be maternal than paternal. Either men or women might force a sexual partner into procreation, or they might mutually consent, but any resultant baby would be at the mercy of its mother who had control over it because she gave birth so that maternity, but not paternity, was certain. Such a birth would face the woman with the choice of nourishing the child, in the prospect of securing its loyalty and help in its maturity, but in a state of nature where contracts could not be enforced this was to place an uncertain future hope against a certain present encumbrance: the burden of care which put her at a disadvantage, other things being equal, to men, and to women who were not mothers. 'Infants would endanger the person who had right over them by giving openings to their enemies in the war of all against all' (Pateman 1988: 49). She also had the choice of killing or abandoning it; there would be no matrimonial, or any other 'laws' in the state of nature. Men and women might contract, or force each other into, 'society of the bed only'.

Critics, like the patriarchalist Sir Robert Filmer accused Hobbes with good reason of contemplating virtually anything in the state of nature, from infanticide through rape and murder to cannibalism, and that this conception of the state of nature must thus be ungodly – much the same reaction that greeted Freud's description of the id two centuries later. For Hobbes, the brutish character of the state of nature simply meant that any authority relations which existed between fathers and children reflected a political order, or commonwealth, formed by social contract, to which all family members were party. It was quite possible for different contracts to be arrived at; he cited the 'example' of the Amazons where, he alleged, women ruled both the family, and the kingdom as a whole, while packing off their male children to neighbouring countries, to whose men they also 'had recourse for issue' (1651/1991: 140). In theory at any rate, Hobbes was prepared to imagine societies where the traffic was in men rather than women.

Thus Hobbes concluded that not only marriage but also the family and sexual relations must therefore be constructed, at least in part, by the establishment of societies, or commonwealths, through contract or political agreement. Families, he argues, are an example of a commonwealth acquired by force. Fathers enjoy a monopoly of right within them because each family can have only one source of authority 'for Powers divided mutually destroy each other' and because 'for the most part Common-wealths have been erected by the Fathers, not by the Mothers of families' (1651/1991: 235, 140). If this relation between father and children is a political one then it implied a contract between infant and father which exchanged obedience for protection.

Hobbes had to insist both that generation did not produce dominion and that men and women were equal in order to attack the patriarchalist argument that the origin of both the rule of fathers, and the divine right of kings was natural; just as fathers produced babies naturally, with the mere assistance of 'the weaker vessel', so too did societies require a 'father'. Hobbes thus argued that both sexual genesis and what we might think of as the private sphere was made by social contract, was a social construction.

In what looks rather like sleight of hand, Hobbes manages to go from assumptions of natural equality to the casual acceptance that men have erected and ruled commonwealths, though his comments on the Amazons suggests he accepted this was not the only logical historical possibility. Hobbes gives no clear explanation, but we might infer that it arises from his argument about the certainty of motherhood. The mother–child bond might put women at a historical disadvantage to men. They must have some such incentive to seek the protection of a husband, for Hobbes is clear that people make contracts in the hope of securing some advantage thereby. They do not sign away their natural rights for nothing (Hobbes, *Leviathan*, 1651/1991: 93): 'Whensoever a man Transferreth his Right, or renounceth it; it is either in consideration of some Right reciprocally transferred to himselfe; or for some other good he hopeth for thereby.'

This sleight of hand has, however, apparently solved the social contract theorists' problem; women and men are formally equal, but in marriage all women consent, either freely or through recognition of superior force, to a particular relation to their husbands which ultimately expresses a natural fact about childbirth. Marriage, the division of labour in the family, and the social position of women as a sex in wider society associated with it could now be seen as social constructs, rather than as a directly natural order – relevant to natural differences between men and women, but acting upon them rather than being determined by them. Putting Hobbes's argument into contemporary language we might even say that: 'The social practices that construct the marriage contract do not express natural patterns, nor do they ignore natural patterns; rather they negate them in a practical transformation.' The formulation is Connell's (1987: 79). I have simply replaced the words 'gender relations' with 'the marriage contract'. It suggests that the essential components for the concept of gender are all there in Hobbes. We could say that he attempted to explain the position of men and women as a function of their gender (socially constructed) rather than their sex (naturally determined). And like all socialization theorists since, he suggested a relationship between the two based on sexual difference: the implications of childbirth for women. This is where Hobbes swings between the penis and the phallus. On the one hand women 'choose' to become feminine, by letting the men erect commonwealths, on the other, some biological explanation of this choice seems necessary to explain its universality.

The mother–infant bond Hobbes posited appeared to explain empirically the inferior position of women, which he had started out by refusing to assume theoretically. This allowed him to slip between a 'natural' and 'social' account of women's position. He refused to assume an original natural inferiority on the part of women, for that would undermine the logic of contract. Yet he had to assume that at the point where the social contract is made to emerge from the state of nature, women have already been 'conquered' by men, for only this explains the different position the two sexes occupy when they come to erect commonwealths that grant political supremacy to the father and fix marriage contracts accordingly. A 'social' account faced the problem of explaining how women pursuing their own self-interests might freely agree to become virtual slaves. Thus an account of their conquest in 'nature' was both necessary yet impossible. His account of motherhood, however, squares the theoretical circle; here is a social relationship that influences the terms of other 'contracts', but which is an expression of natural differences between men and women. It makes females feminine and hence, males masculine.

It is a patently weak argument, however, which we have already dismissed in its modern anthropological variant (p. 108). Hobbes anticipated the argument that the natural obviousness of motherhood makes it more of a natural relationship than fatherhood, and creates the mother–infant unit as the irreducible unit of the family in the state of nature – an original private sphere established by the fact of natural difference between men and women. But why shouldn't fathers seek to exchange protection and obedience with an infant rather than mothers? Why should either care whether they are the genitor or genetrix of the infant concerned? Nor is it clear how being the parent of an infant privileges men over women, rather than adults who are not currently in the advanced stages of pregnancy or charged with the care of infants over those who are, regardless of their sex. If we accept, as Hobbes does at other points in the argument, that motherhood *and* fatherhood are equally social constructions, his attempt to explain the rule of the father falls down. Moreover, if we accept Hobbes's logic fully, we have to accept that no one in the state of nature would rationally choose to produce a child – a problem of which Hobbes was only too aware, leading to his equation of the genesis of persons with mushrooms, springing spontaneously from the ground. Filmer savaged this idea, yet it is one which we accept today, in the more sophisticated form of socialization theories.

The patriarchalists' critique of Hobbes and social contract

It is not just the Lakher of Burma who regard women as containers. Much the same interpretation is found in Genesis, where Eve emerges from Adam's rib to become his 'help meet' and as Pateman points out, it underlay patriarchal constitutional and political theory in England at the start of the modern era in the writings of Sir Robert Filmer (1988: 86ff.). His argument was that political right lay in fatherhood, which ultimately stretched back to Adam, and that if this were the case, it logically entailed that men exercised absolute political right over women, since to become fathers, men first needed unconditional rights of sexual access to women's bodies: male sex-right. Were mothers to be granted any recognition in this process, then fathers would no longer have absolute dominion over their sons, and were this the case, not only patriarchy but society itself would collapse, since parental authority was a natural precondition of human existence. Laslett (1949: 31) summarizes Filmer's critique of Hobbes well:

> It was simply not true that authority was being exercised by consent. How could it be pretended that the son consented to being commanded by his father? . . . If authority could be exercised without consent, if in fact it was perpetually being so exercised, then there must be some other source of obligation. This other sort of obligation could only be by nature, not by choice, and observation showed that it was patriarchal.

Filmer quotes lengthily from Genesis to establish the absolute procreative power of the father, the *patria potestas*, including the origin of Eve in Adam's body, and the absence of any role for women, except as aspects of that original male power. As Pateman argues (1988: 87, my emphasis), for him 'Women are merely *empty vessels* for the exercise of men's sexual and procreative power.' The biological facts of life, which seventeenth-century England knew very well, did not stand in the way of Filmer's argument in the least, for he was concerned to argue about the production of political order rather than the procreation of babies and knew that only if the father was seen as sole genitor could conjugal and parental right be brought together and kinship be made to explain the subordination of women and 'natural' order of society. 'Dominion' *had* to be 'Paternall'. If man could be imagined to be the sole sexual genitor (aided only by a 'help meet') then this sexual difference could be used to argue that he was also (albeit by grace of God, or nature) the sole *political* genitor, the sole maker and therefore ruler of society. The key thing was that he saw both as proceeding from a natural order. He was astute enough to see some of the conclusions which flowed from the contract theorists' approach, which the latter preferred to avoid. Were the entire basis of society truly to be government by contract and consent, rather than submission to a natural order, then this must apply not only to relations between the sexes but also to relations between the generations. If this was the case, what difference was left between man and woman, adult or child, and what limits could logically be posited on any person, male or female, contracting with any other person, for any purpose at all, including any use of their body they chose? What was there left, save complete chaos and anarchy – was not the alternative to a natural order no order at all? Was it not, to use Freud's language, to break the incest taboo, return to polymorphous perversity and accept the collapse of civilization?

The first problem concerned the ability of infants to make contracts. If this were the case, and it is accepted that the population changes as people die and new infants are born, it would follow that:

> it is necessary to ask of every infant so soon as it is born its consent to government, if you will ever have the consent of the whole people . . . There every infant at the hour it is born in, hath a like interest with the greatest and wisest man in the world. Mankind is like the sea, ever ebbing or flowing, every minute one is born another dies. Those that are the people this minute, are not the people the next minute. In every instant and point of time there is a variation. No one time can be indifferent for all mankind to assemble. It cannot but be mischievous always at least to all infants and others under the age of discretion – not to speak of women, especially virgins, who by birth have as much natural freedom as an other and therefore ought not to lose their liberty without their own consent.
>
> (Filmer in Sommerville 1991: 142)

In the seventeenth century Filmer could assume that the irony of his comment on virgins would be self-evident. It was as silly to think of contracts being made by unmarried women as by babies. He saw it as proof of the nonsense of contract theory that it spelt the inevitable death of patriarchy in the private sphere as well as the public. For if both men and women could contract out their bodies as they chose, so too could they refuse to do so. And if virgins could personally decide the terms of sexual access to their bodies – which was surely a direct implication of possessive individualism – then what was left of male sex-right or the traditional conjugal power of men over women? The *patria potestes* would be, literally, fucked.

His conclusion was that 'where there is an equality by nature, there can be no superior power' (Filmer in Sommerville 1991: 142). The social contract theorists like Hobbes were simply choosing to ignore their own presumptions of natural equality when it led to troublesome implications.[1] The main reply to Filmer's case was that children (and by extension virgins and wives) could be considered to be under the protection of their father or husbands to whom they thus owed honour and obedience. This argument was deployed by most contract theorists for the next two centuries, and arguably continues to underpin much liberal political theory today in so far as it bases its analysis on (heads of) households (see Brennan and Patcman 1979). Filmer treated this argument with the contempt its shaky logic deserved:

> But in part to salve this, it will be said that infants and children may be concluded by the votes of their parents. This remedy may cure some part of the mischief, but it destroys the whole cause and at last stumbles upon the true original of government. For if it be allowed that the acts of parents bind the children, then farewell the doctrine of the natural freedom of mankind. Where subjection of children to parents is natural, there can be no natural freedom. If any reply that not all children shall be bound by their parents consent but only those that are under age, it must be considered that in nature there is no nonage. If a man be not born free, she doth not assign him any other time when he shall attain his freedom, or if she did then children attaining that age shall be discharged of their parents' contract.
>
> (Filmer in Sommerville 1991: 142)

Indeed, Filmer identified a crucial weakness in the logic of the social contract theorists. It was hardly consistent to assert that all humans were born free and equal, and then to argue that in practice some were born freer and more equal than others, or required protection on some 'natural' grounds. Indeed, the whole business of imputing contract-making capacities to infants seemed to imply that people entered the world as if they were already mature, as if selves had no limits to their ability, especially their ability to construct and reconstruct their own capacities, as if they indeed sprung out of the ground, ready formed, like mushrooms. If it was accepted that they did not enter the world like this, however, how were they ever to reach a point where they *could* claim autonomy or freedom, especially a freedom claimed to be rooted in nature itself? Thus not only did Hobbes face the problem of explaining how, in the state of nature, anyone would choose to have a child, it was also difficult to explain how anyone had ever *been* a child.

> I cannot understand how this 'right of nature' can be conceived without imagining a company of men at the very first to have been all created together without any dependency one of another, or as 'mushrooms (fungorum more) they all on a sudden were sprung out of the earth without any obligation one to another', as Mr. Hobbes's words are in his book De Cive, chapter 8, section 3: the scripture teacheth us otherwise, that all men came by succession, and generation from one man: we must not deny the truth of the history of creation.

It is not to be thought that God would create man in a condition worse than any beasts, as if he made men to no other end by nature but to destroy one another, a right for the Father to destroy or eat his children, and for children to do the like by their parents, is worse than cannibals (De Cive, Ch. 1 section 10). This horrid condition of pure nature when Mr Hobbes was charged with, his refuge was to answer, that no son can be understood to be in a state of nature: which is all one with denying his own principle, for if men be not free-born, it is not possible for him to assign and prove any other time for them to claim a right of nature to liberty, if not at their birth.

(Filmer in Laslett 1949: 241–2)

Hobbes's two problems

Biological reproduction might, just, be the subject of contract, though that in itself posed problems for possessive individualism. If two free individuals contract to produce an infant, is the result of their labour their property to dispose of as they wish, in the same way that an inanimate product of their labour would clearly be? Was this not a question of the way in which possessive individualism led to the commoditization of social relations? How could children, originally 'possessions' of their parents, come to be possessors of themselves?[2] Hobbes was surely aware of how close he was coming to the traditional patriarchal argument about the natural rights of fathers, so he sought to distance himself from this with two claims: that infants made contracts with their fathers or parents (as we have already seen, Filmer suggested such an argument was implicit in the concept of 'free and equal' birth) and that the authority of parents was given to them by the commonwealth, not the natural fact of their parenthood. This gave him a 'political' basis for obligation of infants to parents.

The right of Dominion by Generation, is that, which the Parent hath over his Children; and is called PATERNALL. And is not so derived from the Generation, as if therefore the Parent had Dominion over his Child because he begat him; but from the Childs Consent, either expresse, or by other sufficient arguments declared.

(Hobbes 1651/1991: 139)

This led Hobbes into deeper trouble. The first was that such an exchange looked like a poor deal from the point of view of the infant. Imagining a powerless infant making contracts made it difficult to see what the limits of the infant's obligations could be, and if they were unlimited, then this contract began to look suspiciously like straight paternal dominion. Hobbes himself discusses the position of servants, slaves and children in remarkably similar terms (1651/1991: 139–42). It also looks suspiciously like a slave contract that reduces the status of the infant to a thing; what was to stop a parent requiring a lifetime's obedience – a state of servitude which would prevent the emergence of contract and undermine the basis of the commonwealth itself? As I suggested in Chapter 2, the only solution to this problem is to see the private sphere as existing in some way beyond contract, beyond social construction. The incest taboo cannot be seen as a contract. It might better be seen as a gift by one generation to the next, of the capacity to be alone.

Conversely, the contract did not look promising from the point of view of the parents. Offspring only gained the capacity to become useful allies to their parents to exactly the same extent as they became strong enough to renounce the basis of this alliance. If they indeed exchanged obedience for protection, what 'obedience' might be expected once that protection was no longer required? If families were examples of 'commonwealths by acquisition' then it was difficult to argue against children's right, once they were powerful enough, to assert their independence. At best, the family looked pretty fragile.

Hobbes thus relied on a political account of the family, and gives us the first account of it as an institution of socialization; the authority of the father was drawn from the state's need to educate citizens in their obligations, including the obligations of boys and girls to develop an appropriate gender identity. But this begged the question of the patriarchal character of states which assigned authority in the family to the father in the first place. Here we find him pursuing a curiously patriarchal and convoluted argument, one moreover which goes against his usual preference for 'feare' over 'generousity' in his suggestion that fathers would secure obedience through gratitude and honour:

> And because the first instruction of Children, dependeth on the care of their Parents; it is necessary that they should be obedient to them, whilest they are under their tuition; and not onely so, but that also afterwards (as gratitude requireth), they acknowledge the benefit of their education, by externall signes of honour. To which end they are to be taught, that originally the Father of every man was also his Soveraign Lord, with power over him of life and death; and that the Fathers of families, when by instituting a Common-wealth, they resigned that absolute Power, yet it was never intended, they should lose the honour due unto them for their education. For to relinquish such right, was not necessary to the Institution of Soveraign Power; nor would there be any reason, why any man should desire to have children, or to take care to nourish and instruct them, if they were afterwards to have no other benefit from them, than from other men. And this accordeth with the fifth Commandment.
>
> (Hobbes 1651/1991: 235)

To safeguard social contract Hobbes had to reject the argument that generation created paternal dominion, but in order not to subvert the position of men as fathers, he had to account for their power, and find some way of requiring children to honour their fathers in order to have any account of reproduction at all. But whatever might give an incentive to the father, by the same measure, must render the infant less than equal to him.

The solution Hobbes found was of inestimable significance: to turn the problem from one of relations between the generations to one between the sexes. If the father had, as Hobbes asserts here, originally held absolute power before the erection of the commonwealth, and the latter had thus drawn upon it, then they might still be due honour for 'their education'. As long as the position of the father was now understood to be a political one rather than a 'natural' one, then the glaring similarity of this argument to the straightforward assertion of natural 'paternall dominion' which it had originally set out to contest might be overlooked. Hobbes swung, as it were, from the penis to the phallus. He replaced an account of the natural superiority of men by virtue of their maleness, with an account of their superiority by virtue of their political role: a role that we would today describe as their masculinity. Hobbes's solution is also important because it inaugurated what was to become a distinguished tradition in the social sciences of ignoring reproduction at the expense of production, while assuming that babies would nevertheless emerge from somewhere. The conclusion I draw from this is that Hobbes could not produce a consistent account of sexual genesis, or the power of the father, except by the patriarchal arguments about sexual difference he had originally set out to challenge. As we shall see however, this defeat could yet be turned into a victory.

Thus the first key weakness in Hobbes, and social contract theory generally, was explaining reproduction. It literally denied the role of sexual genesis. The second key weakness was his account of marriage, together with the status-defined roles of husbands and wives, as a contract. Hobbes had to square a theoretical circle again here; he had to explain how a contract which was made by men and women as social beings nevertheless always resulted in males having powers as husbands which might appear (and certainly did to Filmer and others) to be a consequence of their natural, sexual difference.[3] Contract theorists had some fancy intellectual footwork to do if they wished to deny that society was naturally or divinely ordered but still believed in men's natural exclusive right to govern the public sphere, and women's corresponding suitability to concentrate on the domestic sphere, the rearing of children and the nurturance of both them and their husbands.

The marriage contract was permanent; for two centuries not even the most radical contract theorist countenanced the possibility of routine divorce.[4] Second, status entered directly into the terms of the contract; it had to be between a man and a woman. Even today, gay marriage is controversial, and officially sanctioned in only a few countries. Finally, the status of the man and woman in the contract was fixed in advance and gave virtually all the power to the man, whom the woman was not only to honour but also obey. The woman effectively gave up her power to make contracts on marriage; her 'I' as well as her 'me' became fused with that of her husband. At the time the contract theorists were writing, wives had their entire legal personalities submerged into that of their husbands (the doctrine of 'coverture'); they literally ceased to have possession of their self.[5] Husbands enjoyed the right, within certain limits, to imprison, beat, rape and even sell their wives if they so wished. They had rights to compensation to damage to their property if their wives were injured by a third party, thus depriving them of their services, or if a third party gained sexual access to them (criminal 'conversation') (Pateman 1988). The legally enforced submission of a wife to her husband has been gradually reformed over the last two centuries, but it is striking that rape within marriage was only recognized within the last decade in Britain, and as I mentioned in Chapter 1, only in the 1970s did West German and Spanish husbands lose the right to prevent their wives working without their consent. Pateman describes the marriage contract as akin to a slave contract, for obvious reasons. But perhaps a better comparison is with the parental relationship. The wife is the permanent child, for whom her husband is responsible and upon whose guidance she must depend and to whose authority she must submit.

Like children, the status of women as wives in this contract was unclear. Were they to be mere objects of a contract, gifts given by fathers to husbands (in much the same way as a child might be seen as a gift given by the parents to each other) then they could in no sense be seen as individuals and the society which claimed to be founded on a social contract would have to admit that it was in essence patriarchal after all. It was founded on the natural order of difference between the sexes which reduced the status of women to that of the child or the slave. Worse, if women were mere property, mere gifts rather than givers of themselves, the marriage contract would not be a contract at all. As the mere object of it, how were women a party to it? Logically, the prospective husband should enter a contract not with his future wife but with her father for her use or sale. Were women to be made the full equal of men, what would happen to the marriage contract? Were it to be purely contractual, what eventualities would have to be foreseen? Might spouses contract to provide specific forms of sexual access to their bodies, or particular forms of domestic labour or access to certain amounts of their wealth or income? Could they decide in advance, for example, just what measure of love or faithfulness or charity they promised to deliver?[6]

Here we find, once again, that Hobbes resorts to contradictory statements. We have already seen how fathers emerge as the rulers of families once commonwealths have been instituted, which implies they had an advantage over women in the state of nature, an assumption Hobbes makes explicitly at times (e.g. 1651/ 1991: 163, 'the Father and Master being before the Institution of Commonwealth, absolute Soveraigns in their own families, they lose afterward no more of their Authority, than the Law of the Common-wealth taketh from them'). Yet at other times he implies (through his arguments about motherhood and domination of children) that women might also have power resources. It is difficult to avoid the conclusion Brennan and Pateman reach (1979: 189) that in Hobbes's argument 'the mother silently fades from sight'. Thus although Hobbes commences his argument against patriarchalism by asserting that it takes two parents, not just fathers, to beget children, the solution to the problem of having only one source of power and authority in the family is for the woman to become, socially if not naturally, as empty a vessel as the women in Filmer's account. We find too, that from time to time Hobbes falls foul of his own assertion that men and women are naturally equal, so that, for example in discussing rules of succession we find him explaining male inheritance 'because men, are naturally fitter than women, for actions of labour and danger' (Hobbes, *Leviathan*, 1651/ 1991: 137).

The marriage contract and the family becomes a thoroughly political affair in Hobbes's account, a mechanism for the socialization of all its members into the political order. Obedience is due to the father as the infant's moral and political tutor rather than its sexual genitor. It is determined in large part by the needs of the commonwealth for the education of its infants rather than simply resulting from the wishes of the two immediate parties to it, and these needs in turn are revealed as curiously patriarchal: for the father to have sole authority and for children to be raised to honour fathers. Domestic patriarchy and the terms of the marriage contract become a product of the social contract rather than the natural order, but this social contract itself turns out to have a patriarchal character whose roots look suspiciously 'natural'.

Zvesper (1985: 32) suggests that in so far as Hobbes's view of the family locates the political authority of the father in his role as representative of the state it represents

> the transformation of the family into an instrument of the state, a means of educating humans to make them more political, and therefore less dependent on the family. Children will have less dependence on the family after they are old enough to understand that their protection is secured not by the family but by a greater authority. Adults will now have less incentive to have children in the first place, since they no longer need to raise children as allies.

This seems to me to emphasize both Hobbes's prescience (developments I sketch in Chapter 8 flow in large measure from the politicization of the family and intimate relations, and modernity has produced a spectacular decline in fertility rates) and the core weakness of his theory. If the personal becomes *only* political, it ceases to be personal. Following Arendt (1958) Krouse (1982: 152) argues, and I agree with him, that the preservation of autonomous spheres of private thought and action, including

> 'intimate, stable, nurturant units that promote ties across the generations while they prepare children for the linked responsibilities of citizenship, work, and child-rearing as adults – families or their functional equivalents – would be essential to prevent the subordination of these values to one overarching collective imperative.[7]

What I am suggesting here is that we can imagine the 'I's who make contracts as in some sense autonomous beings only if we see them as, in part, naturally produced rather than culturally determined. Were the 'I's fully constructed by the 'me' we would have not only an oversocialized concept of men, but a determinist social and political science wedded to a totalitarian theory and social reality. This leads to a number of ironic or paradoxical conclusions, for example that the roots of democracy lie in the existence of a naturally defined private sphere and thus in sexual genesis, and that the essence of our 'true' as opposed to 'false' selves, or our 'I' as opposed to our 'me' must lie in that part of our selves which is beyond our conscious regulation or which we can in any meaningful sense 'know' or identify. The essence of our identity is, in some respects, what we cannot identify about it. This is why it makes such a suitable platform for the fetishism of sexual difference, the ideology of gender that it throws up, and the other dimensions of the romance of authenticity, including race, ethnicity and national identity. Given we can never finally fix 'who' we are, we can *imagine* ourselves to inhabit any number of socially produced identities, but this need not imply any actual change in the nature of our self. If this is the case, then it is the essence of the personal that it is not entirely political, that it is not entirely socially constructed, and that no matter how hard we might try, identity can never be reduced to ideology. To say the least, this makes the politics of identity problematic – something I discuss in the following chapter.

The confusion of sexual genesis and sexual difference and the origin of the fetishism of sexual difference

By falling back on a theory of natural sexual difference, the contract theorists were able to produce a conjectural history of the origin of the private sphere which otherwise eluded them, and allowed them to 'explain' where babies came from. Hobbes, and the social contract theorists who followed him, solved the problem of accounting for the sexual genesis of human beings by appealing to a concept of sexual difference between them. He produced an account of what women essentially lacked, and rooted it in sex. But these roots had to be obscured if the principle of social contract was to be maintained, so this sexual difference had to be socially constructed; it had to be a product of socialization, what we would learn to think of as 'gender'. Thus, as we have seen, the power of fathers was seen to flow from the political order of the commonwealth; fathers ruled on its behalf. What was quietly forgotten, as women 'faded from view' as Brennan and Pateman (1979) put it, was that this power was traced back by Hobbes to some original power of men present at the institution of the commonwealth. To make the 'natural' basis of this power more explicit would have been to fall back on the openly patriarchal arguments advanced by Filmer and others about the *patria potestes*. Were this sexual difference, along with the power relation between men and women that it established, to be seen as created by social contract, or at least expressed by it, then the charge of making a patriarchal argument might be avoided. To translate this into modern language, if men and women, male and female, were to be seen as masculine and feminine, and the difference between them viewed in terms of social capacities rather than natural abilities, then a social account could be produced both of sexual genesis or parental authority, and of the social relations (marriage and the family) within which it took place. In so far as a woman was an individual, she possessed herself and could be a party to a contract, but as a female, and therefore feminine one, there would be a limit to the kinds of contracts she would attempt to make. As mothers, women required protection, which the marriage contract afforded them. The nature of this contract facilitated childbirth and the raising of children. If the relative position of men and women in the marriage contract set the terms of all the other contracts they participated in, then this was a fundamentally social expression of their different 'natural' capacities – what in a later age came to called masculinity and femininity. The implicit 'sexual contract' as Pateman calls it, which underlay the marriage contract, both presupposed sex in its natural sense and created 'gender' in its social sense. Societies could be seen as comprising not abstract individuals but a combination of masculine and feminine ones.

These 'natural' capacities which were socially expressed were very strange ones indeed, however. They had to exist in order to form the basis of gender, yet they had also to be denied in order to keep gender as something social rather than simply naturally determined. Most explanations of women's 'need' for men's 'protection' hinged on an explanation of her being the 'weaker' sex, which in turn explained her original subordination to men. But was this weakness primarily physical or mental, and what form could it take which nevertheless allowed women and men to be 'equal' in nature? As Pateman points out (1988: 94ff.) physical weakness was a poor explanation of someone's capacity to make contracts. She quotes Thompson's withering nineteenth-century scorn at such arguments: 'let the simple test for the exercise of political rights, both by men and women, be the capacity of carrying 300 lbs. weight.' If the weakness was mental (Rousseau (1995), for example, fell back on another old patriarchal bogey: men's greater capacity to sublimate their sexual desires) then this amounted either to an admission that the patriarchal argument that the social order was an expression of natural birth-ascribed capacity was correct, or it opened the way for feminists from the seventeenth century onwards to argue that as a socially constructed difference, it could be removed through social change such as equal access to education.

In these arguments we can see the origin of the concept of gender, although the term itself was not used, in the sense of a way of thinking about the difference between men and women that could slip, as the occasion demanded, between the social and the natural, between the penis and the phallus. It solved the problem the social contract theorists faced of claiming that modern society was founded on a purely social contract, when the clear evidence was that relations between the sexes were based on sexually-defined status. It also solved the problem of providing a 'contractual' account of reproduction. Sexual relations were seen as social, but expressing a 'natural' difference. We can also see the origin of three different 'solutions' to sorting out the confusion that surrounded attempts to specify just what such natural sexual difference comprised, which we encounter two and a half centuries later in Freud (1986: 353) (discussed in the previous chapter). There was a search for a 'more definite connotation' to the essence of masculinity, which could be pursued by associating the contrasting capacities any mortal self must have with the two contrasting genders. From the start the debate is recognizable as an early version of what was to be refined three centuries later by Parsons (Parsons and Bales 1956) into instrumentalism versus expressiveness. Kant, for example, argued that men could think rationally but women could only feel. For Rousseau the physical difference between men and women led inevitably to moral differences. There is not a great deal of difference between his account of men's ability to sublimate their passion into the task of constructing society, Freud's account of masculinity as 'activity' and still later Chodorow's and Dinnerstein's account of men's flight from the mother to the task of enterprise. This 'more definite connotation' was in turn connected back to biology through reproduction and childbirth. Ultimately females were closer to nature, leaving males to reproduce societies rather than babies. Nineteenth and twentieth-century positivism and sex difference research progressively refined the casual misogyny of a Kant, Locke or Rousseau, but the theoretical context in which the research was pursued did not change at all. It aimed to 'discover' how women's 'natural' difference to men, even as fellow authors of a social order, might define or explain their place in that order. Finally in Hobbes's attempt to start out from an assumption of natural similarity, but acceptance of the empirical fact of a sexual division of labour in practice as the social contract emerged from the state of nature, we find Freud's 'sociological' option – one also used by Parsons (Parsons and Bales 1956) – in accepting that while there was no theoretical or logical reason to associate males with instrumental activities, empirically, they always seem to have monopolized them historically.

Like the contemporary theorists of gender, the contract theorists embroiled themselves in such tangles because they sought at once to confirm and deny a connection between the character of men and women and nature. They had to confirm it to explain the sexual division of labour between men and women, the status of men and women in the marriage contract, the concentration of all natural parental power in the father and all the other remnants of patriarchy in modern, contract-based society. They had to deny it in order to see women as parties to that contract at all, and as members of a society which claimed to be based on the consent of all of its members – not just the men.

The genius of Hobbes, like Freud three centuries later, was to grasp at the concept that if the assumption was dropped that men and women were naturally different, born with different, naturally fixed feminine and masculine personalities and capacities, then the origin of the wider sexual division of labour in society became extremely difficult to explain. Yet if this assumption was not dropped, then a malignant worm of status continued to threaten the apple of universalist modernity. For Hobbes, like Freud, gender, or a system of concepts very like it, offered the way out. The tragedy of Hobbes and Freud was their failure to follow their logic to its conclusions: sexual relations were as political and socially constructed as any other, and possessive individualism ultimately implied possession of one's sexual identity, orientation and practice as much as possession of any other capacities. The natural limits to the social order came not from sexual difference, but sexual genesis, which meant that since selves were originally natural rather than social products, there were aspects of themselves which they could not simply possess, nor could they choose to construct themselves and their relations in any way they chose, whether that concerned their sexual relations with each other, or their most instrumental business dealings. Possessive individualism was not in the long run compatible with the idea that men and women were naturally different and that this difference ordered sexual and all other relations. To cling to a theory of natural difference meant clinging to a theory of patriarchy. The history of the last 300 years has been the history of the erosion of patriarchy by possessive individualism.

The alternative, which Hobbes refused, and which most social scientists have refused since, was to accept the argument, advanced by patriarchalists like Filmer, that the social order was not, after all, purely social; it did have a natural basis. But the limits set by nature lay not in sexual difference, which could be used by the patriarchalists to argue that men's power had a natural origin, but in sexual genesis. Parental power *did* have a natural origin. It was not created by any social contract between an infant and parent. This meant that any society which claimed to see itself as democratically constructed by contracts between its members had to account for the way in which its members could develop to the stage where they were capable of making such contracts in the first place – where the 'I's come from. This suggests that there lies an area of human experience and the social order which inevitably lies beyond contract and this area concerns the nature of the relationship between parent and infant. This relationship, rooted in the sexual nature of human reproduction, represents an inevitable survival of status or kinship in the modern, contractual, universal world. This means that all social relations, whether in the private or public sphere, whether concerned with enterprise and industry, or intimacy and sexual pleasure, are not simply the conscious, sovereign creations of their authors, who are free to make and reform them by an effort of conscious will. To use Freud's language, if the ability to be perverse paradoxically demonstrates the civilized nature of human beings through the symbolic focus of their sexuality and its emancipation from natural instinct; their inability to 'choose' their perversions (or for that matter, to choose other aspects of their 'identity') demonstrates that, as adults who were originally infants, as possessors of an unconscious, their civilization has a natural basis. The paradox here is that this natural basis makes a democratic civilization possible in the first place.

Accepting such a natural dimension to parental power might at first appear conservative in its implications, but here lies a profound and inescapable paradox. The theoretically independent authors of contracts had all to start out as utterly dependent. Were their development then understood as determined entirely by their social relations with the social order they arrived in, then their 'independence' could ultimately be little more than an illusion; their biography would be little more than the inscription of socialization on *tabulae rasae* – rather like the selves we might imagine being produced by the political family theorized by Hobbes, or the citizens of Orwell's *Nineteen Eighty-Four*. Conversely, the possibility of seeing society as more than the revelation of God's mysterious workings lay in seeing this development as partly natural, something that proceeded beyond the comprehensive conscious control of either parent or infant, something that, by definition, could not be rationally understood. The unconscious, or at least the existence of a private sphere beyond the public, as I suggest in the next chapter, might be the royal road to democracy.

The relation between genetrix, genitor and infant stands at the centre of all the arguments made in this book. It is because human beings as a species reproduce sexually that male and female persons exist (so we have the material basis for even beginning to imagine that such a thing as masculinity or femininity could exist). These persons are mortal; both the species, and the culture into which they are born, will outlast them (though this is not to deny that it may change dramatically over the course of their lives). It means that every member of any society which has ever existed starts out with a biological relation to a genitor and genetrix and an initial total dependence on a parental figure or figures for the first few years of its existence. Sociology, however, because of its origins in social contract theory, and its resulting emphasis on social constructionism, has been nervous about the natural genesis of human beings, and preferred to ignore it. This has led, in turn, to what O'Neill (1994) has termed 'the missing child in liberal theory' or what I have discussed here as the question of the origins of our human agency, self and personality.

Fixing this relationship properly, and untangling the confusion between sexual genesis and sexual difference enables me to answer the three questions I earlier posed of Rubin (1975) in Chapter 6. First it suggests that we cannot look to sexual difference as such to account for patriarchy, or why women rather than men were originally gifts. If we did, we would have to conclude that patriarchy was inevitable. But we might be able to produce an account in terms of the changing historical context of sexual genesis, and how this particular sexual division of labour relates to others. This is what I suggested in my account of patriarchy and the demographic transition in Chapter 2.

Second, it suggests that the paradoxical position of women as both gift and giver, simultaneously object of a contract and party to it, represents a real contradiction in modernity at both ideological and material levels between the legacy of patriarchy and its historical defeat – between the sexual contract and the social contract. The possessive individualism of modernity could be described in Rubin's language as the right for everyone to become a giver of themselves, and to decide with others on the traffic regulations. Men have fought against this assault on patriarchy, but have faced the problem that it was, in part, unleashed by their own claims for equal rights. It has consistently proved impossible to produce good arguments for the equality of all men that do not also imply the equality of all men *and women*. Gender is a good example. Starting out as a way of thinking about sexual difference developed by the social contract theorists to defend patriarchal privileges, it became used by feminists to demonstrate their incompatibility with true equal rights.

Third, I think Rubin's concerns about the connection between patriarchy and culture and symbolism, and about the survival of kinship in modernity now appear as a particular example of the false choice. Universalism is compatible with the survival of kinship in the sense of sexual genesis, and with the survival of the incest taboo, and need not imply a flight to adult polymorphous perversity if we maintain a separation between the private and public spheres and recognize that this separation does not imply sustaining patriarchy in the private sphere because the latter is founded on sexual genesis, not sexual difference. Parental authority over infants need not imply paternal authority over either wives or daughters.

I have concentrated on the ideas of Hobbes and social contact theory because they were important for the subsequent development of social and political thought. Hobbes answered the critique of the patriarchalists that nature played a role in relations between fathers and children by arguing, in effect, that the self was an entirely social construction. It drew its character from the family, which was in turn a political institution which socialized its members into accepting the necessary constraints of a stable political order. While the role of sexual genesis was thus overlooked, the fact of sexual difference was brought in to explain the sexual division of labour, and make inequality between men and women appear to be one such necessary constraint. But again, in order to counter the arguments of the patriarchalists that this was to recognize the role of nature in erecting the social order, this sexual difference itself had to be theorized as something which was itself socially or politically constructed rather than naturally determined. The concept of gender was born. Hobbes's argument with Filmer was that generation did not imply dominion. But the patriarchalism of the patriarchalists was not rooted in this argument. It flowed only from the assumption that parental dominion was essentially paternal.

It is difficult to overestimate the subsequent impact of this way of thinking on modern social scientific thought. Debates in the seventeenth and eighteenth centuries about social contract became debates in the twentieth century about social construction and socialization. As I discuss in the final chapter, it has perhaps three contemporary legacies. The first is the idea that our identities are purely social constructions, that we can thus come to control them, and that identity is reducible, ultimately, to ideology; what Craib (1994a) has called the 'powerful self'. The second is the idea that any limits to this process are to be found in our sexual difference rather than our sexual genesis – the fact that we are male or female rather than the fact that we have all been reproduced from a male and a female. The third is the 'false choice' which this approach presents us, between an over-socialized but non-patriarchal view of the self, and a view which gives the self autonomy, but assumes that this autonomy itself must have a patriarchal character.

Notes

1 Elsewhere Hobbes contradicted himself, clearly arguing that babies could not make contracts, and that their ability to enter society depended on 'education' or what we might today call socialization:

> But civill Societies are not meer Meetings, but Bonds, to the making whereof, Faith and Compacts are necessary: The Vertue whereof to Children, and Fooles, and the Profit whereof to those who have not yet tasted the miseries which accompany its defects, is altogether unknown; whence it happens, that those, because they know not what society is, cannot enter into it; these, because ignorant of the benefit it brings, care not for it. Manifest therefore it is, that all men, because they are born in Infancy, are born unapt for Society. Many also (perhaps most men) either through defect of minde, or want of education remain unfit during the whole course of their lives; yet have Infants, as well as those of riper years, an humane nature; wherefore Man is made fit for Society not by nature, but by Education.
>
> (Hobbes 1651/1983: 44)

2 My argument could be seen as advancing a parallel criticism of Marx from the point of view of reproduction which I have earlier made from the point of view of production (Cressey and MacInnes 1980): if labour itself can never be entirely commoditized in the process of production, then neither can the process of its reproduction.

3 We can recognize this problem of Hobbes as being exactly parallel to the one faced by Freud when he tackled the same issue. How could he square his demonstration that masculinity was socially produced rather than naturally determined, with his explanation of how only males could acquire masculinity? Both Hobbes and Freud solved their problems by swinging between the penis and the phallus.

4 Although, as Shanley (1982) points out, Milton advocated divorce.

5 Brennan and Pateman (1979: 197) quote from Blackstone's *Commentaries on the Laws of England*, first published in the 1760s: 'a man cannot grant any thing to his wife, or enter into covenant with her, for the grant would suppose her separate existence'.

6 Precisely what some couples, particularly in the United States, now appear to try to write into their marriage contracts. It is, of course, a logical implication of the concept of a pure relationship.

7 Krouse (1982) quotes from W. Connolly (no date) 'The State and the private interest'. Washington: American Political Studies Association. There is an unintentional irony in the quotation; the main purpose of the autonomy of families from politics is nevertheless a political one! It is assumed to be a civically correct one, however – facilitating democracy, rather than authoritarianism. This line of political argument goes back to Arendt's (1958) classic and persuasive study, *The Human Condition*.

8

Why the personal is not political

'I don't mean confessing. Confession is not betrayal. What you say or do doesn't matter: only feelings matter. If they could make me stop loving you – that would be real betrayal.'

She thought it over. 'They can't do that,' she said finally. 'It's the one thing they can't do. They can make you say anything – *anything* – but they can't make you believe it. They can't get inside you.'

'No,' he said a little more hopefully, 'no, that's quite true. They can't get inside you. If you can *feel* that staying human is worth while, even when it can't have any result whatever, you've beaten them.' . . .

They could not alter your feelings: for that matter you could not alter them yourself, even if you wanted to. They could lay bare in the utmost detail everything that you had done or said or thought; but the inner heart, whose workings were mysterious even to yourself, remained impregnable.

(Orwell 1949: 136)

What I do not like is that if the fate of a great passion comes over a person, he fashions from it a 'right' of himself to act in such and such a way instead of simply taking it 'humanly' – simply as a 'fate' with which one must cope, and often cannot cope, because one is only human.

(Weber, cited in Gane 1993: 165)

The paradoxes of the politics of identity

If 'workers of the world unite' was the essential political aphorism of the world for a century after Marx proclaimed it in 1848, surely the 'personal is political' has replaced it in the 50 years since then. This slogan is a slippery one, however, because it both expresses the core recognition of modernity that people rather than God or nature make societies, but does so in a way that conveys most clearly the core illusion of modernity, expressed in the concept of gender, that personal identities create political social structures and social structures create identities. In contrast to the old adage that all is fair in love and war, perhaps the key conviction of contemporary industrial capitalist societies is that it is possible and desirable to 'democratize' private, intimate and personal relations, including those between sexual partners and between parents and children, and to do this by perfecting the reflexive conscious control of the self, emancipating it, for example, from traditional ideologies about gender and allowing it to form 'pure' relationships (Giddens 1992).

This assertion is the basis of the various forms of the politics of identity, and could be seen as the extension of the concept of public 'rights' to the private sphere, and in particular the notion of a right, supported by public political arrangements, to discover, realize, inhabit or express one's authentic identity. If modernity originated in the claim that independent selves now consciously created society in their own image rather than God's, and that this was best expressed in the concept of the equal public rights of persons, we could perhaps describe late modernity as the era in which those same selves now claim private rights to a true self. Where before public conflicts and struggle took place over the right to vote, strike or work, there are increasing conflicts over the right to a particular identity, or conversely, the social obligation to develop a particular form of identity (Goldstein and Rayner 1994). These conflicts often focus on gender, and are articulated in its terms. Men are called upon to reform what is imagined to be their (hegemonic) masculinity; other men claim the right to express what they imagine to be their 'deep masculine' (Bly 1991, Thompson 1991). I argued above (pp. 94ff.) that some forms of essentialist feminist argument have tried to make direct connections between the nature of gender identity (understood as masculinity or femininity) and social relations of exploitation or oppression. Masculinity, for example, has been seen as an identity which creates a hierarchical and oppressive social division of labour.

This politics of identity, which takes many diverse forms, has as its common core, the assumption that the self or identity is essentially socially constructed, and that political and social progress can be achieved by the reflexive reconstruction of the self along the right lines. In this sense the politics of identity and this emphasis on the social construction of the self is the contemporary intellectual descendent of the tradition of Hobbes and the other social contract theorists who first tried to see the self as a *tabula rasa*, made by contract rather than defined by nature. But my argument has been that this way of thinking about the self arose out of the need to legitimate men's dominance in an era where simple appeals to natural superiority could no longer work. It depended upon the confusion of sexual genesis and sexual difference. The personal was imagined as directly political, in order to explain how infants could acquire a gender identity that was not reducible to natural sexual difference. Generation became imagined as gender socialization. Because it is rooted in this tradition of thought, the politics of identity remains a prisoner of the ideology of patriarchy, because the essence of this ideology in modernity, is the idea that the development of the self is a process of gender socialization whereby male and female infant selves become masculine and feminine ones.

The social and political essence of my thesis could be summarized as *the personal is not political; the personal is what makes the political possible.* What we have tried, hitherto, to understand as the political results of the socialization of sexed members of society into gender identities via the Oedipus complex, we should understand instead as the sexual genesis of persons who become autonomous selves, capable of social relations, through the development of a capacity to be alone produced by the ambivalences of attachment. The existence of this process, in part naturally determined, defines the existence of a private sphere and its distinction from the political or public one. If my distinction between generation and socialization is correct, and aspects of identity and intimate personal relations are not socially constructed, it can make no sense to call for their rationalization, modernization or democratization. The democratization of personal life, or the rise of the 'pure' relationship will not be what they might appear to be – an advance in sexual egalitarianism, but something less desirable – the totalitarian politicization of the self in late modernity (Craib 1988). This might also be seen as part of the privatization of how we envisage social change and reform; the picket line has been supplanted by the psychotherapist's couch. We come to believe that our life chances are more significantly determined by our identity, formed by our parenting, than by the social structure and division of labour shaped by the axes of class, race and sex. Instead of being drawn to social mobility, centred around material resources and opportunities, our attention is drawn to personal growth centred around identity. It is drawn towards the emotional poverty caused by dysfunctional parents, for example, rather than child poverty caused by increasing material inequality. Within sociology, it is as if C. Wright Mills' (1970) famous dictum has been turned on its head and the watchword of our understanding is henceforth to be the discovery of the origin of public issue in the aetiology of private trouble.

Whereas the politics of identity implies that the personal itself is a key site of political struggle (for example against sexism or racism) my argument is that perhaps the most important political battle of the contemporary era is that to defend personal and private space from politicization and rationalization. This is not a conservative, individualist or narcissistic approach, but on the contrary the only means of avoiding one. It is about reasserting what politics is properly about: the collective struggle against material exploitation and inequality to achieve equal public rights for private citizens, using the sort of material which classic sociology provides. An example is the struggle against a division of labour still based on sex, and gender ideologies that sustain this, for instance against claims that there are differences between the social capacities of men and women – differences often described as their gender identities. To argue against the politicization of the personal appears at first sight to defend patriarchal relations, but this is because patriarchal ideology itself leads us to assume that the essence of the personal or private sphere is sexual difference (and hence power relations between men and women) rather than sexual genesis (and power relations between adult carers and infants). If we make this mistaken assumption we are led to make the false choice I discussed in Chapter 3 between the personal as *either* political *or* patriarchal.

Asserting that the personal is political appears, at first sight, to bring what had previously been dismissed as the merely personal further up the political agenda and make it more important. As Phillips (1991: 93) comments, the slogan 'was initially a riposte to male politicos in the civil rights and socialist/radical movements: activists whose conception of politics was far too grand to admit the pertinence of merely sexual concerns.' It emphasized the political and public relevance of relations in the personal or private sphere (domestic and personal labour, childcare, emotional support) *in so far* as they had an impact on or resulted from men and women's participation in the public spheres of politics, employment, education, other aspects of the division of labour beyond the family, and civil society generally, for example access to the public sociability of the street or public places of entertainment. As Carole Pateman (1983: 295) put it:

> Feminists have emphasised how personal circumstances are structured by public factors, by laws about rape and abortion, by the status of 'wife', by policies on childcare and the allocation of welfare benefits and the sexual division of labour in the home and workplace. 'Personal' problems can thus be solved only through political means and political action.

In these senses the slogan highlighted women's relative exclusion from the public sphere and their patriarchal subordination in the private sphere, that such 'private trouble' was rooted in the 'public issue' of the survival of patriarchy. In this sense the slogan describes the central argument of this book that the heart of patriarchy comprises the denial of equal public political rights to women which flow from the material and ideological legacy of the era of patriarchy, the lingering feudal remnants of male sex right.

Another interpretation of the slogan has become important and influential, however. Cohen (1996: 5) for example suggests that

> Feminist theorists have long argued that the 'personal is political', meaning that the apparently 'natural' private domain of intimacy (the family and sexuality) is legally constructed, culturally defined and the site of power relations.

This too can be seen as endorsing another argument I have made in this book: that modernity is about recognizing that societies (including social relations between men and women) are made by people, not ordained by God or nature. It can also be seen as suggesting an argument which I have tried to refute, however: that nature plays no part in social relations, including those in the private sphere, so that everything that appears 'natural' is actually a product of the social. This in turn has given rise to two arguments, both of which I wish to challenge. One is that the personal (including everything about the personal which appears to be 'natural') is created by the political, and that modernity is fundamentally about this recognition, in contrast to premodern ideologies about a spirit or soul that might exist beyond the social in God or nature. We have seen Hobbes struggling after this idea, in the way that he came to see the family as a creation of the Commonwealth. It haunted Marx too. In the *Communist Manifesto* he imagined that the transformation of all social relations into market transactions would logically extend to sexual relations between adults and the reproduction of children: 'The bourgeoisie has torn away from the family its sentimental veil, and has reduced the family relation to a mere money relation' (Marx and Engels 1968: 38). It finds contemporary expression in Giddens's (1992) theory of 'the reflexive project of the self' and the 'pure relationship':

> a situation where a social relation is entered into for its own sake, by what can be derived for each person from a sustained association with another; and which is continued only insofar as it is thought by both parties to deliver enough satisfactions for each individual to stay within it . . . it is part of a generic restructuring of intimacy.

The other argument is that the personal, and especially aspects of the personal such as the gender identity of the self, directly creates the political. The personal, in the sense of the self or individual identity, is an important or even fundamental site of social and political change. These arguments are simply the two sides of inevitably circular socialization theories. In the first the personal is the product of the political, while in the second the political comes to be seen as a product of the kind of identities or selves which society comprises. Both these arguments depend upon effacing a crucial distinction between the private and public spheres which it is vital to maintain; the personal and the political are collapsed into each other. Thus Anne Phillips writes (1991: 102):

> Many [feminists] had thought of the problems they had with husbands or lovers in terms of individual psychology – maybe we're not compatible? maybe I want what's impossible? maybe he just doesn't care? – but in the process of exploring individual experiences, they came to identify general patterns of power . . . The personal was as political as anything else and as devastatingly destructive of our human development as anything that governments could do.

In so far as Phillips is suggesting that intimate relations are in part structured by power inequalities between men and women, which they inevitably bring with each other from the wider social world, and that this causes problems for couples who believe in equality, I am with her. In so far as she is discussing political activists whose 'activity' doesn't stretch to a fair share of childcare or domestic labour, I am with her. But at the point where the argument suggests that all problems here are a function of the political construction of the personal or family relations, or of a particular kind of self or identity conceptualized as masculinity, or that intimate relations are possible without 'problems', then I part company from it.[1] The key point is to distinguish the social political or public aspects of the self and its relations from its personal and private ones.

The idea that the self is only social and can therefore be consciously constructed and reconstructed makes the idea of the democratization of personal life thinkable. It makes therapy in its manifold forms possible, as the 'scientific' analysis and development of the self (personal growth) and of children who might thus be rationally parented. Only with such a self is a sociology of emotions possible, both from the point of view of the sociologist able to analyse the emotional labour undertaken by the subjects she or he studies, and from the point of view of the application of the results of such analysis, in terms of the decision by individuals to do emotional labour of various kinds, whether on themselves or others around them. This is what Craib (1994a) calls the 'powerful self', what Dennis Wrong (1961) criticized as the 'over socialized conception of man'. This can be seen as the final meaning of 'the personal is political': our post-enlightenment belief that not only do we make history and the social order, we make our selves and inner personal order too. All this can be achieved, however, only by denying our sexual genesis together with the mortality that implies and collapsing public ideologies about what we might aspire to become into what we imagine our actual identities or selves to actually be. Let me briefly review the implications of such ideas for the rearing of children and the public discussion of emotion and identity.

A difficult time to be a parent?

They fuck you up, your mum and dad.
They may not mean to but they do.
They fill you with the faults they had
And add some extra, just for you.
>   (Philip Larkin, This Be The Verse, *High Windows*)

We know many people who are 'screwed up' – in a few cases they may actually have cracked up altogether – but we prefer to think of ourselves as having had a 'reasonably normal childhood' and as being 'reasonably well balanced'. The truth is more interesting.
    The truth is that it is now normal to be screwed up. Philip Larkin was right. Nearly all of us come from families which have to some degree abused and deprived us.
>   (James 1996: 3)

While there has probably always been plenty of advice directed at men and women about how to be good fathers and mothers, not least from their own fathers and mothers, the modern period brought a great change in the status of childhood (Aries 1973). More recently the public control of its organization has increased, both directly through state regulation of education and welfare, and legislation about minimum standards of parenting, and indirectly through the massive expansion of public discussion (based on the 'scientific' advice of professionals) *both* about how children ought to be raised safely and well, *and* about the injuries, wounds and injustices suffered by those who are not 'correctly' parented, those who come from 'dysfunctional' families or who suffered an 'abusive' father, mother or guardian.[2] Perhaps the single clearest evidence of this is the rise of psychoanalysis and psychotherapy as scientific and professional disciplines (Craib 1989,

1994a) with mass popular influence, as evidenced by the best-seller status of intellectually robust works such as *Families and How to Survive Them* (Skynner and Cleese 1983) authored by a respected academic and a comedian, and endorsed by the *Sun*. Their very existence is predicated on an ability to analyse the nature of the parent–infant relationship in a scientific and rational way – in much the same way as we might analyse economic laws or the engineering of buildings.

It could be argued that behind these changing conceptions of the relationship between parents and infants lies an implicit demand, if not for the right to be happy, then at least for the demand for such parenting as produces adults who are unhindered by the particular psychological dynamics of their family of origin, and have been emancipated from – or to use the jargon, survived – its legacy. Here lurks the conviction that we can grow to become the type of person we aspire to be, to develop into the type of self we want to have, and that, if we are conscious enough, we can grow or socialize our children in the same way, often according to a blueprint that has emerged from public or political discussion, or according to the pressing material demands of everyday life. This is a Utopian conviction because it imagines that we could escape from the limits of our sexual genesis, from the fact that we are born of particular parents, and that this inevitably creates aspects of our self or identity which we can never transcend, as opposed to accept as our mortal human fate. It is ultimately a pernicious conviction because it devalues the importance of the real physical or sexual abuse of children by suggesting that anyone who has not realized what they imagine to be their full potential must be in some sense a victim, as James (1996) does in the article quoted at the start of this section. This invites us to leave our humanity behind, by suggesting that we can, if we only try, bring our own identity, or that of those we care for, into line with what public ideologies suggest they should comprise. If we are only conscientious enough, and extend our supervision far enough, we can socialize our children into androgynous identities.

There is an increasingly far-ranging public discussion of every conceivable aspect of relations between parents and children with an increasing tendency to suggest that parents face fairly clear choices between right (or functional) or wrong (dysfunctional) behaviour towards their children and that it is these choices that most affect their children's future. This may indeed have progressive aspects – why leave childhood to superstition, ritual, tradition and ignorance? It is valuable to rid children's books of sexist imagery, or challenge sex stereotyping of infants' toys and activities. But to imagine that we might thus create egalitarian infant gender identities is not only misconceived but also profoundly conservative. It puts the cart of identity before the horse of the existing sexual division of labour. Any parent knows that their own attempts at sexual egalitarianism are inevitably overwhelmed by the ubiquitous impact of the sexual division of labour and its ideological legitimation in contemporary culture. Children are alert to these messages, which they understand as adult and thus enthusiastically embrace.

There is something deeply disturbing here too, however – the spectre of Frankenstein, and the hatcheries of *Brave New World*. We would rightly reject any science which pretended to tell us how we must live. Why embrace a science which tells us how to create perfect children? Is there not something sinister about a society where there is consensus between the two main political parties about the value of testing 5-year-olds? Ironically, much of this discussion has proceeded within a political context where it has become *more legitimate* for parents to insist on the right to unequal access to the social and public provision of education for their children through the expansion of private schools and selection, and where the number of children living in poverty has risen steadily. Debates over imaginary private rights to a non-screwed-up childhood have obscured the threat to more fundamental public rights to a decent education and minimum standard of living for children.

If we can disentangle sexual genesis and sexual difference, it is possible to resist the inexorable socialization of intimate relations, and defend the autonomy of the modern self from the threat of what we could see as the bureaucratization of the soul, without simply encouraging a return to conservative and patriarchal 'family values' as a 'haven from a heartless world' (Lasch 1977). We may also be able to propose strategies which help emancipate girls and boys from the straitjacket of gender stereotypes, without resorting to imposing blueprints on either children, their parents or their teachers, about how they must be raised. We can do this if we realize that the political is not produced by the character of our selves, including what we think of as our gender identities, nor do we possess gender identities which are produced directly by the political order, including the sexual division of labour, in which we live. We can only do this if we refuse to reduce the personal and the political to each other, and recognize that how we think of the personal, including the idea that we possess gender identities at all, is part of an ideology which has developed to legitimate a particular form of the political, namely a society in which men were still dominant, but in which they could no longer logically appeal to claims of natural superiority to rationalize that dominance. We can then propose strategies that tackle sexual inequality in society directly, while we leave aspects of the personal that do not have any connection to this alone.

Such strategies would take us to two main questions. One is the sexual division of labour and its ideological legitimation. What circumstances most effectively force or encourage men to do a more equal proportion of childcare and domestic labour, so that the expansion of women's employment does not simply become 'the double shift'? How can sexual segregation in the public sphere be most effectively reduced, so that girls and boys face less powerful stereotypes about what men and women do, and more equal career opportunities and domestic obligations themselves? How might we achieve as much public concern about working fathers as about working mothers? The other is the way in which capitalism avoids the material costs of the reproduction of children. It is not just Hobbes who liked to imagine that people might spring up like mushrooms; rational capitalist organizations, so long as they can obtain a labour supply from somewhere, would prefer it too. Since the rearing of children is costly – in terms of time, money and emotional commitment – it is hopeless to leave it to the market. Any social system of reproduction requires transfers of resources from those currently without dependent children to those who have them. The more meagre these transfers, the more childcare depends on the unpaid labour of women, and the more unequal the sexual division of labour at this stage in the life cycle becomes. It is a scandal, for example, that young fathers in Britain now work longer hours than a decade ago, not because they want to escape their domestic obligations more, but because they need to pay for their children.

The politicization of the soul?

Unhappy that I am, I cannot heave my heart into my mouth.
                                    (Cordelia, *King Lear*, I. i. 90)

The secret thoughts of a man run over all things, holy, profane, clean, obscene, grave, and light, without shame, or blame; which verball discourse cannot do, farther than the Judgement shall approve of the Time, Place and Persons.
                                    (Hobbes 1651/1991: 52)

It is not only about how to raise our children that we are increasingly counselled, but on how to 'grow' our selves and raise our 'inner' child. The personal – in the sense of our innermost feelings, our intimate lives, our private sexual relationships, our hearts, our souls, what we might choose to think of as our true selves or what Hobbes describes as our 'secret thoughts' – has become relentlessly political in that it has become a focus for public analysis and discussion. Although this trend might be traced back to the dawn of modernity and beyond – is the novel in essence a private biography with a public moral? – it has assumed particular force over the last three decades. Our identities are steadily less private and increasingly something of political and public relevance which it is our responsibility to control and direct appropriately. In any imaginable society, there will be a difference between the inner individual and their outer, public face; we will be anxious about the latter (and the necessary distance between that and our hearts' darker fantasies and desires) and others will be interested in what might go on in our private self. But in earlier times these others, particularly when they are not intimate with us, neither a lover, confidante or close kin, might be able to resist the temptation either to ask us what we really 'feel' or indeed, tell us how we ought to be feeling. Cas Wouters (1987, 1991) is surely correct to argue, both that there has been a development of what he calls 'mutually expected self restraint' which makes it possible for people to assume that the articulation of a feeling will be kept separate from acting it out, so that we can confess our sexual desires or violent impulses without tearing off our clothes or raising our fists; and that the articulation of such appropriately detached emotion has become a mark of status.

Nowadays it is hard to grasp just how relentlessly politicized and publicized our personal selves, emotions or identities have become. This includes the increase in popular discussion of private experience, the analysis of that experience in sociological and political terms, and the explanation of social and political problems as the results of that experience. This ranges from the ubiquitous confessional prurient television shows and magazine and newspaper articles about every conceivable aspect of private lives or feeling states, to the mushrooming of the problem page (and its grim shadow, the obituary) to the explosion in counselling, psychotherapy and social work, of 'self help' and 12-step programs for 'survivors' of every imaginable predicament to trends in scientific disciplines. As I noted in Chapter 3 the 'sociology of emotions' is a fast growing area. Jean Duncombe and Dennis Marsden (1995: 150) have suggested that emotional labour may constitute 'the last frontier of gender inequality' while Ulrich Beck and Elizabeth Beck-Gernsheim have claimed that 'love is the new centre round which our detraditionalized life revolves' (1995: 2) while the back cover blurb for their book asserts that 'The struggle to harmonize family and career, love and marriage, "new" motherhood and fatherhood, has today replaced class struggle.'

The outer public world, it seems, has mounted an invasion of the inner, private one, and it is we who are inviting it in, as we sit in the psychiatrist's chair (if we are especially fortunate, with a radio or television audience joining in), watch *The Oprah Winfrey Show*, read Susie Orbach's psychotherapy column in *The Guardian* or do our *Meditations for Men* (or women) *Who Do Too Much* (Lazear 1992). This may appear to us as a process of increasing our conscious, reflexive mastery over our own selves. But its essence may be something quite different. Late, flexible, capitalism needs resourceful, flexible, selves. Selves perhaps who are prepared to invite the public world into their souls. Selves perhaps which are not so much powerful, as to be insecure enough, or have weak enough boundaries to be incapable of keeping the public world out.

This has a sexual dimension in that gender ideology has associated men and masculinity with emotional inarticulacy. Now they are increasingly being urged to get in touch with their feelings, whether by participating in drumming sessions and replicating traditional initiation rituals from other cultures, or more prosaically, by lifting the telephone. 'It's good to talk', announces Bob Hoskins – an icon of masculine instrumentalism – and in case men don't get the message British Telecom has run a series of newspaper adverts urging men to talk more, particularly to other members of the family, and even teaching them how to do it.

Encouraging men to articulate their emotions may be positive, but is unlikely to produce much social change, because it confuses identity and ideology once more, this time by confusing the personal experience of an emotion with the public expression of it. It is not just that there is an inevitable difference between these two things; it is that one of the most effective ways to avoid experiencing an emotion or being aware of an aspect of our identity is to focus our attention on expressing it or discussing it, or better still, on demanding that others tell us about theirs (Craib 1995). The public discussion of emotion, and the sociology

which imagines that it analyses it, does not therefore constitute either the liberation of the self, or the political struggle to change oppressive identities. It is the
voyeuristic invasion of the private space of others by weak selves without enough
capacity to be alone. To the extent that sociology has become focused on identity,
emotion and the subjective, without reflecting critically enough on its material
basis in social relations, it has become a part of the development of the mass
culture of modernity which it ought to be analysing rather than uncritically
adopting. It has become part of the problem instead of the solution. It would do
well to note the caution and irony implicit in a poem by D.H. Lawrence:

> *To Women, as far as I'm concerned*
>
> The feelings I don't have, I don't have
> The feelings I don't have, I won't say I have
> The feelings you say you have, you don't have
> The feelings you would like us both to have, we neither of us have
> The feelings people ought to have, they never have
> If people say they've got feelings, you may be pretty sure they haven't got
>   them
> So if you want either of us to feel anything at all
> You had better abandon any idea of feelings altogether.

In order to pursue sexual equality, we should not seek to change men's private
identities. We should demand their public support for sexual equality in material
and ideological terms. We should demand that men challenge the sexual division
of labour wherever its continued existence is not related to the biologocial division of labour in reproduction. We might want to accept, for example, that most or
all midwives are female. We would expect the development of health care services to reflect the fact that only women become pregnant. We should demand
that they challenge ideas which sustain the belief that there are differences –
social or natural – between men and women which explain or legitimate the
existing sexual division of labour. And we should demand that they challenge all
the other social consequences that flow from sexual inequality, from all the forms
of sexual violence to sex stereotyped imagery. We should demand selves that are
publicly responsible but personally autonomous.[3]

Imagination and sociology

There is an essential paradox, which is seldom noticed, at the heart of the politics
of identity. The notion of a right to an identity that is claimed to be authentic
implies a right to demand the political arrangements which make that possible,
usually through abolishing or reforming political structures which have hitherto
repressed authenticity. But from the 'other' side, this same politics of identity
appears as the demand that personal identities are politicized and fall into line.
The personalization of the political envisages the expansion of the political to

comprehend private subordination and exploitation. But it can also mean the domination of the political and the public over the personal and the private. In *Nineteen Eighty-Four* (Orwell 1949) when Winston Smith learns to love Big Brother rather than obey him, the personal becomes political in a sense feminism never intended. Ironically it is the personal (my current 'gender identity') which comes to be suppressed by the political (publicly and politically produced models of what an unoppressive masculinity might comprise) under the guise of subordinating the latter to it.

Thus (following Craib) we might draw a more pessimistic conclusion: self-reflexivity in fact comprises the further development of what Weber thought of as the 'iron cage' of modernity (Weber 1930) that I briefly discussed in Chapter 1. The danger we therefore face today is that thinking of the personal as political simply represents the bureaucratization of personal life, the rationalization and hollowing out of the soul, the overwhelming of the 'pianissimo' of life by the cold skeletal embrace of the remorseless extension of the iron cage of bureaucratized disenchanted modernity and the scientific knowledge (such as psychotherapy) it creates. This is not the liberation of the true self, but its final surrender. What starts out as the romance of authenticity ends up as the revenge of history. Walter Benjamin produces a memorable image of it (1973: 259–60):

> This is how one pictures the angel of history. His face is turned towards the past. Where we perceive a chain of events, he sees one single catastrophe which keeps piling wreckage upon wreckage and hurls it in front of his feet. The angel would like to stay, awaken the dead, and make whole what has been smashed. But a storm is blowing from Paradise; it has got caught in his wings with such violence that the angel can no longer close them. This storm irresistibly propels him into the future to which his back is turned, while the pile of debris before him grows skyward. This storm is what we call progress.

Just how remorseless the onward march of contract and instrumentalism can appear is demonstrated by the increasing demands which corporations feel able to place on their employees, to the extent for example, that outward obedience to the demands of the office is no longer sufficient; officeholders are expected to give their soul, or at least, possess the right kind of soul. For example a report in *The Guardian* (21 October 1995) claimed that 75 per cent of large companies in Britain now use psychometric testing which aims, *inter alia* to 'hire people who are manageable, who will fit in comfortably to the company culture'.[4]

The self-control we may crave or be exhorted to develop, and which we prefer to imagine as the realization of our true or authentic or mature self, together with its victory over our false or oppressed, subordinated or socially constrained or distorted self, is much more likely to represent the reverse: the development of a self able to consciously flex and adapt itself to the increasingly strident demands of rationalized abstract systems. Our models of our 'true' self, if it is the product of conscious reflection and social discussion, are inexorably political.

Giddens (1992: 52) writes of reflexivity as involving 'an emotional restructuring of the past in order to project a coherent narrative to the future'. This seems to me to contain one vision of personal change and growth, a conscious revision of the previous meaning of my life and identity undertaken to make my future life more meaningful and satisfying. Another description of the same process could be rewriting history, while denying that it had been thus rewritten, to avoid inexorable and potentially disappointing losses and turning such past defeats into imagined future victories, rather like Winston Smith's work with the memory hole in *Nineteen Eighty-Four*. Here is the powerful and self-reflexive self hard at work! Here is emotional labour being done! Freud used to speak of the ego as a fortress of civilization in the self. We might come to think of its late modern expression as more of a wooden horse; the agent whereby the self, all the while imagining that it is making itself stronger, submits itself to ever more elaborate forms of public regulation and actively cooperates in its hollowing out by consciously attempting to make itself into the publicly and politically produced image of what it should properly comprise. No wonder narcissism is the illness of the age – on *both* sides of the couch (Lasch 1979).[5]

The very distance between ideology and identity which makes the politics of identity a poor strategy for achieving sexual equality also renders impossible the final political subordination of the self. We face a contrast between what is only a *fantasy* of a pure self beyond any social constraint – the 'authentic identity' demanding the right to realize itself – and what is equally a fantasy of an enslaved, 'false' self utterly subordinated to social control. The first fantasy is produced by the idea that the personal creates the political. The self which can imagine itself to be entirely socially constructed, which can change at will, which can emancipate itself from disappointments and loss by emotionally reconstructing itself to put its narrative back on course, which is, in a sense, all ego, is the other side of the authentic, natural, socially unconstrained incarnation of id. If we take an optimistic gloss, the pure relationship becomes a combination of the final stage of the enlightenment (private rights to match public ones) and the ultimate orgasm: a kind of mystical union of the Declaration of Independence and the *Joy of Sex*. This is a fantasy of final, total psychic security, delivered by the liberation of authenticity from its social constraint.

The second fantasy (as in the images of Weber or Benjamin) stresses the reverse aspect of the relationship, a fear of the violation of psychic security so total that the self dies, even if the body lives. Here the very heart of the self becomes nothing but a lifeless prisoner of social constraint. As Orwell put it (1949: 215) 'If you want a picture of the future, imagine a boot stamping on a human face – for ever.' But his greatest insight is relevant here. *Nineteen Eighty-Four* is satire, and its basis is the recognition that, though we might fear the possibility, the political can never entirely turn the self into its willing servant, precisely because we ourselves cannot make it so. As mortal products of sexual genesis we cannot always alter our feelings and identity, whether we have the loftiest or basest reasons for doing so. Winnicott (1965a: 179) describes such a fantasy in graphic terms: 'Rape and being eaten by cannibals are mere bagatelles as compared with the violation of the self's core, the alteration of the self's central elements by communication seeping through the defences.' This captures well the depths of our fear of the violation of our psychic security and explains the emotional charge we invest in the fetish of sexual difference and our images of masculinity and femininity. The challenge in the disenchanted era of modernity is to recognize that this is a violation we can only attempt to perform upon ourselves, in part through the construction of these images which we feel publicly obliged to inhabit, in a hopeless attempt to pursue a more perfect psychic security. The challenge is to realize that there is no authenticity, in our sex or elsewhere, to provide such security, and that such potential for psychic security as we develop comes in large part from our earliest attachment experiences, rooted in our sexual genesis. Weber (1949: 57) expressed this well:

> The fate of an epoch which has eaten of the tree of knowledge is that it must know that we cannot learn the meaning of the world from the results of its analysis, be it ever so perfect; it must rather be in a position to create this meaning itself.

One variant of these fantasies is that we can 'democratize' or rationalize our personal or intimate life, in the same way in which the public sphere has been democratized. This seems to retreat to the Hobbesian idea that the self is socially constructed, however, that this process is conscious and that therefore everyone, even infants, can be imagined to make contracts with each other which govern their personal relations. What might a really 'pure' relationship comprise? Would it be one which was entirely politically or socially constructed and free of any traditional prescriptions, devoid of the drag of attachment and based purely on contract relations? Presumably consenting adults can bargain to do anything to each other which gives them pleasure, and end the relationship when they no longer feel they derive benefit from it. Nothing can be specified in advance about what the content of that relationship might comprise; there need be neither rules, nor the anticipation of future obligations. Indeed if the latter becomes problematic, then an appropriate 'emotional reconstruction' can be undertaken. But why stop at adults, if in an era of true universalism, as Hobbes argued, every infant was free to give or withhold its consent? Why not embrace polymorphous perversity for all? If nothing is natural, then nothing can be perverse. This opens up the prospect not just of sexual relations we might endorse (female initiative, gay or lesbian homosexuality, open relationships as alternatives to traditional heterosexual marriage) but those we might not: paedophilia, incest, sadism, rape, violence, denial of bodily integrity, cannibalism. Under the logic of contract individuals have property in their own persons and as part of that, in their labour power (their capacity to labour to produce a useful result) and in the product of that labour power if they have not previously alienated or sold it. The product of the consensual labour of two individuals, using means of production owned or rented by them is theirs to consume, sell or otherwise dispose of as they wish. Does the full democratization of personal life therefore entail the parental right to sell, abuse, exploit or kill children?

Clearly advocates of the pure relationship do not advocate child abuse. But what makes relations with children abusive that we might accept for adults is our recognition that infants do not enter the world as adults, and that they therefore require the protection and nurturance of carers – the 'gift' of attachment. This inevitably goes well beyond a right to bodily integrity, to a quality of intimate relations that lies beyond the logic of contract and rationalization, and which cannot be described in terms of this logic.

The academic division of labour between psychology and sociology

If by defining the existence of a private sphere we can see the personal and the political as distinct, then we need a division of academic labour between sociology and psychology such that the latter deals with persons and the former deals with societies. Connell (1987, 1994, 1995) and Segal (1990) have called for such a division of labour to be overcome, but unless we separate the two disciplines we must surely produce either oversocialized models of persons, seeing them as the products of societies, or, on the contrary, models of societies which reduces their complexity to 'applied psychology' by seeing them as the products of persons. We risk falling into the same trap as all the attempts to sociologize Freud from Adler (1992) to Horney (1964), Fromm (1942), Laing (1960) or Sartre (1958). If we seek to reduce the person to a product of their socialization and its particular social context, no matter how elaborate our analysis, we cannot help but end up with a determinist theory with authoritarian implications, even though it will appear as something more radical, critical or progressive. Sociology and psychology need to understand each other. Clearly it is only because there *is* some connection between societies and the people who comprise them that either discipline is possible. But sociology and psychology must also keep themselves distinct as disciplines, because they analyse two distinct kinds of subject matter: societies and persons.

The self is something that can never be perfectly socialized, that in part lies beyond the public, that in other words contains an 'unconscious'. It is, as such, a thing that is a fundamental element of any democratic politics. We can only pursue equality of individual interests to the extent that we assert that identities (as fundamentally incommensurable entities, perhaps ultimately incommunicable essences) are things that it makes no sense to equalize. Thus trying to go *beyond* a politics of equal rights, paradoxically retreats *from* them. We should leave people's selves alone, while at the same time insisting on all the ramifications of a proper material politics of equal rights: who does the housework, who has the employment opportunities, who gets to develop which practical or psychological skills, who does the childcare, where do the resources for this come from and so on. Only under a much more egalitarian *material* sexual division of labour is it possible to explore freeing up gender identities without suspicion and recriminations about people's motives for developing different aspects of their personality.

Through such things as the findings of sex difference research, psychology offers us the message, should we choose to hear it, of the relative irrelevance of sex to our social capacities as selves or identities. Through the work of Freud and others on the unconscious and psychodynamics, and the work of Winnicott, Bowlby and others on what I have called sexual genesis, it offers us a wealth of insight into the complexities of the self and identity. Such work should convince us that, even if it promised desirable changes in the social structure, we cannot either invite or compel men to reform their masculinity, because it is not something which they possess as such in the first place. We may well teach them to change how they think of their selves, but that is something very different indeed, a question of developing ideologies that legitimate or question different material practices.

To focus on reforming masculinity (whether as calls for anti-sexism, gender vertigo, refusing to be a man, or on the contrary, finding the 'deep masculine') or analysing masculinities seems to me to be a fruitless endeavour. Men simply do not possess such a thing as 'masculinity' as an aspect of their self produced by conscious socialization processes of which people could become fully aware and that they might therefore reform under the guidance of a politics of identity. Instead of chasing the shadows of gender identity by analysing what is imagined to be men's masculinity or attempting to re-engineer how the people in a patriarchal society think of their selves, we may challenge the legacy of patriarchy more effectively by tackling the public ideologies which rationalize any sexual division of labour beyond that inevitably created by actual sexual differences between men and women, such as the latter's capacity to breastfeed infants. Rather than writing manifestos for masculine or feminine selves, which hold out the illusory prospect of finding a path to wholeness, integration and freedom from anxiety, limit or disappointment, we should pay more attention to equalizing the material contexts of the development of males and females.

This means that rather than seeking to androgynize the self in line with a variety of political programmes, we ought to reflect on ways in which we value our selves as persons, regardless of our sex, and on publicly available assumptions about what our sex ought to mean for us symbolically. Of course, that value will inevitably be something social, developed in large part in relation to our peers. But stressing our inner worlds rather than their public faces also involves a certain capacity for honesty about the self, which a politicized ideal image of the self systematically obscures in a dangerous way. If men try too hard to be new men, they risk doing so by denying and splitting off from their awareness all those really existing parts of themselves that do not fit with this image or which they prefer to think they do not like and wish to change. If we do this we are likely, paradoxically, to ensure that just these parts of ourselves will find new ways to express themselves. This leads, I suspect, to the passive aggression of the 'new' men who constantly monitor themselves in the way that Christian (1994) describes, and which most women, old or new, intuitively recognize and treat with suspicion.

Since there is no direct connection between the political and the personal, psychology can also tell us that while equal public rights are desirable, they need not have immediately personal consequences for the private self. It is important that men and women in intimate relationships have an equal chance to 'exit' them, and it is desirable that there is not such an imbalance of material power that allows one partner to dominate the other, should they so choose. But it would be very foolish indeed to imagine that such public equality was either a necessary or sufficient condition for a good intimate private relationship, or that it ushers in other personal consequences. That depends on other things. For millennia genuine heterosexual love has been possible across a dramatic material divide. To suggest otherwise would be to condemn virtually all women who have hitherto lived and loved as guilty of false consciousness – a sort of 'complicit' femininity. It would also be to ignore the total material powerlessness that is the very foundation of the first experience of love which we all share in attachment. On the contrary, as Bell and Newby (1991) point out, relationships of deference may be tenacious and strong, precisely because both sides 'believe' in them.

If we take the defence of the private sphere to its logical conclusion, then we must imagine a self that is allowed to exist beyond social surveillance and regulation – whether by companies using psychometric testing to find loyal employees or by agony aunts or uncles urging us to 'express' our emotions. We should resist such monitoring even by the person who is that self. One might say that the essence of the strong self is to have inappropriate feelings, in the sense of an ability to withstand the experience, whether it is consciously desired or not, of feelings or aspects of 'identity' which are not socially sanctioned or approved. It implies the capacity to sulk and be mean, to be the disloyal self, the disorganization man, the bad father or envious brother together with the ability to own such feelings, rather than deny or repudiate them without demanding the 'right' to such an identity. The strong self can accept responsibility for itself, a responsibility which also recognizes its aspects as partial and transitory and contradictory states, not final whole identities (which could be caught by sociologists defining masculinities). It can do this without either demanding that other selves cater to it, or projecting its split-off, unwanted and denied feelings onto others, especially onto others of a different sex by imagining them as gendered. This is the kind of self which I think Weber contemplated when he wrote of the ability to cope with fate. The capacity to be alone is ultimately the capacity to tolerate difference, the capacity to enter imaginatively into the life worlds of others, while accepting that such imagination, and the communication it makes possible, is always limited and distorted, so that any claim we can ever have on the belief of others is partial. From this perspective, what Winnicott saw as the capacity to be alone, appears as what Weber (1948b) envisaged in his insistence on value freedom. He argued that social science can help a person clarify what their ultimate values are (by tracing through the interconnections, consequences and contradictions of their various beliefs and actions), so that they can clarify just what claims they make on the belief of others. It can never, however, tell us whether that belief is just. The human heart itself lies beyond science. Winnicott himself approaches this idea in a late and rather speculative article (1975b).

The challenge facing an adequate sociology of sex and gender, and an emancipatory feminist politics based upon it in the twenty-first century, is to defend the autonomy of the private sphere and the legitimacy of the sovereignty of the self, its inner world and private experience against ever more comprehensive and invasive public ideologies of what selves should be like. It should thus be critical and unromantic about claims to 'authenticity' while at the same time being unromantic about the nature of the private sphere, and especially the family, and see it as a site of social relations *between* selves with public and political aspects which are worthy of scrutiny and political intervention. Defending the autonomy of the self does not mean defending private misogyny. On the contrary, it offers us a more powerful critique of misogyny by allowing us to demonstrate the full range of social consequences that flow from realizing that there is no difference between male and female selves. It allows us to demonstrate how our imagination of masculinity and femininity is ultimately an ideological rationalization of the illegitimate survival of men's power. It allows us to concentrate on the central problem: the survival of a material sexual division of labour.

Politically, my analysis here suggests (and it is reflected in the actual tactics used by the women's movement in its fight against male domestic violence) that tackling material inequalities in the relative position of men and women is more likely to bring about change (through making it possible for women to be independent of abusive partners, or removing men's power over women which makes their continued abuse possible) than attempts to reform men's selves, personalities or identities to make them less likely to choose to abuse women.

From sociology, we can study the ways in which capitalism both undermines the sexual division of labour it has inherited and creates new ones, without trying to understand these as effects caused by the changing gender identities of men and women. We can see, as the study by Siltanen (1994) shows for example, how what we imagine to be gender gets located in the material positions men and women find themselves in as they juggle their changing labour market opportunities and domestic responsibilities across the life cycle, mobilizing ideologies of gender along the way. A liberal politics of equal rights can be taken to radical lengths, if we simply pose the question of why *any* sexual division of labour ought to survive the end of patriarchy. It may be that there are some activities in which it is desirable to have a concentration of one sex or the other. Many women, for example, might prefer female midwives. But such activities must be few indeed. Where we do not find a long-run tendency for the number of men and women in different activities to equalize, we should look for the material and ideological blockages responsible. This does not mean demanding that any individual man or women take up non sex-typical activities, but it does mean refusing to let them cite their sex as a reason; it does mean demanding that both material and ideological structures lead over time to the sex of persons in the social division of labour becoming increasingly irrelevant.

In Chapter 2 I suggested that patriarchal ideology has presented us with a 'false choice' between seeing the private sphere as distinct from the public sphere, but as the natural and patriarchal site of sexual difference, and seeing the private sphere as non-patriarchal but socially determined by the public sphere. Our 'real' choice is between a politics of identity which imagines the self to be purely socially constructed, and which ultimately has its roots in the confusion of sexual genesis and sexual difference first established by Hobbes, and a radical politics of equal rights which embraces the full consequences of universalism in the public sphere but explicitly refuses to embrace the personal, which accepts that there are aspects of the self that are not socially constructed, and therefore aspects that are not answerable to society in any way, which recognizes that people make society but also that they are not themselves entirely social products and which therefore can draw a definite distinction between the personal and the political, together with an appropriate division of labour between the two disciplines – sociology and psychology – which properly analyse these spheres. The politics of identity appears radical, but it has its roots in a set of ideas developed to resist sexual equality and draws its strength from authoritarian material trends in society which threaten the autonomy of the private self. Our private troubles are not the source of our public issues.

I think we can see Weber's idea of 'unprecedented inner loneliness' (1930: 104) as the basic condition of both men and women in a disenchanted era. It is the challenge of the capacity to be alone. Having eaten of the tree of knowledge, they are faced with almost unbearable knowledge that they face personal responsibility for creating meaning in life, and what amounts to the same thing, making sense of their own death and their own mortality and the limits and disappointments that inevitably imposes on them. The difference between priests and therapists is that the latter, if they are any good, reveal the patient's own answers to him or herself. As Phillips (1995) describes it, there are terrors, but no experts. This terror is in essence an absence of certainty, a future that is unknown, cannot be known, and by virtue of that is also open. A life free of anxiety, risk or failure would hardly be worth living, any more than one impoverished by a lack of any security or moments of triumph.

Just as a good therapist can only show the patient their own self, and do so by sharing something of their own lack and vulnerability, so too can the good sociologist only show members of a society the unanticipated consequences of their actions and beliefs, the compatibility or otherwise of various values and actions and the difficulty of reaching firm conclusions. Sociology can reveal, for example, the full implications of a value that holds men and women to be equal, that this must imply, ultimately, the abolition of a sexual division of labour and the ideologies that sustain it, that this is quite compatible with a heterogeneous range of identities for males and females and that different gender capacities we have imagined men and women to possess depend upon, rather than cause, the existing sexual division of labour and its legitimation.

I am thus suggesting that one aspect of the capacity to be alone is to re-appropriate our gender-based projections about masculine and feminine capacities, and realize that what we thus imagine as gendered and social are but our own and unavoidable potentials as mortal beings. Our fantasies of gender are ultimately a neurotic displacement of our terror of our mortality – an ingenious way to hide both from our responsibilities for our lives, and the limits of the control over them which our conscious self can exert. I am also suggesting that the other aspect of the capacity to be alone is to pay less attention to these projections, to our 'identities', and to stop seeing in them all the roots of our social troubles. The capacity to be alone implies an ability to tolerate difference rather than insist on the perfect environment in the form of a society of fully emancipated selves.

Weber's vision of personal and moral loneliness is a rather bleak one. Like Benjamin, he sees progress overwhelming the individual, who discovers that they have traded their spiritual emancipation from magic and dogma for the 'iron cage' of bureaucratic rationalization. But Winnicott's vision of the capacity to be alone is a warmer one. He emphasizes that this capacity can only ever have developed in the presence of another. Its precondition is some sense of trust and security: what we might call faith in the meaningfulness of the world, even as we accept that it can have no final meaning. Such faith is born of the gift of attachment, and such attachment makes the final triumph of a dead rationalism impossible, even though the price of disenchantment is the certain knowledge of our personal mortality.

In a teasing aside Craib (1994a: 134–5) has suggested that, 'I sometimes think that the lasting scandal of human life is that we cannot reproduce by parthenogenesis.' Given the manifold and frequently violent ways sexual dimorphism has been used to oppress women and gays across the millennia it is difficult to disagree. But the challenge that modernity and the rise of universalism offers us is to fulfil our capacity to be alone. One of the most important barriers to fulfilling that capacity is now the concepts of gender, masculinity and femininity, and the ideologies of sexual difference which sustain them. Challenging those ideologies will play a key role in the further erosion of the sexual division of labour which modernity has commenced. If we can take responsibility for the possession of a body that is of one sex only, was produced by our parents and will thus never fully transcend the manifold consequences of its particular origins and which will inexorably die, and make the most of it, in the presence of, and actively with, others, then we may turn a lasting scandal into what it has always also been, a source of real pleasure, a testament to the noblest aspirations of human creativity and the ultimate proof of our human lust for life in the very face of death.

Notes

1 I understand Phillips herself to reject this suggestion; compare the following passage from Elshtain (1981: 301) which she uses approvingly:

> Part of the struggle involves reflecting on whether our current misery and unhappiness derive entirely from the faulty and exploitative social forms that can, and therefore must, be changed or whether a large part of that unhappiness derives from the simple fact of being human, therefore limited, knowing that one is going to die.

2 Let me emphasize here, lest I be misinterpreted, that I am not suggesting that the sexual and physical abuse of children has been exaggerated or constitutes a moral panic. The reverse is true. Appalling levels of cruelty to children challenge modernity's claim to the status of 'civilization'. What I am criticizing here is the misuse of the term 'abuse' through a confusion between public right and private relations. All persons, including infants, have a public right to bodily integrity, which physical and sexual abuse violates. In so far as it is required for the defence of this public right, surveillance of the private sphere by the state is legitimate. I would also argue that defence of this right extends to the public organization of good, safe, accessible and cheap childcare, free universal and universally good education and income guarantees for parents which tackle child poverty. What children do not have is either a private capacity or right, equal to their parents, to decide on how they should be, or should have been reared. Yet such a right seems implicit in many of the loose, contemporary uses of 'abuse', of which the quotation heading this section is an example.

3 Mitchell Duneier (1994: 168) puts this well: 'When we stop trying to feel good about ourselves, or to increase our own power by asserting our innocence, we can begin to look for answers by searching for truth.'

4 'Selection by prying', Graham Wade. The quotation is from Professor Linda Dickens of Warwick University Business School.

5 I do not mean that all psychotherapy is of this form – but much of its popular expression in the mass media has this character.

Bibliography

Adler, A. (1992) *Understanding Human Nature*. Oxford: Oneworld.

Adorno, T. (1968) Sociology and Psychology. *New Left Review* 47: 79–97.

Anderson, B. (1991) *Imagined Communities: Reflections on the Origin and Spread of Nationalism*, revised edition. London: Verso.

Arendt, H. (1958) *The Human Condition*. Chicago, IL: University of Chicago Press.

Aries, P. (1973) *Centuries of Childhood*, translated by Robert Baldick. Harmondsworth: Penguin.

Barnes, J.A. (1973) Genitrix: genitor: nature: culture? In J. Goody (ed.) *The Character of Kinship*. Cambridge: Cambridge University Press.

Barrett, M. (1987) The concept of 'difference'. *Feminist Review*, 26: 29–41.

Bauman, Z. (1991) *Modernity and the Holocaust*. Oxford: Polity Press.

Beck, U. and Beck-Gernsheim, E. (1995) *The Normal Chaos of Love*, translated by M. Ritter and J. Wiebel. Cambridge: Polity Press.

Bell, C. and Newby, H. (1991) Husbands and wives: The deferential dialectic. In S. Allen and D. Leonard (eds) *Sexual Divisions Revisited*. London: Macmillan.

Benjamin, J. (1990) *The Bonds of Love*. London: Virago.

Benjamin, W. (1973) *Illuminations*. London: Fontana.

Bly, R. (1991) *Iron John: A Book About Men*. Shaftesbury, Dorset: Element Books.

Boon, J. (1974) Anthropology and nannies. *Man*, 9: 137–40.

Bordo, S. (1990) Reading the slender body. In M. Jacobus, E. Fox-Keller and S. Shuttleworth (eds) *Body/Politics Women and the Discourses of Science*. London: Routledge.

Bowlby, J. (1951) *Maternal Care and Mental Health*. Geneva: WHO.

Bowlby, J. (1971) *Attachment and Loss. Vol. 1: Attachment*. Harmondsworth: Penguin.

Bowlby, J. (1975) *Attachment and Loss. Vol. 2: Separation, Anxiety and Anger*. Harmondsworth: Penguin.

Bowlby, J. (1981) *Attachment and Loss. Vol. 3: Loss, Sadness and Depression*. Harmondsworth: Penguin.

Brecht, B. (1980) *Life of Galileo*. London: Eyre Methuen.

Brennan, T. and Pateman, C. (1979) 'Mere auxiliaries to the Commonwealth': Women and the origins of Liberalism. *Political Studies*, 27, No. 2: 183–200.

Brod, H. and Kaufman, M. (eds) (1994) *Theorising Masculinities*. London: Sage.

Brownmiller, S. (1976) *Against Our Will: Men, Women and Rape*. Harmondsworth: Penguin.

Carrigan, T., Connell, R. and Lee, J. (1987) Towards a new sociology of masculinity. In H. Brod (ed.) *The Making of Masculinities: The New Men's Studies*. London: Allen and Unwin.

Carter, A. (ed.) (1990) *The Virago Book of Fairy Tales*. London: Virago.

Chodorow, N.J. (1978) *The Reproduction of Mothering*. Berkeley, CA: University of California Press.

Christian, H. (1994) *The Making of Anti-Sexist Men*. London: Routledge.

Cockburn, C. (1991) *In the Way of Women: Men's Resistance to Sex Equality in Organisations*. London: Macmillan.

Cohen, J. (1997) Rethinking Privacy: Autonomy, Identity and the Abortion Controversy. In J.A. Weintraub and K. Kumar (eds) *Public and private in thought and practice: perspectives on a grand dichotomy*. London: University of Chicago Press.

Condy, A. (1994) *Families and Work. International Year of the Family Factsheet 3*. London: IYF UK Office.

Connell, R.W. (1987) *Gender and Power*. Cambridge: Polity.

Connell, R.W. (1994) Psychoanalysis on masculinity. In H. Brod and M. Kaufman (eds) *Theorising Masculinities*. London: Sage.

Connell, R.W. (1995) *Masculinities*. Cambridge: Polity.

Corrigan, P. (1977) Feudal relics or capitalist monuments? *Sociology*, 11.

Craib, I. (1987) Masculinity and male dominance. *Sociological Review*, 34: 721–43.

Craib, I. (1988) The personal and political. *Radical Philosophy*, 48: 14–15.

Craib, I. (1989) *Psychoanalysis and Social Theory: The Limits of Sociology*. London: Harvester Wheatsheaf.

Craib, I. (1994a) *The Importance of Disappointment*. London: Routledge.

Craib, I. (1994b) Going to pieces or getting it together? Giddens and the sociology of the self. *Sociology Review*, November: 12–15.

Craib, I. (1995) Some comments on the sociology of emotions, *Sociology*, 29.

Cressey, P. and MacInnes, J. (1980) 'Voting for Ford': Industrial democracy and the control of labour. *Capital and Class*, 11: 5–33.

Crick, B. (1982) *George Orwell: A Life*. Harmondsworth: Penguin.

Daly, M. (1984) *Pure Lust: Elemental Feminist Philosophy*. London: Women's Press.

Davis, H. and Joshi, H. (1990) *The Foregone Earnings of Europe's Mothers*, Discussion Papers in Economics no. 24. London: Birkbeck College.

de Beauvoir, S. (1972) *The Second Sex*. Harmondsworth: Penguin.

Dinnerstein, D. (1987) *The Rocking of the Cradle and the Ruling of the World*. London: Women's Press. Previously published in 1976 as *The Mermaid and the Minotaur*. New York: Harper and Row.

Duindam, V. (1995) 'Mothering and fathering: Socialisation theory and beyond'. Mimeo. Utrecht: Department of Social Sciences, University of Utrecht.

Duncombe, J. and Marsden, D. (1993) Love and intimacy: The gender division of emotion and 'emotion work'. *Sociology*, 27: 221–41.

Duncombe, J. and Marsden, D. (1995) 'Workaholics' and 'whingeing women': Theorizing intimacy and emotion work – the last frontier of gender inequality? *Sociological Review*, 43: 150–69.

Duneier, M. (1994) *Slim's Table*. London: University of Chicago Press.

Dunning, E. (1986) Sport as a male preserve: Notes on the social sources of masculine identity and its transformation. *Theory, Culture and Society*, 3: 79–90.

Dworkin, A. (1981) *Pornography: Men Possessing Women*. London: Women's Press.

Elshtain, J.B. (1981) *Public Man, Private Woman*. Oxford: Robertson.

Elshtain, J.B. (ed.) (1982) *The Family in Political Thought*. Brighton: Harvester.

Elshtain, J.B. (1984) Symmetry and soporifics: A critique of feminist accounts of gender development. In B. Richards (ed.) *Capitalism and Infancy*. London: Free Association Books.

Engels, F. (1968) The origin of the family, private property and the state. In *Marx and Engels: Selected Works in One Volume*. London: Lawrence and Wishart.

Fairweather, H. (1976) Sex differences in cognition. *Cognition*, 4: 231–80.

Fausto-Sterling, A. (1985) *Myths of Gender*. New York: Basic Books.

Firestone, S. (1971) *The Dialectic of Sex*. London: Paladin.

Flax, J. (1990) *Thinking fragments: psychoanalysis, feminism, and postmodernism in the contemporary West*. Oxford: University of California Press.

Foucault, M. (1984) *The History of Sexuality. Volume 1 An Introduction*. Harmondsworth: Peregrine Books.

Fox, A. (1974) *Beyond Contract: Work, Power and Trust Relations*. London: Faber.

Freud, S. (1986) Three essays on sexuality. In *The Essentials of Psycho-Analysis*. Selected, with an introduction and commentaries by Anna Freud. Harmondsworth: Pelican.

Friday, N. (1980) *Men in Love: Men's Sexual Fantasies*. New York: Arrow Books.

Fromm, E. (1942) *The Fear of Freedom*. London: Routledge and Kegan Paul.

Frosh, S. (1987) *The Politics of Psychoanalysis: An Introduction to Freudian and Post Freudian Theory*. London: Macmillan.

Fuchs Epstein, C. (1988) *Deceptive Distinctions: Sex, Gender and the Social Order*. New Haven, CT: Yale University Press.

Gane, M. (1993) *Harmless Lovers? Gender Theory and Personal Relationships*. London: Routledge.

Gatens, M. (1996) *Imaginary Bodies: Ethics, Power and Corporeality*. London: Routledge.

General Household Survey (1994) London: HMSO.

Gershuny, J., Godwin, M. and Jones, S. (1994) The domestic labour revolution: A process of lagged adaption. In M. Anderson, F. Bechhofer and J. Gershuny (eds) *The Social and Political Economy of the Household*. Oxford: Oxford University Press.

Gerth, H.H. and Mills, C. Wright (eds) (1948) *From Max Weber*. London: Routledge and Kegan Paul.

Giddens, A. (1976) *New Rules of Sociological Method*. London: Hutchinson.

Giddens, A. (1991) *Modernity and Self Identity: Self and Society in the Late Modern Age*. Cambridge: Polity.

Giddens, A. (1992) *The Transformation of Intimacy: Love, Sexuality and Eroticism in Modern Societies*. Cambridge: Polity.

Gilligan, C. (1982) *In a Different Voice: Psychological Theory and Women's Development*. London: Harvard University Press.

Goffman, E. (1963) *Stigma*. Hemel Hempstead: Prentice Hall.

Goffman, E. (1977) The arrangement between the sexes. *Theory and Society*, 4: 301–32.

Goldstein, J. and Rayner, J. (1994) The politics of identity in late modern society, *Theory and Society*, 23: 367–84.

Gray, J. (1992) *Men Are From Mars, Women Are From Venus*. London: Thorsons.

Griffin, S. (1971) Rape: The All-American Crime. *Ramparts*. September, 26–35.

Harding, S. (1981) What is the Real Material Base of Patriarchy and Capital? In Lydia Sargent (ed.) *Women and Revolution. The Unhappy Marriage of Marxism and Feminism*. London: Pluto.

Harding, S. (1991) *Whose Science? Whose Knowledge? Thinking from Women's Lives*. Buckingham: Open University Press.

Hartsock, N. (1983) The Feminist Standpoint: Developing the Ground of a Specifically Feminist Historical Materialism. In S. Harding and M.B. Hintikka (eds) *Discovering Reality: Feminist Perspectives on Epistemology, Metaphysics, Methodology, and Philosophy of Science*. Dordecht: Reidel Publishing Co.

Hartsock, N. (1985) *Money, Sex and Power: Toward a Feminist Historical Materialism*. Boston, MA: Northeastern University Press.

Hearn, J. (1996) Is masculinity dead? A critique of the concept of masculinity/masculinities. In M. Mac an Ghaill (ed.) *Understanding Masculinities*. Buckingham: Open University Press.

Hirschman, A.O. (1970) *Exit, Voice, and Loyalty: Responses to Decline in Firms, Organizations, and States*. Cambridge, MA: Harvard University Press.

Hobbes, T. (1651/1983) *De Cive*, English version, Volume III of the Clarendon Edition of the Philosophical Works of Thomas Hobbes, edited by H. Warrender. Oxford: Clarendon Press.

Hobbes, T. (1651/1991) *Leviathan*. Cambridge: Cambridge University Press.

Horney, K. (1964) *The Neurotic Personality of Our Time*. New York: W.W. Norton.

Horney, K. (1967) *Feminine Psychology*. New York: W.W. Norton.

Horrocks, R. (1994) *Masculinity in Crisis: Myths, Fantasies and Realities*. London: Macmillan.

Huxley, A. (1994) *Brave New World*. London: Flamingo.

Jaggar, A.M. and Bordo, S.R. (eds) (1989) *Gender/Body/Knowledge: Feminist Reconstructions of Being and Knowing*. New Brunswick, NJ: Rutgers University Press.

James (1996) The Larkin Syndrome: How your parents ****ed you up. London: Observer Newspapers.

Jensen, J., Hagen, E. and Reddy, C. (eds) (1988) *Feminisation of the Labour Force: Paradoxes and Promises*. Cambridge: Polity.

Jong, E. (1974) *Fear of Flying*. London: Martin Secker and Warburg Ltd.

Jukes, A. (1993) *Why Men Hate Women*. London: Free Association Books.

Kaufman, M. (1994) Men, feminism, and men's contradictory experiences of power. In H. Brod and M. Kaufman (eds) *Theorising Masculinities*. London: Sage.

Keesing, R. (1981) *Cultural Anthropology: A Contemporary Perspective*. Harcourt Brace Jovanovich.

Kessler, S.J. and McKenna, W. (1978) *Gender: An Ethnomethodological Approach*. New York: Wiley.

Kimmel, M.S. (1987) The contemporary 'crisis' of masculinity in historical perspective. In H. Brod (ed.) *The Making of Masculinities: The New Men's Studies*. London: Allen & Unwin.

Klein, M. (1957) *Envy and Gratitude: A Study of Unconscious Sources*. London: Tavistock.

Krouse, R.W. (1982) Patriarchal liberalism and beyond: From John Stuart Mill to Harriet Taylor. In J.B. Elshtain (ed.) *The Family in Political Thought*. Brighton: Harvester.

Kundera, M. (1984) *The Unbearable Lightness of Being*. Translated by Michael Henry Heim. London: Faber.

Laing, R.D. (1960) *The Divided Self*. London: Tavistock.

Lasch, C. (1977) *Haven in a Heartless World: The Family Besieged*. New York: Basic Books.

Lasch, C. (1979) *The Culture of Narcissism*. New York: W.W. Norton.

Laslett, P. (1949) *Patriarcha and Other Political Works of Sir Robert Filmer*. Oxford: Basil Blackwell.

Lazear, J. (1992) *Meditations for Men Who Do Too Much*. London: The Aquarian Press.

Le Guin, U. (1969) *The Left Hand of Darkness*. London: Panther.

Lerner, G. (1986) *The Creation of Patriarchy*. Oxford: Oxford University Press.

Lévi-Strauss, C. (1969) *The Elementary Structures of Kinship*. Translated from the French by James Harle Bell, John Richard von Sturmer and Rodney Needham. Revised edition. London: Beacon Press.

Lloyd, T. (1994) *Analysis of Newspaper Coverage of Fathers and Men as Carers* (Carried out in June 1994), mimeo.

Locke, J. (1924) *Of Civil Government: Two Treatises*. London: Dent.

Mac an Ghaill, M. (ed.) (1996) *Understanding Masculinities*. Buckingham: Open University Press.

MacFarlane, A. (1986) *Marriage and Love in England: Modes of Reproduction 1300–1840*. Oxford: Basil Blackwell.

Maine, H.S. (1982) *Ancient law: its connection with the early history of society and its relation to modern ideas*. Birmingham, Ala.: Legal Classics Library.

McMahon, A. (1993) Male readings of feminist theory: The psychologisation of sexual politics in the masculinity literature. *Theory and Society*, 22: 675–95.

Macpherson, C.B. (1962) *The Political Theory of Possessive Individualism: Hobbes to Locke*. Oxford: Clarendon Press.

Mann, M. (1994) Persons, households, families, lineages, genders, classes and nations. In *The Polity Reader in Gender Studies*. Cambridge: Polity.

Marsh, C. (1991) *Hours of Work of Women and Men in Britain*, Research Series, Equal Opportunities Commission. London: HMSO.

Marx, K. (1976) *Capital*, volume 1. Harmondsworth: Penguin.

Mauss, M. (1970) *The Gift: Forms and Functions of Exchange in Archaic Societies*. Translated by I. Cunnison. London: Routledge and Kegan Paul.

Middleton, C. (1988) The familiar fate of the *Famulae*: Gender divisions in the history of wage labour. In R.E. Pahl (ed.) *On Work*. Oxford: Basil Blackwell.

Mill, J.S. (1982) *On Liberty*, edited with an introduction by Gertrude Himmelfarb. Harmondsworth: Penguin.

Mills, C. Wright (1970) *The Sociological Imagination*. Harmondsworth: Penguin.

Mitchell, G. (1962) *The Role of The Father*. Programme 12 of Parents and Children, The First Five Years. BBC Radio Broadcast, 18 June.

Moore, H.L. (1988) *Feminism and Anthropology*. Cambridge: Polity.

Morgan, D.H.J. (1986) Gender. In R. Burgess (ed.) *Key Variables in Sociological Research*. London: Routledge and Kegan Paul.

Morgan, D.H.J. (1992) *Discovering Men*. London: Routledge.

Morgan, D.H.J. (1993) You too can have a body like mine. In D. Morgan and S. Scott (eds) *Body Matters*. London: The Falmer Press.

Nairn, T. (1977) *The Break-up of Britain: Crisis and Neo-nationalism*. London: NLB.

Oakley, A. (1972) *Sex, gender and society*. London: Maurice Temple Smith Ltd.

O'Brien, M. (1981) *Politics of Reproduction*. London: Routledge and Kegan Paul.

O'Neill, J. (1994) *The Missing Child in Liberal Theory*. London: University of Toronto Press.

O'Neill, J.M. (1982) Gender role conflict and strain in men's lives. In K. Solomon and N.P. Levy (eds) *Men in Transition: Theory and Therapy*. New York: Plenum Press.

Organisation for Economic Cooperation and Development (OECD) (1996) *Historical Statistics 1960–94*. Paris: OECD.

Ortner, S.B. (1974) Is female to male as nature is to culture? In M.Z. Rosaldo, and L. Lamphere (eds) *Women, Culture and Society*. Stanford, CA: Stanford University Press.

Orwell, G. (1949) *Nineteen Eighty-Four*. Harmondsworth: Penguin.

Ostner, I. (1993) Slow motion: Women, work and the family in Germany. In J.C. Lewis (ed.) *Women and Social Policies in Europe*. Aldershot: Edward Elgar.

Pahl, R.E. (1995) *After Success*. Cambridge: Polity.

Parsons, T. and Bales, R.F. (1956) *Family, Socialisation and Interaction Process*. London: Routledge and Kegan Paul.

Pateman, C. (1983) Feminist critiques of the public/private dichotomy. In S.I. Benn, and G.F. Gauss, *Public and Private in Social Life*. London: Croom Helm.

Pateman, C. (1988) *The Sexual Contract*. Cambridge: Polity.

Phillips, Adam (1988) *Winnicott*. London: Fontana.

Phillips, Adam (1989) Making a mess. *London Review of Books*, 2 February.

Phillips, Adam (1995) *Terrors and Experts*. London: Faber and Faber.

Phillips, Anne (1991) *Engendering Democracy*. Cambridge: Polity.

Pietila, H. (1990) The daughters of the Earth: women's culture as a basis for sustainable development. In J.R. Engel and J.B. Engel (eds) *Ethics of Environment and Development: Global Challenge, International Response*. London: Belhaven Press.

Pufendorf, S.F. von (1991) *On the Duty of Man and Citizen According to Natural Law*. Edited by James Tully and translated by Michael Silverthorne. Cambridge: Cambridge University Press.

Rich, A. (1984) Compulsory heterosexuality and lesbian existence. In A. Snitow, C. Stansell and S. Thompson (eds) *Desire. The Politics of Sexuality*. London: Virago.

Richards, B. (1984) *Capitalism and Infancy*. London: Free Association Books.

Rousseau, J.J. (1968) *The Social Contract*. Translated and introduced by Maurice Cranston. Harmondsworth: Penguin.

Rousseau, J.J. (1995) *Emile*. Translated by Barbara Foxley. London: Dent.

Rowbotham, S. (1979) The trouble with 'patriarchy'. In R. Samuel (ed.) *People's History and Socialist Theory*. London: Routledge and Kegan Paul.

Rubin, G. (1975) The traffic in women: Notes on the political economy of sex. In R.R. Reiter (ed.) *Towards an Anthropology of Women*. New York: Monthly Review Press.

Sartre, J.P. (1958) *Being and Nothingness*. London: Methuen.

Sayers, J. (1986) *Sexual Contradictions: Psychology, Psychoanalysis and Feminism*. London: Tavistock.

Sayers, J. (1992) *Mothering Psychoanalysis*. Harmondsworth: Penguin.

Scott, J. Alwin, D.F. and Braun, M. (1996) Changing sex-role attitudes. *Sociology*, 30, 471–92.

Segal, L. (1987) *Is the Future Female?* London: Virago.

Segal, L. (1990) *Slow Motion: Changing Masculinities, Changing Men*. London: Virago.

Segal, L. (1993) Changing men: Masculinities in context. *Theory and Society*, 22: 625–41.

Segal, L. (1994) *Straight Sex*. London: Virago.

Seidler, V.J. (1989) *Rediscovering Masculinity: Reason, Language and Sexuality*. London: Routledge.

Seidler, V.J. (1990) Men, feminism and power. In J. Hearn and D. Morgan (eds) *Men, Masculinities and Social Theory*. London: Unwin Hyman.

Shanley, M.L. (1982) Marriage contract and social contract in seventeenth-century English political thought. In J.B. Elshtain (ed.) *The Family in Political Thought*. Brighton: Harvester.

Siltanen, J. (1994) *Locating Gender: Occupational Segregation, Wages and Domestic Responsibilities*, Cambridge Studies in Work and Social Inequality 1. London: UCL Press.

Siltanen, J. and Stanworth, M. (1984) The politics of private woman and public man. In J. Siltanen and M. Stanworth (eds) *Women and the Public Sphere*. London: Hutchinson.

Skynner, R. and Cleese, J. (1983) *Families and How to Survive Them*. London: Methuen.

Smith, A. (1976) *The Theory of Moral Sentiments*, edited by D.D. Raphael and A.L. Macfie. Oxford: Clarendon Press.

Sommerville, J.P. (1991) *Patriarcha and Other Writings*. Cambridge: Cambridge University Press.

Stoller, R. (1968) *Sex and Gender*. London: The Hogarth Press and Institute of Psychoanalysis.

Sydie, R.A. (1987) *Natural Women, Cultured Men: A Feminist Perspective on Sociological Theory*. Buckingham: Open University Press.

Temperley, J. (1984) Our own worst enemies: Unconscious factors in female disadvantage. *Free Associations*, Pilot Issue.

Thompson, K. (ed.) (1991) *To Be a Man. In Search of the Deep Masculine*. Los Angeles, CA: Jeremy P. Tarcher.

Threlfall, M. (1996) Feminist politics and social change in Spain. In M. Threlfall (ed.) *Mapping the Women's Movement*. London: Verso.

United Kingdom Men's Movement (1995) *Discrimination Against Men in the UK*. Cheltenham: The United Kingdom Men's Movement.

Weber, M. (1930) *The Protestant Ethic and The Spirit of Capitalism*. London: Allen and Unwin.

Weber, M. (1948a) Politics as a vocation. In H.H. Gerth and C. Wright Mills (eds) *From Max Weber*. London: Routledge and Kegan Paul.

Weber, M. (1948b) Science as a vocation. In H.H. Gerth and C. Wright Mills (eds) *From Max Weber*. London: Routledge and Kegan Paul.

Weber, M. (1948c) Religious rejections of the world and their directions. In H.H. Gerth and C. Wright Mills (eds) *From Max Weber*. London: Routledge and Kegan Paul.

Weber, M. (1949) *The Methodology of the Social Sciences*, translated and edited by E.A. Shils and H.A. Finch. New York: Free Press.

Weber, M. (1978a) *Economy and Society: An Outline of Interpretive Sociology*, edited by Guenther Roth and Claus Wittich. Berkeley, CA: University of California Press.

Weber, M. (1978b) Freudianism. In W.G. Runciman (ed.) *Max Weber: Selections in Translation*. Cambridge: Cambridge University Press.

Weeks, J. (1995) *Invented Moralities*. Cambridge: Polity.

Wilkinson, H. (1994) *No Turning Back: Generations and the Genderquake*. London: Demos.

Winnicott, D.W. (1965a) *The Maturational Processes and the Facilitating Environment*. London: Hogarth Press.

Winnicott, D.W. (1965b) Some Thoughts on the Meaning of the Word Democracy. In *The Family and Individual Development*. London: Tavistock Publications.

Winnicott, D.W. (1975) *Through Paediatrics to Psycho-analysis*. London: Hogarth Press and The Institute of Psychoanalysis.

Wouters, C. (1987) Developments in the behavioural codes between the sexes: The formalisation of informalisation in the Netherlands, 1930–85. *Theory, Culture and Society*, 4: 405–27.

Wouters, C. (1989) The sociology of emotions and flight attendants: Hochschild's managed heart. *Theory, Culture and Society*, 6: 95–123.

Wouters, C. (1991) On status competition and emotion management. *Journal of Social History*, 24: 699–717.

Wrong, D. (1961) The oversocialized conception of man in modern sociology. *American Sociological Review*, 26: 183–93.

Yeandle, S. (1995) 'Change in the gender composition of the workforce: Recent analyses and their significance for social theory'. Conference paper. European Sociological Association conference, Budapest, 2 September.

Young, I.M. (1984) Is male gender identity the cause of male domination? In J. Trebilcot (ed.) *Mothering*. NJ: Rowman and Allenheld (Littelfield Adams and Co.).

Zilboorg, G. (1944) Masculine and feminine: Some biological and cultural aspects. *Psychiatry*, 7: 257–96.

Zvesper, J. (1985) Hobbes' individualistic view of the family. *Politics*, 5: 28–33.

Index

abuse, 47, 49, 79, 139–40, 147, 151,
    154n, *see also* violence
activity, 62, 86–8, 90, 92–8, 129, *see*
    also agency, subjectivity, identity,
    self
Adler, A., 32, 148
Adorno, T., 56
agency, 15, 19, 67, 87, 131, *see also*
    activity, subjectivity, identity, self
Amazons, 9, 23n, 117
Anderson, B., 40
anxiety, 12–13, 18, 31, 35, 142, 148–9,
    152, *see also* psychic security,
    ontological security
Arendt, H., 126, 133n
Aries, P., 139
Astell, M., 1
attachment, 17–23, 29, 32, 37, 94, 96,
    109, 147, 150, 153
    ambivalent character of, 19, 136
    aspect of all social relations, 22, 34–5
authenticity, 32, 67, 89, 135, 144–7,
    151
    romance of, 2, 13, 36–9, 127

baby *see* infants
Bales, R.F., 99n, 129
Barnes, J.A., 108
Barrett, M., 73
Bauman, Z., 4, 58
Beck, U., 38, 143
Beck-Gernsheim, E., 38, 143
Bell, C., 75, 150
Benjamin, J., 58, 94
Benjamin, W., 145–6, 153

Big Brother, 22, 145
Bly, R., 55, 68, 135
body, 13, 15, 17, 20, 28–30, 35, 38–9,
    46, 65–7, 70, 75, 83, 91, 93–5,
    115, 119, 120, 146, 153
Boon, J., 109
Bordo, S., 65
Bowlby, J., 18, 98, 149
Brave New World, 34, 139–40
Brecht, B., 5
Brennan, T., 8, 121, 125, 127, 133n
Brod, H., 61, 63
Brownmiller, S., 73
bureaucracy, 4, 46, 57–8
    bureaucratization, 12, 22, 37, 141,
        145, *see also* rationalization
    'iron cage' of, 5, 36–8, 145, 153
Burns, R., 1

cathexis, 72, *see also* love
cannibalism, 9, 117, 122, 146, 147
capacity to be alone, 17, 20, 28, 35, 99,
    106, 123, 136, 144, 150–53
capital
    general law of capitalist accumulation,
        22
    primitive accumulation of, 6
capitalism, 3, 8, 16, 37, 42–3, 48, 51–5,
    57, 59, 76, 113, 134, 141, 143,
    151, *see also* modernity
Carrigan, T., 15
Carter, A., 99n
Chodorow, N.J., 58, 75, 78–80, 82n, 91,
    94–7, 129
Christian, H., 14, 150

Cleese, J., 139
Cockburn, C., 80
Cohen, J., 137
commoditization, 12, 122, *see also*
    markets, capitalism
commodity, 3
Condy, A., 51
Connell, R.W., 9, 14, 55, 56–7, 58,
    61–2, 63, 64, 66, 67, 70–72, 76,
    80, 85, 86, 88, 94, 100, 106,
    118, 148
contract, 3, 4, 5–6, 19, 26, Ch. 7 *passim*,
    145, 147–8, *see also* social
    contract theorists, marriage
    contract
    sexual, 28, 73, 99, Ch. 6 *passim*, 128,
    131
    and sexual reproduction, 27, 108
Corrigan, P., 14
Craib, 1, 14, 15, 22, 31, 33, 60n, 65,
    88, 91–2, 99n, 132, 139, 143,
    145, 153
Cressey, P., 133n
Crick, B., 44n

Daly, M., 69
Davies, H., 48
death *see* mortality
de Beauvoir, S., 1
Declaration of Independence, 8, 112, 146
democratization of personal relationships,
    34–5, 134–6, 138–9, 147–8, *see
    also* pure relationship
demographic transition, 41–3, *see also*
    infant mortality, fertility rates
dependence, 13, 21, 96–7, 110, 130–31,
    see also attachment, infants:
    relationship with adults
Dickens, L., 154n
difference, 73, 77–9, 95, 128, 144, *see
    also* sex difference research, sexual
    difference
Dinnerstein, D., 18, 42, 43, 56, 58, 75,
    78–80, 82n, 94–5, 97–8, 129
disenchantment, 3, 12, 89, 98, 145,
    147, 152
divine right of kings, 8, 11, 117
divorce, 49, 124, 133n

domestic labour, 48–9, 53, 125, 137–8,
    141–2, 151
doublethink, 24, 32
Duindam, V., 75
Duncombe, J., 56, 143
Duneier, M., 154n
Dunning, E., 39
Dworkin, A., 95–7

education, 53, 117, 123–6, 128, 137,
    139, 141
Elshtain, J.B., 154n
emotional inarticulacy, *see*
    instrumentalism
employment, 49–53, 137, 140–41,
    149
    feminization of, 51–2
Engels, F., 49, 108, 137
Enlightenment, 3, 36, 83, 146
envy, 20, 21, 29, 93
    penis envy, 94–9, 104
    womb envy, 12, 63, 86–7, 94–9,
    106–7
equal rights, 3, 24, 26, 46, 59, 76, 79,
    99, 115, 131–2, 147–8, 151–2,
    see also sexual equality
    in employment, 53
existential anxiety *see* anxiety
existential contradiction, 20
exit, 19, 114, 151
expressiveness, 12–13, 22, 31, 32, 36–8,
    53, 56, 80, 95, 129, *see also* self:
    contradictory nature of

Fairweather, H., 66
false choice, 34, 58, 74, 101, 110, 132,
    136, 152
family, 19–20, 35, 55, 71, 74–5,
    102–10, 112, 117–19, 123–7,
    130, 132, 137–8, 140–41, 143,
    151, *see also* infants: relationship
    with adults
fate, 12, 22, 134, 147
father, 15–16, 26, 27, 47, 53, 64, 79,
    97, 104–8, 113, 139, 141–2
    rule of, 7, 11, 48, 49, 60n, 116–32,
    see also patriarchy
Fausto-Sterling, A., 66

feminism, 1, 7, 9, 15, 39, 42, 45, 72,
    73, 77–80, 83, 93, 94–6, 105,
    128, 131, 135, 137–8, 145, 151
  backlash against, 47–8
fertility rates, 41–3, 126
fetishism, 3, 44n
  of commodities, 30, 31, 43n
  of sexual difference, 9, 13, 17, 23, Ch.
    2 *passim*, 85, 97–8, 100, 112,
    127–32, 147
Filmer, Sir Robert, 7, 26, 117, 119–25,
    127, 130, 132
Firestone, S., 73
Flax, J., 94
Foucault, M., 35, 39
Freud, S., 6, 9, 10, 11, 15, 32, 37, 38,
    58, 60n, 61, 62, 68, 71, 80, 81n,
    82n, Ch. 5 *passim*, 101, 102, 104,
    109, 110–11n, 115–17, 120,
    128–30, 133n, 146, 148, 149
Friday, N., 58
Fromm, E., 148
Frosh, S., 99n
Fuchs Epstein, C., 66, 67

Galileo, 3, 5
Gane, M., 22, 134
Gatens, M., 67
gender, 7, 10
  confusion with generation, 27–33, Chs.
    5–7 *passim*, 135–6, *see also* sexual
    difference: confusion with sexual
    genesis
  as 'doublethink', 24–6, 76
  as fetishistic ideology, 3, 98, 100, 127,
    152–3, *see also* fetishism of sexual
    difference
  'historical consciousness of', 10, 64,
    85–6
  origin of, 12, 25–6, 27–33, 39, Ch. 4
    passim, Ch. 6 *passim*, 128–9, 132,
    see also socialization
  and sex, 16, 25–6, 32, 40, Ch. 4
    passim, 86–93, 100, 118, 128–9
gender identity, 31, 83, 88–9, 101, 102,
    127, 135, 138, 140, 145
  non-existence of empirically, 2, 64, 149
gender vertigo, 30, 56–7, 58, 106, 149

General Household Survey, 51
generation *see* sexual genesis
  confusion with gender, 17, 28–33, 74,
    Ch. 5 *passim*, 135, *see also* sexual
    difference: confusion with sexual
    genesis
  and dominion, 11, 101, 108,
    116–32
Gershuny, J., 53
Giddens, A., 3, 12, 20, 23n, 34, 38, 56,
    94, 135, 138, 145
gift, 20, Ch. 6 *passim*, 112–13, 123–5,
    131, 148, 153
Gilligan, C., 23n
God, 3, 6, 12, 13, 26, 27, 30, 69, 84,
    113, 122, 131, 134–5, 137, *see
    also* religion
Goffman, E., 14, 67, 70
Goldstein, J., 135
Gray, J., 68
Griffin, S., 73

Harding, S., 97
Hartsock, N., 94–5
Hearn, J., 63–4
Hemingway, E., 15
Hirschman, A.O., 19, 114
Hobbes, T., 3, 6, 7, 9, 11, 19, 23n, 26,
    33, 85, 99n, 100–102, 105–10,
    Ch. 7 *passim*, 135, 137, 141–2,
    147, 152
Horney, K., 88, 94, 148
Horrocks, R., 15
Huxley, A., 34, 73

identity *see* gender identity
  national, 40, 127
  politics of, 33–5, 98–9, 101–2, Ch. 8
    passim
  that which cannot be identified, 22,
    23, 127, 130, 136, 145–6, *see
    also* personal and political
incest taboo, 7, 20, 37, 65, 84, 95,
    97–8, Ch. 6 *passim*, 116, 120,
    122, 132, *see also* attachment
independence, 13, 20–21, 87, 95–7,
    123, 130–31
individuation, 17–23, *see also* attachment

infanticide, 9, 117, 147
infants, 9, 17–19, 85, 97, 133n, 154n
  men's nurturance of, 42, 53
  relationship with adults, 17, 26, 27,
    94, 97, 101, 105, 108–110,
    116–19, 120–24, 130–32,
    135–6, 140–41, 147, *see also*
    attachment, sexual genesis,
    polymorphous perversity, Oedipus
    complex
infant mortality, 41–3
instrumentalism, 12, 22, 31, 32, 47, 56,
  see also self: contradictory nature
  of
iron cage *see* bureaucracy: 'iron cage' of

Jackson, C., 81n
Jaggar, A.M., 65
James, O., 139–40
Jensen, J. *et al.*, 51
Jong, E., 36
Joshi, H., 48
Jukes, A., 60n

Kaufman, M., 56, 61, 63
Keesing, R., 103, 107–8
Kessler, S.J., 65
Kimmel, M.S., 11, 62
kinship, 3, 41, Ch. 6 *passim*, 112, 120,
  130, 132
Klein, M., 97
Krouse, R.W., 126, 133n
Kundera, M., 13

Laing, R.D., 148
Lasch, C., 141, 146
Laslett, P., 119, 122
Lawrence, D.H., 144
Lazear, J., 143
Le Guin, U., 73
Lerner, G., 107
lesbian, 23n, 147
Leviathan, 6, 23n, 108, 116, 117, 122,
  123, 125, 142
Lévi-Strauss, C., 82n, 102–4, 107, 113
libido, 32, 86–8, 102
lifestyle magazines, 14, 31, 36, 56, 68
Lloyd, T., 47

Locke, J., 7, 11, 112, 129
Lorber, J.
love, 20, 22, 32, 37–8, 84, 94, 102,
  125, 134, 138, 143, 145, 150,
  see also attachment, cathexis,
  gift
loyalty, 19, 114

Mac an Ghaill, M., 63
MacFarlane, A., 60
MacInnes, J., 133n
Macpherson, C.B., 111n, 112
Maine, H.S., 112
male breadwinner ideology, 53–5
male gaze, 47, 49
male sex-right, 7, 73, 104, 106, 111n,
  119–20
Mann, M., 46, 48, 115
markets, 3, 30–1, 36, 100, 106, 137–8,
  141, *see also* employment
  impersonality of, 12, 46, 58, *see also*
    rationalization, universalism
marriage, 71, 103, 107, 117–19, 124–9,
  143, 147
  bars in employment, 49
  contract, 8, 25, 106, 117–19, 124–9
Marsden, D., 56, 143
Marsh, C., 53
Marx, K., 3, 4, 5, 6, 23n, 30, 43n, 49,
  114, 133n, 134, 137–8
masculinity, 2, 7, 10, 27–8, *see also*
  gender, sociology of masculinity
  crisis of, 11, 45–55
  definitions of, 2, 14–16, 45, Ch. 4
    passim, Ch. 5 *passim*, 127–8
  hegemonic, 14, 30, 55, 62, 76, 86,
    90, 135
  historical conditions giving rise to, 3,
    39
  as incarnation of evil, 69, 95–7
  as identity, 2, 57, 91–2, 135, 138
  as ideological legitimation of patriarchy,
    2, Ch. 7 *passim*
  as ideology, 1, 2, 24–5, 39, 76, 94,
    98–9
  literature about, 1, 61–2, 77, 87, 90,
    see also sociology of masculinity
  strategies for reform, 2, 149

Mauss, M., 103
McKenna, W., 65
McMahon, A., 62
Middleton, C., 75
Mill, J.S., 114
Mills, C.W., 136
Mitchell, G., 106
modernity, 2–7, 11, 12, 13–14, 16–17,
    35–8, 42–3, 56–9, 64, 107, 110,
    113, 126, 129, 131–2, 134–8,
    142, 145, 147, 153
Moore, H.L., 109
Morgan, D.H.J., 63, 64, 65, 81n, 93
mortality, 12, 13, 17, 18, 20, 29–31, 36,
    69, 95–8, 114, 152–3, 154n

Nairn, T., 40
nature, 3, 8–9, 11, 13, 18, 20, 26–7,
    32, 39, 42, 45, 56, 66–7, 69, 77,
    84, 88–9, 96, 101, 107, 113,
    115–22, 129–32, 137, *see also*
    state of nature
Newby, H., 75, 150
Nineteen Eighty-Four, 22, 32, 74, 131,
    144, 146

Oakley, A., 81n
O'Brien, M., 94, 108–9
Oedipus complex, 7, 29, 83–5, 97, Ch. 6
    passim, 135
O'Neill, J., 14, 131
ontological security, 12, 17, *see also*
    psychic security
Orbach, S., 143
Organisation for Economic Cooperation
    and Development, 51, 52
orgasm, 13, 36–8, 74, 95, 146
Ortner, S.B., 77
Orwell, G., 22, 24, 32, 44n, 74, 131,
    134, 144, 146
Ostner, 51
over-socialized conception of the
    individual *see* self: as a social
    construction

Pahl, R.E., 56
Parsons, T., 58, 71, 99n, 129
passivity, 62, 86–8, 92, 95–7

Pateman, C., 4, 6, 7, 23n, 28, 49, 73,
    93, 94, 99n, 100, 104, 106, 108,
    110, 111n, 112–13, 116, 119,
    121, 124–5, 127–8, 133n, 137
patriarchalism, 7, 132
patriarchalists, 6, 26, 27, 109, Ch. 7
    passim
patriarchy, 1, 7, 16, 17, 137, 151
    definition of, 7
    historical origin of, 41–3, 72–7, Ch. 6
    passim, 119, 131
    material and ideological legacy of, 3, 7,
    11, 30, 48, 129
    undermined by modernity, 1, 2, 16,
    46, 49, 55–9, Ch. 6 *passim*, 130,
    149
penis, 15, Ch. 5 *passim*, 103–5, 107, *see
    also* envy: penis envy
    swinging between the penis and the
    phallus, 11–12, 16, 30, 72–7, 97,
    100–101, 105, 118, 124, 128
personal and the political, the, 2, 18, 22,
    33–4, 57, 97–9, 114, Ch. 8
    passim
    distance between and democracy, 23,
    33–5, 74, 114–15, 126–7,
    130–31, 148–9
persons and societies
    distinction between, 18, 33, 105, 148
phallus, 16, 30, 41, 94, 97, 104
Phillips, Adam, 13, 21
Phillips, Anne, 137–8, 154n
Pietila, H., 69
polymorphous perversity, 4, 6, 29, 71,
    72, 83–4, 89, 91, 97, Ch. 6
    passim, 116, 120, 132, 147
private sphere, 18, 94–6, 107–8, 117,
    127, 131, 132, 134, 136–8,
    142–4, 148
    constitution by sexual genesis and
    attachment, 18, 33–4, 105,
    109–10, 114–15, 122–3, 126–7,
    136
projection, 3, 12–3, 29, 36, 38, 39, 44n,
    69–70, 92, 98–9, 105, 150, 153
psychic security, 2, 12, 28–31, 89, 97,
    146–7, *see also* ontological
    security

psychoanalysis, 59, 75, 84, 87, 91, 92, 94, 103–4, 136, 139–40, 143, 145
psychology, 56, 57, 83, 88, 148–52
public sphere, 4, 18, 94–6, 107–8, 114–15, 137–8
Pufendorf, S.F. von, 7, 115
pure relationship, 36, 38, 58, 133n, 138, 146–8

race, 40, 75, 127, 136
rape, 4, 16, 49, 72, 93, 106, 117, 124–5, 137, 146, 147, *see also* abuse, violence
rationality, formal and substantive, 4
rationalization, 3, 12, 22, 37–8, 46, 153
of the self or soul, 58, 98, 102, 136, 138–47
Rayner, J., 135
reflexivity, 3, 38, 67, 145–6
religion, 3, 10, 13, 17, 31, 89, *see also* God
reproduction, 17, 18, 71–4, 106, 109–10, 122–3, 129, 137, 141–2, *see also* sexual genesis
responsibility (for social relations), 3, 5, 12, 20, 22, 39, 71, 84, 89–90, 113, 142, 150–52
Rich, A., 72, 111n
Rousseau, J.J., 7, 11, 112, 128–9
Rowbotham, S., 73
Rubin, G., 70–2, 81n, 82n, 95, Ch. 6 *passim*, 112, 131–2
rule of offices not men, 5, 12, 55, 57, *see also* bureaucratization

Sartre, J.P., 148
Sayers, J., 12, 66
Scott, J.F., 53
Segal, L., 15, 36, 58, 62, 66, 68, 69, 77, 81n, 93, 94, 99n, 148
Seïdler, V.J., 56
self, 18–22, 87, 96, 124–5, 131, 148–53, *see also* agency, identity, personal and political, private sphere
contradictory nature of, 18, 96, 98, 127–8

'I' and 'me', 22, 114–15, 124, 126–7
imagined in gendered terms, 29, 31–3, 39, 95–6, 101, 135
powerful self, 22, 33, 36–7, 101–102, 121, 127, 132, 133–4, 138–43
as a social contruction, 2, 26, 35, 105–6, 126, 129–30, 132, 135, 148
threatened by rationalization *see* rationalization: of the self or soul
true self, 22, 38, 39, 114, 126, 127, 134–5, 142, 145
sex, 1–2, 14, 26, 37, 39–40, 46, 49, 53, 58, 83–4, 103, 105, 107, 136, 146–7, 149–53, *see also* gender and sex
as religion, 10, 13, 31, 35–8, 68
solidarity of, 41–3, 70–72, 74–5, 80, 107
sexual contract *see* contracts: sexual
sexual difference, 1, 9, 16, 45, 58, 64–5, 66–8, 107, 116, 127, 128, 149, 150–53
confusion with sexual genesis, 17, 27–9, Ch. 5 *passim*, 100–101, 104, 110, Ch. 7 *passim*, 135, 136, 141
sex difference research, 15, 66–8, 88, 129, 149
sexual division of labour, 1, 7, 8, 11, 47–55, 78–80, 94, 95, 102, 104, 108, 110, 129, 131–2, 137, 142, 144, 151–3
and gender identity, 2, 25, 30, 32, 89, 140–41, 149
sexual equality, 2, 11, 24, 58, 102, 136, 141, 144, 146, 152
sexual genesis, 2, 11, 17–23, 26–30, 33, 64–5, 74, 96, 98, 107–10, 115, 124, 129, 132, 135–6, 146–9, *see also* sexual difference: confusion with sexual genesis, attachment, reproduction
sexual intercourse, 71–2, 92–3, 105, 108
sexual relations as social constructions, 9, 33, Ch. 7 *passim*
Shanley, M.L., 115, 133n
Siltanen, J., 151

Skynner, R., 139
Smith, A., 114
Smith, Winston, 22, 145, 146
social construction, 83–4, 101, 104,
        113, 117, 119, 131–2, *see also*
        self: as a social construction
    natural limits to, 18, 27–8, 30, 33,
        114–15, 119–23
social contract, 4, 96, 104–6, 112,
        115–32
social contract theorists, 6–10, 26, 27,
        29, 70, 77, 80, 83–4, 99, 106,
        110, Ch. 7 *passim*, 135
socialization, 18, 28, 58–9, 75, 78–80,
        132
sociology, 57, 65, 83, 88, 100, 106, 112,
        131, 136, 148–53
    of emotions, 55–6, 138, 143–4
    of masculinity, 55–9
Sommerville, J.P., 26, 120, 121
state of nature, 6, 84, 108, 115–19,
        121–2, 125, 129
status, 3, 4, 6, 100, 103–5, 110, 112,
        124, 129–30, 137
Stoller, R., 81n
subjectivity, 15, 19, 56, *see also* agency,
        identity, self
swinging between the penis and the
        phallus *see* penis: swinging
        between the penis and the phallus
Sydie, R.A., 95, 99n

Temperley, J., 69
The Second Sex, 1

Thompson, K., 135
Threlfall, M., 51
transitional societies, 3, 17, 24–6, 31,
        59, 100

unconscious, 12, 21–3, 31, 32, 33–4,
        65, 68, 95, 98, 149
United Kingdom Men's Movement, 47
universalism, 3, 11, 17, 46, 59, 77, 105,
        Ch. 7 *passim*, 152–3
unprecedented inner loneliness, 13,
        28–9, 31, 152–3, *see also* capacity
        to be alone

violence, 14, 49, 57–8, 72–4, 93, 97,
        107, 142, 144, 147, 151, 153
voice, 19, 114

Wade, G., 154n
Weber, M., 3, 4, 5, 6, 13, 22, 23n, 36,
        37–8, 57, 134, 145, 146, 147,
        149–50, 152–3
Weeks, J., 13
Winnicott, D.W., 18, 20, 21, 22, 98,
        114, 146–7, 149, 150–3
womb envy *see* envy: womb envy
Wouters, C., 44n, 142
Wrong, D., 17, 22, 44, 139

Yeandle, S., 51
Young, I.M., 57, 60n, 75, 78

Zilboorg, G., 93, 99n
Zvesper, J., 23n, 126